bank marketing:

a guide to strategic planning

R. Eric Reidenbach

Associate Professor
and Phil B. Hardin Chair of Marketing
Department of Management and Marketing
University of Mississippi
University, Mississippi

Robert E. Pitts

Professor and Chair of Marketing
Department of Marketing
DePaul University
Chicago, Illinois

A Reston Book, Prentice-Hall
Englewood Cliffs, N.J. 07632

Library of Congress Cataloging-in-Publication Data

Reidenbach, R. Eric.
Bank marketing.
"A Reston book."
1. Bank marketing. I. Pitts, Robert E.
II. Title.
HG1616.M3R45 1986 332.1'068'8 85-25621
ISBN 0-8359-0408-3

A Reston Book
Published by Prentice-Hall
A Division of Simon & Schuster, Inc.
Englewood Cliffs, NJ 07632

10 9 8 7 6 5 4 3 2 1

PRINTED IN THE UNITED STATES OF AMERICA

contents

preface

This is a book about bank marketing. Bank marketing is not new. Sophisticated bank marketing, however, is. As the banking industry moves from a highly controlled industry to an industry characterized by more aggressive competition, pervasive uncertainty, and unlimited opportunity, banks will have to change the way they do business.

Driving this change is the realization that consumers do not want or need banks! What consumers want and need is a financial distribution system that is convenient and secure. This distribution system can take different forms and names. The ensuing years will tell us what that form and what that name will be.

Banking has a big stake in the changes that will take place in the next several years. Because of its tradition, banking has a head start, but the security provided by this tradition may be a false security. Today, and at an increasing rate, competitors who have survived the challenges of hypercompetition in the retail industry may prove a significant competitive force for traditional banks. Retailers understand consumer wants and needs, and they understand distribution, promotion, and pricing. Insurance companies, stock brokers, and thrifts and even retail store chains such as K-Mart and Sears will all be vying for market share for profitable products that were the exclusive "property" of banking in years past.

This book deals with these challenges and offers bankers a way of coping with these challenges. We are by no means so conceited as to offer that what is on these pages is a panacea or a guarantee for survival. What we do offer is what will be, for many smaller and medium-sized bankers, a different way to look at competition in the banking industry. This different perspective, coupled with the imagination, creativity, and experience of the reader, will prove helpful in adapting to the problems and opportunities of the next few years.

The topical outline follows what we have learned and experienced as instructors in banking seminars and as consultants to the industry. Chapter 1 offers, for those without the marketing vocabulary and background, some basic but extremely important marketing concepts. The more knowledgeable reader may choose to skip this chapter.

Chapter 2 describes the strategic marketing planning process as applied to banking. The remaining chapters examine each step from environmental monitoring (Chapter 3), target marketing and segmentation (Chapter 4), and positioning (Chapter 5) to assembling the marketing mix (Chapters 6 to 10). We have dedicated a special chapter to new product development (Chapter 7) because of what we believe will be the increasing importance of this activity. In the next two chapters we offer some thoughts on organization with a marketing perspective (Chapter 11) and controlling the marketing activity (Chapter 12). Chapter 13 concludes the text with some observations on key public policy issues facing the banking industry in the 1980s and some thoughts on how to deal with these issues.

Our plan in each chapter has been to introduce the concepts and provide examples from both the consumer goods industry and banking. In some cases the latter has been difficult, because banks have not utilized some of these concepts and approaches.

Some readers may naturally ask why we are using the consumer goods industry for examples for a text directed at the banking industry. Over the years this industry has taken the lead in American and, in fact, international business in the adoption of marketing techniques that focus on ever-changing consumer motives and perceived needs in an extremely competitive environment. They are pros. Further, we are all familiar with the products and have experienced many of the techniques.

Overall our approach in this text is strategic. That is, we have frequently and purposely not examined detailed tactics such as specific how-to's and examples for advertising/promotional ads for television.

What we do offer is a strategic marketing approach through which you can evaluate your own products and services for your present and potential customers in the appropriate business and cultural environment. An understanding of the material in this book should assist you in making those right decisions and avoiding the wrong ones in the complex days ahead in the banking industry.

A book like this required the efforts of others besides Bob and myself. Special mention must be made of Linda Wilkinson, my secretary, who worked long and hard on the manuscript. The book was made so much easier to write because of her. Janet Reidenbach, whose experience in banking was valuable to this project, deserves special mention also. She kept us on track and real-world oriented throughout the long months of preparing the manuscript. A special thanks goes to Mr. Ray Grubbs, Vice-President of Marketing at the Bank of Mississippi, for his contributions concerning the chapter on public policy issues facing the banking industry.

R. ERIC REIDENBACH
ROBERT E. PITTS

1

introduction to key marketing concepts

A STRATEGIC MARKETING ORIENTATION

There are many definitions of marketing, those which describe it as a business activity, as a trade phenomenon, as a group of related business activities, and even as a frame of mind. All these definitions lack an essential strategic managerial orientation that today's financial leaders must possess. With this in mind we have chosen to define marketing from a strategic managerial perspective:

> Marketing is an integrated business activity directed at identifying, creating, and servicing demand.

There are several aspects of this definition which merit closer examination. First, marketing is an integrated business activity. Successful competitive firms have found that marketing activities cannot be isolated from other company activities and used only to *sell* a finished product or service. Marketing activities must be integrated throughout the entire planning process, and should permeate every facet of a bank's activities, from receiving deposits to corporate planning. Marketing focuses on the consumer. To the extent that a bank is capable of satisfying consumer wants and needs profitably, its success is more probable. What this means is that all banking activities (accounting, research and development, finance, etc.) are undertaken with the consumer's wants and needs in mind.

The profitable satisfaction of wants and needs is the driving force behind a marketing orientation. Wants can be satisfied in any number of ways, and conversely, a single product or service may satisfy a number of different wants and needs. For example, most individuals have a need for security. One important aspect of this need for security is the need for financial security. In response to this need, the financial services industry has evolved a number of diverse security-satisfying products and services. Products and services such as time deposits, IRAs, and trusts are just a few examples. Most consumers will utilize several of these products in satisfying their financial security needs.

A second aspect of this consumer-need-satisfying process is that each product or service offering has the potential for satisfying different needs for different individuals. Not all consumers will be content with a basic time deposit or demand deposit account. Financial services and products, along with a number of different consumer products, have the ability to make statements about who we are or, perhaps equally important, who we want to be. A number of financial planners have recognized this aspect of their product and service offerings and have "upscaled" them by providing ancillary packaged services or positioning the offerings as something special. A good example is the gold MasterCard, which is designed not only to provide the individual with credit and convenience but also to satisfy a prestige or status need. While this may appear frivolous to the more traditional banker, the need-satisfying capabilities of such products are well documented and can provide a powerful base for consumer loyalty.

This latter point brings out a second aspect of the definition we are using in this book. That is, marketing involves identifying and creating a demand. The demand is in response to a need. Identifying the opportunity to satisfy a consumer need is the first step in successfully marketing a product or service and that which essentially differentiates a marketing effort from selling. Identifying a potential demand presents the strategic marketing planner with the opportunity to develop and successfully market a need-satisfying product or service. In so doing, (s)he must understand the nature of the need. Once understood, the strategic marketing planner can then develop a mix of price, product, promotion, and distribution that will create a demand-satisfying product or service offering.

Figure 1–1 shows, in economic terms, the effects of this identification and creation of demand process. Figure 1(a) shows a hypothetical demand curve for DDAs in a given market area. The flat demand curve is indicative of an undifferentiated product; in the consumer's opinion,

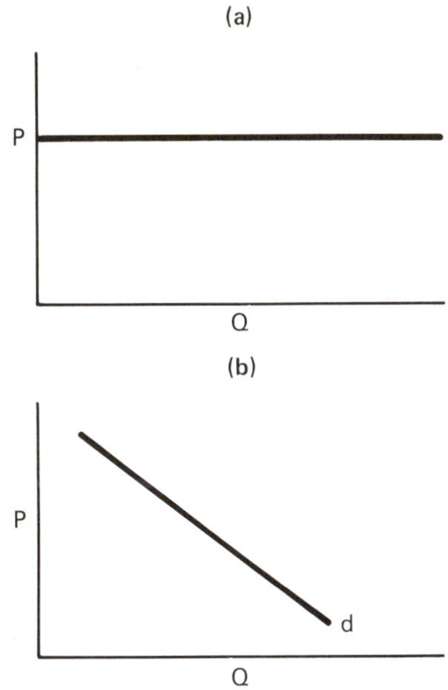

FIG. 1–1. The effects of demand creation.

all DDAs are essentially perceived as being the same. Figure 1(b) demonstrates the effect of identifying and creating a demand for a unique DDA offering—one that is perceived as being different from all the others. This demand creation could have resulted from a number of different tactics, perhaps most typically through the promotion and positioning of the DDA as being different. Some banks have even gone so far as to offer special options. By creating this difference, a firm or bank has greater control over its market and the way it chooses to compete. We should emphasize that marketers work to create demand, but they do not create need. This is a key component of the marketing concept. The consumer's needs are shaped by cultural and personal forces far beyond the control of the marketer. Demand, however, is created when product or service offerings are offered which match the consumer's perceived needs.

A final aspect of our definition involves the servicing of the demand. This is an important aspect of marketing that many marketers of consumer goods have learned the hard way. Once the demand has been created and a market developed, that market must be served. This is particularly true for an industry such as banking, where some studies have equated trips to the bank with such onerous tasks as changing a flat tire on the car or sweeping the house. Today's markets demand service and lots of it. This service means different things to different markets, and it is incumbent upon the strategic planner to understand how the market expects to be serviced. In an industry where many alternatives exist, loyalty can be extremely evanescent and loss of market costly. The strategic planner must be capable not only of identifying and creating a demand but also of providing the service necessary to maintain market loyalty as the needs of the market change. This is what the rest of this book is about.

WHAT IS A MARKET?

The word *market* has numerous meanings. To many it is a place where an exchange of value is consumated. This meaning of market is too limited for our use. Because of the national and international scope of financial transactions, defining a market as a "place" is too confining. Instead we will describe a market as being composed of three components, each of which is a necessary but, unto itself, insufficient condition for the existence of a market. It is not until all three components are simultaneously present that a market is said to exist (Figure 1–2).

The first component is obvious. A market is composed of people. Not all people, however, are included in a market. These people must have two qualities. They must have an *ability* to buy and perhaps more importantly, a *willingness* to buy. The ability to buy is a factor that many unsuccessful marketers have focused on in the past. The mere presumption that consumers can afford a product or service offering has been the undoing of many marketers. Many high-priced, and, for that matter, moderately priced or low-priced products, while easily affordable by a large proportion of the population, have been abysmal marketing failures. What the marketer failed to take into account was the consumer's willingness to buy the product. This brings us back to our previous discussion of the need-satisfying capabilities of the product or service. If consumers perceive no need-satisfying capability of the product, the probability that they will be willing to buy the product

People
+
An ability to buy = A market
+
A willingness to buy

FIG. 1–2. Components of a market.

is greatly reduced. This again points out the importance of identifying a need and creating a product that will satisfy that consumer need.

MARKET SEGMENTS

Marketers also speak of market segments. These are subdivisions of the overall market that represent slightly different marketing opportunities than those presented by the overall market. For example, when marketers focus on one or more of these segments they are said to be *targeting* markets. Such a strategy has positive benefits and will be discussed in much greater length in Chapter 4.

Most financial institutions, depending on the scope of their activities, can speak of a number of different markets. These might include the market for IRAs, time deposits, demand deposits, loans, or trust services, to name just a few. What they are really saying and, that which is crucial to a strategic marketing orientation, is that there exist *individuals with an ability to buy* and *willingness to buy IRAs, time deposits, demand deposits, loans,* and *trust services.*

The potential for a specific market or market segment can be expressed either in terms of the number of products or services that can be sold or in terms of the dollar value of these products or services. The *market potential* of a segment represents the total number of product sales (or dollar value) that would result if *everyone* in the market were to purchase the product or service. Banks must also recognize that they are in constant competition for these potential individuals. Not only do other banks and savings and loans represent competition but so too do investment houses, financial boutiques, insurance companies, credit unions, and some of the larger nontraditional financial service institutions such as retailers.

The market(s) or portions of a market *(market share)* that a firm controls represents its most important asset. It does not show up directly on the balance sheet or the bank's profit and loss statement, but its effects do. The amount of time, effort, and dollars spent in developing a market for a bank's product and service offering is proportional to the amount of market share the bank enjoys. Statistically speaking, the greater the market share, the greater the long-term profitability of the bank. Unfortunately, the greater the market share, the more tempting a target the bank may become as larger money centers or regional banks attempt to undermine its market position. The surest guard against such erosion of market share is a strong product-market match. In other words, the better a bank can satisfy the financial needs of its target markets, the greater will be its ability to withstand competitive onslaught from those who would invade its market.

An example from the consumer goods market will provide an illustration of this last point. For a number of years Procter & Gamble controlled a very profitable segment of the toothpaste market with its Crest entry. So dominant was its position that many felt it was impregnable to competitive intrusion. A competitor saw this lucrative position and developed a flanking strategy which left a big cavity in Crest's market. Aqua-fresh was a product which was designed not only to satisfy the decay-prevention needs of the market but also to satisfy the need for white teeth and fresh breath as well. This was an emerging need that an inattentive P & G overlooked. The product broke into Crest's vaunted position and in addition pushed around a couple of other entries in the "sensory segment," resulting in a significant market position for Bristol Meyers's Aqua-fresh. Bristol Meyers understood the changing needs of the market and was better able to capitalize on this need identification by creating a demand for their Aqua-fresh product, which P & G has now imitated with its Crest Gel version.

The banking industry is experiencing similar problems. The attractiveness of the banking business has proven extremely inviting to competitors from outside the industry. At the writing of this book, some of the first retailers are invading the markets established by traditional banks.

Another way of looking at a market is to equate the market(s) that a bank serves with a life support system. The larger the life support system, the more freedom that bank has to grow. The smaller the life support system, the more likely the bank's growth will be constrained. Both instances (large market vs small market) will require different types of marketing strategies to accomplish specified objectives.

CONSUMER SATISFACTION AT A PROFIT

Present-day marketing has evolved from a series of different orientations (Figure 1–3). Originally, marketing was governed by what has been referred to as the *production concept*. This is a marketing management orientation which, as the name implies, focuses on the production of the product. The underlying premise is that consumers will favor those products that are both available and affordable. Such an orientation is prevalent in a sellers' market where the demand for the product is greater than the supply. Management's task under this orientation is to increase and maintain production and distribution efficiency. Although a production orientation has proven successful for a number of different firms in the past, it can leave the company open to criticisms of consumer insensitivity and nonconcern.

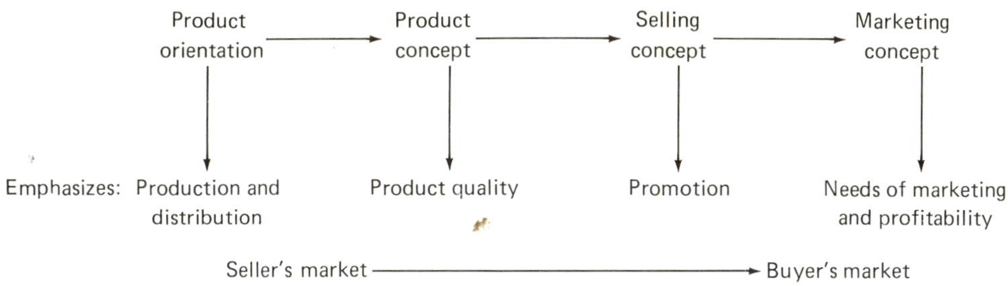

FIG. 1–3. The evolution of the marketing concept.

Next in the evolutionary sequence of marketing is what is known as the *product concept.* This type of orientation places emphasis on product quality and differs from the production concept in that the former concentrates more on product quantity. Such an orientation is manifest in the erroneous idea that if you build a better mousetrap, the world will beat a path to your door. Unfortunately, as a number of firms have found out, this marketing philosophy has not been adequate to sustain a competitive position in the market place. The charge of having a "product concept" has been leveled at Chrysler and is, in some circles of marketing thought, felt to be responsible for their loss of market share and near collapse. Product quality is important, but if the product does not satisfy consumer needs, the quality of the product is irrelevant.

Many banks have adopted a product orientation in their current marketing activities. Products and services are offered to match any and all banks and other financial institutions in the market area regardless of how they fit either the needs of current customers or the bank's marketing strategy. For example, the customer today is offered a bewildering array of nontraditional banking products such as N.O.W. accounts, multiple CDs, and the like with little regard as to how each fits the needs of specific customer groups.

The selling concept places marketing emphasis on the idea that consumers can be induced to buy a company's product even if that product does not really satisfy a need. This philosophy of marketing dominated the 1950s and has, in part, been responsible for the pushy, brash, and callous image that was associated with salesmen and marketers and has fostered the *caveat emptor* warning so often heard. The problem of putting the sale before the consumer is that nonsatisfied consumers do not make loyal customers. While they may succumb to the initial sales pressure and effort, the likelihood of their repurchasing or continuing to use a product or service that does not satisfy a need is low. This can be extremely harmful for an industry like banking, which is dependent upon loyal consumers. In addition, consumers talk to each other and, in so doing, provide one of the most powerful sources of product or service promotion. When this information is positive, it can be extremely influential in developing new customers and clients, but when it is negative, it becomes a potent dissuasive force.

The banking industry has historically viewed "selling" as an unnecessary activity, but as competition has increased in today's deregulated environment, many banks are emphasizing selling activities. As you will see, the industry must not adopt a sales mentality, but must turn to marketing to meet the challenge of this new business environment. More recently, firms have begun to embrace what is called the *marketing concept.* Essential to this marketing management philosophy is that *it is the task of the firm to identify the needs of the target market and then to adapt the organization in a manner that will satisfy those needs while making a profit.* In a sense the marketing concept says, "Satisfy consumer needs at a profit." Gwain Gillespie, senior vice president for R. J. Reynolds Food and Beverage Group, urged bankers to "go and find out what your customers want . . . (then) . . . consider adopting a *consumer-products* marketing and strategic planning approach."[1] In essence, what Mr. Gillespie is telling bankers is to adopt the marketing concept.

The marketing concept and its importance to the banking industry is even more compellingly articulated by Rayburn S. Dezember, chairman of the board, Bank Administration Institute, and chairman and president, Central Pacific Corporation in Bakersfield, California:

> Today customers control our destiny and shape our strategies. They are compelling bankers to ask and answer the most fundamental questions. What is a bank and what can it be? Who are our potential customers and which of them do we want to serve? What products and services do they want? Which services do we have the capital, geographic reach, structure, operational capacity and marketing acumen to offer successfully? And how do we bring these things together?[2]

McDonald's recognizes the importance of a consumer emphasis and even goes so far as to make the customer the center of their Basic Beliefs:

McDonald's Believes that our Customer

. . . is the most important person in our business.

. . . is not dependent on us. We are dependent on him.

. . . is one who brings us his wants. It is our job to fill them.

. . . is not an interruption of our work. He is the purpose of it.

. . . does us an honor when he calls.

. . . is part of our business, not an outsider. He is our guest.

. . . is not a cold statistic. He is flesh and blood, a human being with feelings and emotions like our own.
. . . is deserving of the most courteous and attentive treatment we can give him.
. . . is not someone to argue with or match wits with.[3]

Some confusion exists concerning the difference between the selling concept and the marketing concept. Theodore Levitt differentiates the two in the following manner:

> Selling focuses on the needs of the seller; marketing on the needs of the buyer. Selling is preoccupied with the seller's need to convert his product into cash; marketing with the idea of satisfying the needs of the customer by means of the product and the whole cluster of things associated with creating, delivering and finally consuming it.
>
> The selling concept begins with the product and asks the question "How can we stimulate a profitable volume of sales?" Essential to this approach is the heavy use of promotion and sales effort. The marketing concept begins with the consumer and asks "What consumer needs in this target market are not being satisfied and how can I satisfy them?"[4]

Once these needs have been identified, management must adapt the organization in such a way so that this need- and want-satisfying orientation is integrated throughout all functional areas. It does little good for the marketing department to embrace a marketing concept philosophy which is not and cannot be translated into want-satisfying products through its trust services and operation and in the delivery of these products.

Peter Drucker makes the distinction between the selling concept and the marketing concept even more definable:

> Indeed, selling and marketing are antithetical rather than synonymous or even complementary. There will always, one can assume, be a need for some selling. But the aim of marketing is to make selling superfluous. The aim of marketing is to know and understand the customer so well that the product or service fits him and sells itself. Ideally, marketing should result in a customer who is ready to buy. All that should be needed then is to make the product or service available, i.e., logistics rather than salesmanship, and statistical distribution rather than promotion.[5]

It is evident that a number of companies claim to embrace the marketing concept but in reality still hold with the more traditional selling concept. These companies may say they are consumer-oriented, but one look at their organizational chart tells you otherwise. What is missing is the integration of the marketing function and a marketing orientation throughout the different functional areas of the firm. While there may exist a marketing department, the major function of this department is selling or advertising. One needs only to look at the organizational chart of most banks to see that the existence of the selling concept is alive and well. Many banks have an "advertising department" instead of a marketing department. Moreover, the ad department is in a staff position rather than an integrated line function. Such selling orientation is particularly visible in less competitive industries. However, as the competition in these industries intensifies, more and more of these firms turn from selling to marketing. We will discuss the integration of marketing in the bank's organizational structure and the development of a marketing culture structure in Chapter 11.

THE MARKETING MIX

Reference has been made several times to some of the tools that marketers use to achieve their objectives. These tools comprise what is referred to as the *marketing mix,* which is composed of the product, the price variable, promotion, and distribution. Aspects of these variables are shown in Table 1–1. The marketing mix comprises the set of variables under the control of the marketer. Manipulation of the product, its price, and the way it is promoted and distributed comprises one of the major decision stages in the strategic marketing process. It may be useful at this time to take a closer, yet brief look at each of these marketer-controlled variables, beginning with the product.

The Product

Companies that best understand the marketing concept have a more sophisticated view of what a product actually is. They recognize that the product is much more than just a tangible good. For example, consider the following question, "What is an individual buying when (s)he is buying a drill bit?" The uninitiated marketer may respond, "A piece of metal that fits into the end of a drill." The more consumer-oriented marketer realizes that the individual is buying holes or the ability to make holes. When viewed in this way the product or service, for that matter, becomes a bundle of want- and need-satisfying benefits. Consumers then will continue to use that product or service as long as it continues to satisfy their wants and needs.

In a similar fashion, an individual is not buying a checking account when (s)he pays his or her monthly service charges. (S)He is buying

TABLE 1–1 Elements of the Marketing Mix

Strategic Decision Areas			
Product	*Place*	*Promotion*	*Price*
Features	Channels Market exposure Kinds of middlemen	Promotion blend Kind of salespeople Selection	Flexibility Level Introductory pricing
Instructions Service		Motivation Kind of advertising	
	Service levels	Media type	
Product lines Package Brand name		Copy thrust	

Adapted from: Philip Kotler, *Marketing Management* (Englewood Cliffs, N.J.: Prentice-Hall, Inc., 1980), p. 89.

convenience, security, freedom, prestige, and perhaps a host of other benefits unknown to the individual in charge of new accounts who sold the checking account.

As we said before, it is the task of marketing management to identify, understand, and deliver want- and need-satisfying products and services. This is often a complex process and a most difficult task, because most consumers will not be able to verbalize their wants and needs in a sufficiently articulate manner to allow marketing to respond. Rather, it is incumbent upon marketing management to uncover and identify what these unsatisfied wants and needs are. This will be dealt with in greater detail in the following chapters. For now it is sufficient to understand that the essential aspect of products or services is their want- and need-satisfying capabilities. From this perspective, consumers no longer buy savings accounts or checking accounts; what they buy is security, convenience, prestige, freedom, and a number of other want- and need-satisfying extensions that are packaged in the form of basic banking services.

Promotion

Most people think of advertising when they think of promotion. As Table 1–1 shows, advertising is just one part of the promotional mix available to marketers. Each one of the variables in the promotion mix is designed to accomplish certain marketing and persuasive tasks. Not all marketing tasks will require the use of advertising, or perhaps more accurately, there will exist a specific time in the accomplishment of the marketing objective when advertising may be more effective. Each of these variables differ as the following definitions indicate:

- *Advertising.* Any paid form of nonpersonal presentation and promotion of ideas, goods, or services by an identified sponsor.
- *Personal Selling.* Oral presentation in a conversation with one or more prospective purchasers for the purpose of making sales.
- *Sales Promotion.* Short-term incentives to encourage purchase or sale of product or service.
- *Publicity.* Nonpersonal stimulation of demand for a product, service, or business unit by planting commercially significant news about it in a published medium or obtaining favorable presentation of it upon radio, television, or stage that is not paid for by the sponsor.[5]

Each of these promotional tools has found ready acceptance and use in the banking industry, some more than others. For example, advertising is one of the more used promotional tools in the industry. Unfortunately, in many cases a bank's entire marketing effort seems to be manifested in its advertising campaigns. The use of sales promotions in the form of free gifts with the minimum deposit of a specified sum was, and to a more limited extent still is, a common practice. Banks have discovered what many consumer goods firms had previously learned, that sales promotions may have limited short-term effects and, in fact, may not be sound promotional investments. Personal selling is relied upon heavily in the banking industry through the use of tellers and customer service representatives. This is an important aspect of bank promotion, since it represents a personal interface between the bank and the customer. Indications are that, for the typical bank, personal selling will take on increasing importance in the future. Some banks, however, are now limiting the personal selling effort to their more lucrative and upscale customers with varying results. Finally, the publicity variable is used with varying degrees of intensity. Publicity is a relative newcomer to the promotion mix, and many accomplished marketing organizations are still learning how to effectively use this tool.

Each of these variables has certain capabilities and advantages that the others do not and will be effective at different stages of the strategic marketing process. What these capabilities and advantages are and how they can be used is the topic of Chapter 8. For now it is important to understand that these are the principal means by which the business organization communicates with its target markets. How, when, and where it communicates and what is communicated is essential to the successful accomplishment of marketing objectives.

Distribution

If promotion is the means of verbally communicating with a target market, distribution is the vehicle for delivering the product to the customer. Current psychographic changes have put a premium on convenience. The proliferation of fast food outlets, convenience stores, and in banking, branch banks (where permitted) and ATMs attests to the importance of this variable. Recent distribution developments have proven extremely profitable for firms which had previously discounted the potency of this component of the marketing mix. For example, L'eggs Pantyhose pioneered a distribution breakthrough by distributing their products through supermarkets and convenience stores, although previously these garments were sold almost exclusively through department stores. The upswing in catalog sales and distribution further attests to the importance of convenience and the response of marketers to this need. Products such as computers, software, audiovisual equipment, and other products traditionally purchased in retail outlets are now purchased at home. Other products and services such as insurance, investments, and other financial services are finding their way into the home, where the consumer can decide at his or her leisure. Moreover, the way in which a product or service is distributed says a lot about the product itself.

Banks have been quick to recognize the important aspect of this variable. Branch banking is in part a response to this convenience need, as are the automated teller machines and home computer banking. Changes in the way in which bank services are distributed on a national basis are beginning to manifest themselves. Issues of interstate banking will continue to pose difficult and important distribution decisions long after the legality of interstate banking is decided.

How these decisions are made is more fully discussed in Chapter 9. Again, it is important at this point to understand the important role that distribution plays in the overall marketing effort of the firm.

Price

This is perhaps one of the more difficult of the marketing variables to manipulate. The price of the product or service has a strong impact upon the image of the product as well as an economic impact on the bank. Marketers have been quick to recognize this fact and have used price, both low and high, to successfully differentiate their products and services.

Consider how beer brewers use price to distinguish between brands of beers. A higher price has the ability to convey a more prestigious image than a lower-priced brand. Add a European name and the picture is complete—a high-quality, premium, prestigious beverage. Studies have shown that most beer drinkers probably cannot differentiate between the brands but instead rely on such cues as the price of the product to guide their decision.

Marketers also realize that the price a consumer pays for a product or service includes such factors as the time spent looking for the product, the amount of effort expended, and the satisfaction one gets from shopping for alternatives. These factors must be taken into consideration when planning the marketing mix in the strategic planning process.

Price in the banking industry had been regulated for a long time, and banks were forced to compete on a nonprice basis. The loosening of regulations concerning the interest rates paid, costs of participating in different plans and accounts, and service charges have more recently come under the control of the individual bank, as has the notion of fee-based services. In addition, competition has brought to the front the idea of opportunity costs that the potential customer must also take into account. By investing in a CD with a five-year maturity date and a substantial early withdrawal penalty, the consumer may forgo a perhaps better investment at a competing bank. This "opportunity cost" becomes an additional price factor for the consumer. While complete flexibility in such decisions is not practical from the bank's point of view, banks that understand and embrace the marketing concept can do much to mitigate the consumer's cost of doing business with a bank. Actual pricing strategies and considerations are the subject of Chapter 9.

EXCHANGE—THE CORE IDEA OF MARKETING

It can be said that marketing exists to facilitate exchanges. The potential for an exchange exists when two or more parties each have something desired by one or more of the other parties. Typically in our society the marketer has a want- or need-satisfying product or service while the consumer has money. It is marketing's role to facilitate the exchange between the two parties. It does this by first understanding the components of the exchange, the wants and needs of the consumers, designing a product or service that will satisfy these wants and needs, putting a value on it, communicating information to the consumer, and finally making it available to the consumer. In other words, the marketer manipulates the product and its price, promotes it, and distributes it. The better it does this and is able to satisfy the consumer, the more profitable the organization will be. Consumating profitable exchanges is the task of marketing management.

The nature of this exchange is complicated by the number and intensity of competing firms as they attempt to reach the same consumers. Those organizations which can more closely provide the consumer with the want- and need-satisfying product or service are more likely to effect the exchange. Firms can choose to make only certain kinds of exchanges. For example, some banks can choose to offer trust services or correspondent banking services, while others may not. These types of exchanges offered depend upon the needs of the different markets that a bank chooses to serve. Traditionally banks have almost been forced to engage in all types of banking exchanges. This full-service policy will likely change as some banks better understand the needs of their market, understand that some exchanges may be more profitable than others, and choose to concentrate only on those it can do well.

SUMMARY

This chapter has focused on providing some of the key concepts of marketing. It began by providing a strategic marketing management perspective and proceeded to discuss such aspects of marketing as what a market is, the marketing concept, and what the marketing mix is and concluded with the nature of exchanges. While many of these concepts may appear elementary to the more advanced bank marketer, they are intended as a base on which some of the more sophisticated notions of strategic marketing planning can be developed. Understanding the importance of the marketing concept is a crucial first step toward developing a proficiency as a strategic marketing planner.

Footnotes

[1]Steven Mintz, "Banking in Marketing," *Sales and Marketing Management,* June 6, 1983, p. 44.

[2]Rayburn S. Dezember, "Customers are Shaping Bank Strategy," *The Magazine of Bank Administration,* Vol. 9, No. 7 (1983), p. 22.

[3]McDonald's Corporation, Oakbrook, Illinois.

[4]Theodore Levitt, "Marketing Myopia," *Harvard Business Review,* July–August, 1960, pp. 45–56.

[5]Peter Drucker, *Management: Tasks, Responsibilities, Practices* (New York: Harper & Row Publishers, 1973, pp. 64–65.

[6]Philip Kotler, *Marketing Management* (Englewood Cliffs, N.J.: Prentice-Hall, Inc., 1980), p. 468.

2

the strategic marketing process

INTRODUCTION

Strategic marketing planning is the process of developing action plans for achieving the banks's goals. Although frequently associated with quantitative operations research techniques, strategic marketing is simply an analytical process for shaping the direction of the bank. According to Peter Drucker, this strategic approach to the operation of a business is not future planning but rather planning how today's actions will affect the future. Further, the strategic approach is a means through which risks may be evaluated.[1] A detailed conceptualization of the strategic planning process is shown in Figure 2–1.

The strategic planning process may take many forms, but perhaps the most straightforward view of the process is offered by Benton E. Gup's three-question approach:

- Where are you going?
- What is the environment?
- How do you get there?[2]

The biggest hurdle for many banks, however, is not the actual application of the process that we shall discuss in this chapter, but

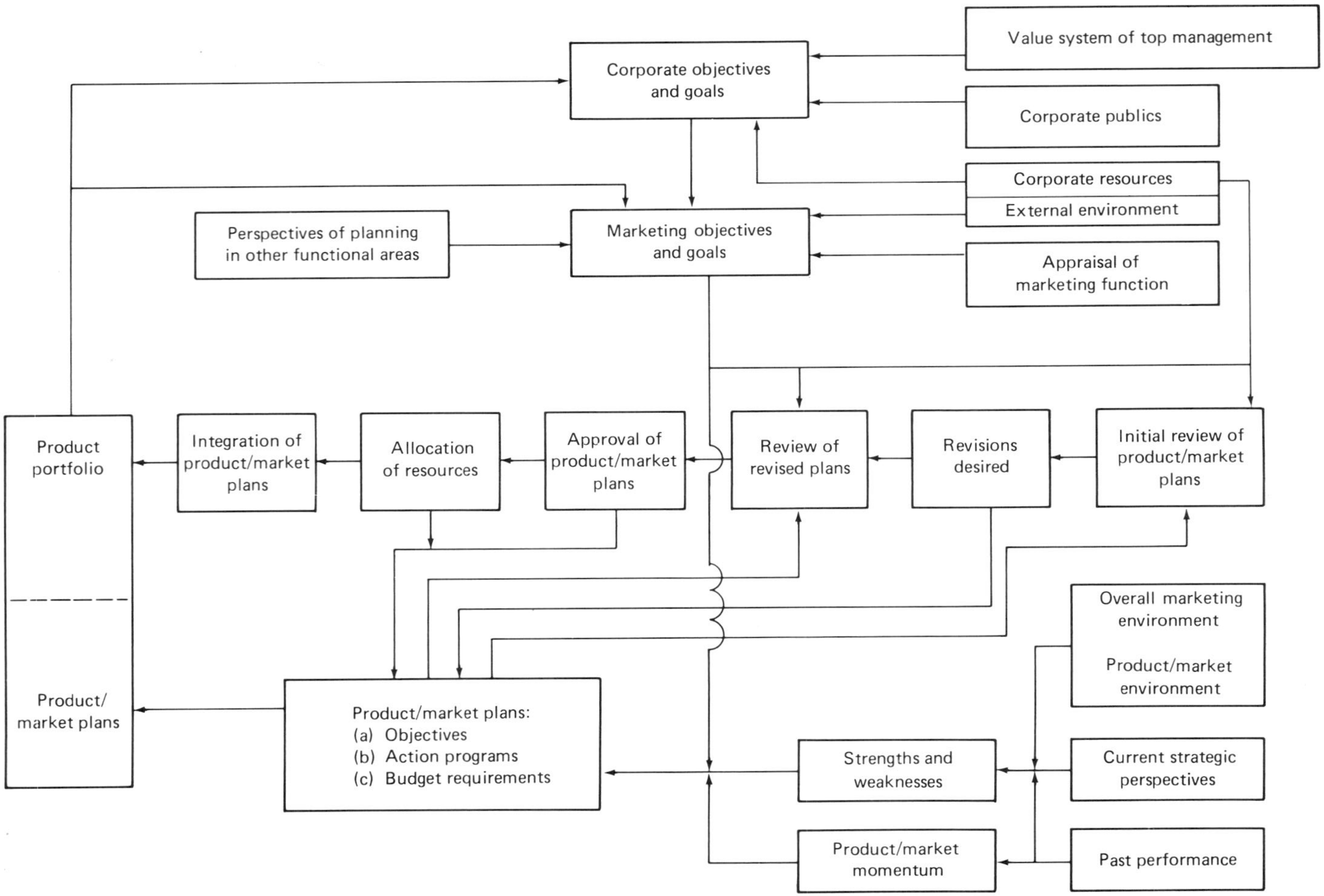

FIG. 2–1. The strategic planning process. *Source: Subhash C. Jain, Marketing Planning and Strategy (Cincinnati: South-Western Publishing Co., 1981), p. 13. Used with permission.*

rather realizing the importance of strategic planning in banking. In most relatively mature industries, firms may appear to offer basically undifferentiated products and services and to face a generally stable environment. This, of course, is not an accurate assessment of either the product/service or of the environment in which the development of effective business strategy takes place. Not only does each bank have a unique set of goals, each faces a unique environment shaped in part by its own strengths and weaknesses. In today's business environment, desirable innovations are quickly copied by competitors. The obtaining of a sustainable competitive advantage requires that the bank find a way of maximizing its strength relative to competitors in the financial marketplace. Blindly copying every competitor, attempting to be everything to every possible customer, and hiding behind a facade of comfortable past practices are not substitutes for evaluation and strategic planning.

OVERVIEW OF THE STRATEGIC MARKETING PLANNING PROCESS

The primary objective of the strategic marketing approach is the development of a comprehensive marketing plan to lead to the achievement of the firm's long-term business goals. This plan should define a course of action for expected business conditions and should encompass all relevant areas of the organization.[3]

In most organizations it is desirable to develop marketing strategy at the strategic business unit level.[4] A strategic business unit (SBU) is an autonomous profit center with a definable product/service or customer orientation, such as a bank's trust department. The SBU can be made up of several departments or facilities which are managed as a unit. Thus, while a basic concept of the strategic approach, the SBU is also a useful concept for both organizational and financial analysis. Depending on the firm, an SBU may encompass divisions with hundreds of millions of dollars in sales or only a separate introductory product/service, which the firm wants to single out because of its potential. The SBU should be established in keeping with the nature of the product(s)/service(s) involved and the market to be served.

Once the firm has established the SBU as the unit of analysis for strategy planning, the next step is the development of a framework within which to study the marketplace.

The tools of the strategic marketing process are market segmentation, environmental analysis, the selection of target markets for the firm's segmentation efforts, (Chapter 4) and the development of unique marketing mixes for each segment targeted, as shown in Figure 2–2.

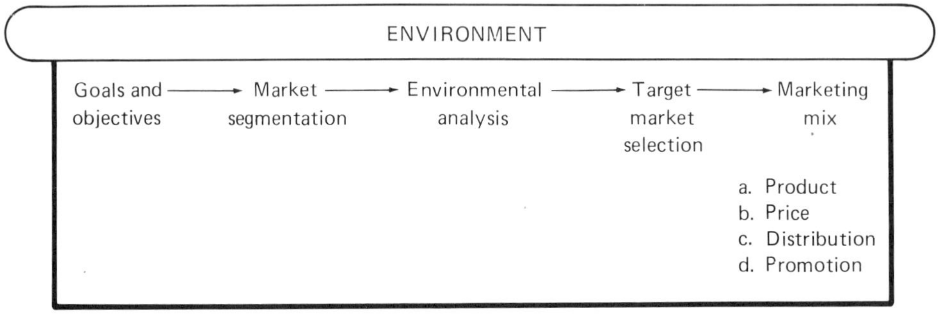

FIG. 2–2. Strategic marketing.

After the development of the firm's goals, the process proceeds to market segmentation. Market segmentation involves the division of what is a heterogenous market for products or services into segments that are as homogenous as possible along the dimensions which are of the most significance for the bank and SBU.

Market segmentation has become one of the primary tools in contemporary marketing practice. From the various segments identified, the marketing manager selects target markets at which the marketing mix will be aimed. The marketing mix consists of the product or service offered, the price attached to the product, the manner in which the product will be delivered or provided to the customer, and finally, an integrated promotional program.

The strategic marketing process provides a procedure through which these strategic tools may be best applied. It provides a framework through which the strategic planner may examine the firm, the environment, and the marketing strategy. Using the general steps proposed earlier (Figure 2–1), the first element of the strategic marketing process is the delineation of appropriate objectives.

DETERMINING MARKETING OBJECTIVES

One should remember that objectives must be established for the SBU department or division for which the strategic marketing plan is being developed. This means that while the goals and objectives will always be in keeping with the bank's overall mission and overall plan, goals and objectives may be very different for different SBUs. In order to provide this specific direction for the firm, the objectives must have several characteristics, as shown in Table 2–1. First a *hierarchy* should exist within the firm's objectives from generalized statements for the firm to specific operational objectives at the SBU, product, and market levels.

TABLE 2–1 Objectives

1. Hierarchical	
Generalized ⟷	Specific
2. Obtainable	
3. Quantifiable	
4. Approach	

This hierarchical concept includes the idea that some objectives have a primary importance to the bank, while others are secondary.

Next, objectives must be *atttainable.* The objective should provide the direction for marketing strategy and not be a pie-in-the-sky dream. Unobtainable objectives can be extremely detrimental to morale in the firm at the operational level, and at the top of the objective hierarchy they may cause misdirection of the bank's activities. For example many experts feel that Chemical Bank's "Pronto" home-banking service using home-based personal computers may be too far ahead of the market. In 1984 Chemical had spent $2000 on each of 10,000 Pronto users and was expecting a pretax operating loss of $30 to $40 million for the program over the next several years. This attempt to gain prominence as a leader in a new technologically based retail customer service area can prove successful only if large numbers of home computer owners learn to use their computers for financial transactions, something most consumers have yet to accept.

Good objectives should be as *quantifiable* as possible. Broad qualitative statements such as "increased market share" or "growth in profits" are simply not objectives, since they provide no real direction and no yardstick against which to measure success. An objective of a 10 percent return on investment assets or a 25 percent market share in total deposits in a market are quantifiable goals toward which strategy may be shaped. Moreover, quantified objectives provide a diagnostic basis for control purposes. Most firms' objectives will generally be stated in some combination of profits, sales, market share, or risk.

Finally, objectives should be *appropriate.* Profits are the "bottom-line" approach which are generally thought to drive every business venture. Many firms, however, select objectives such as market share and sales, which may emphasize revenue, rather than profits. The nation's top ten income-producing banks for 1981 are shown in Table 2–2. In fact, profit maximization and revenue maximization are incompatible goals in most situations. In order to achieve increased revenues and market share, the firm may have to accept lower levels of profit for a given level of sales. In extreme cases, a goal of increased market share can even cause a reduced level of total revenue if extensive price competition takes hold between the firms in a market characterized by non-elastic demand.

TABLE 2–2 Top Ten Income-Producing Banks 1981

	Net Income (000)		*Average Total Assets*
	1981	*1980*	*1981 (millions)*
1. Citibank, N.A.	$673,775	$649,377	$104,612
2. Chase Manhattan Bank, N.A.	441,029	371,440	78,373
3. Bank of America, N.T. & S.A.	429,804	594,535	115,587
4. Morgan Guaranty Trust Co.	314,637	332,649	54,053
5. Manufacturers Hanover Trust Co.	285,144	224,498	54,363
6. Continental Illinois National Bank & Trust Co.	231,284	219,264	43,304
7. Security Pacific National Bank	208,630	181,326	29,083
8. Chemical Bank	199,988	176,934	44,509
9. Bankers Trust Company	174,874	202,480	34,207
10. United California Bank	121,881	108,022	18,829

Source: Barrett F. Binder, "The Top 50 Profit Producing Banks," *The Magazine of Bank Administration* (August, 1982), pp. 16–24, used with permission.

While most businesses use measures such as return on invested capital as a measure of true profit performance, net income is the basic profit measure in the banking industry. Also, rather than sales, the bank will generally use measures of average and year-end return on assets and specific assets (loans and investments) and liabilities (time deposits and CDs).

In a similar fashion, the level of risk that a bank incurs will often increase if a goal of maximum profit is established and maximum profit-oriented strategies are developed. Acceptable risk, producing reasonable levels of profit for a particular type of SBU, is the approach used most frequently in goal setting.

This idea of risk, sales or deposits, and profit as joint goals should not be a new idea in the banking industry. The concept of varying rates for loans of differing levels of risk, and that of increased demand for funds at lower levels of return over funds costs, are the same as those one would apply in setting goals for the SBU and the firm.

Environmental Analysis

The next step in activating the strategic marketing process is the examination of the environment in which the SBU will be operating (Chapter 3). An effective examination of the environment requires that both the internal and the external environment be studied in detail, as shown in Table 2–3. While this is discussed as if it were a discrete step, environmental monitoring is an ongoing process, at least for those successful adaptive organizations. Introspection or self-examination of the SBU should cover a wide range of management, marketing, and financial areas. The strategic planner is attempting to review honestly the strengths and the weaknesses that exist in the SBU.

The *external environment* also must be examined across a number of dimensions. Cultural, economic, political, demographic, technological, and competitive conditions as they currently exist and as they may be expected to exist all bear directly on the strategies that should be employed. This will be discussed in detail in Chapter 3.

Marketing Strategies

The next step in the strategic marketing process is the actual development of the plans that will allow the bank to achieve its goals for a given internal and external environment. The bank must decide on the most appropriate manner to approach its potential market. This process involves the idea of market segmentation. With market segmentation, an important concept is that of market opportunity analysis. In other words, if this is the way we view our marketplace, where are the real opportunities for growth and profits (Figure 2–3)?

Market opportunity analysis leads to the selection of a target market for the SBU and its products and services, and sometimes leads to a direction for the entire institution. While many banks have chosen to target either the commercial or consumer markets as an overall strategy, the target concept can and should be taken much further to the SBU and the product/service level.[5] Banks which have restructured their operations to appeal to the needs of a particular income/social class of retail customers are an extreme example of such targeting. In

TABLE 2–3 Environmental Analysis

Internal	*External*
Finance conditions	Economic conditions
Customer data	Political conditions
Employee skills	Demographic trends
Facilities	Cultural trends
Product/service analysis	Technology
Marketing strengths & weaknesses	Competition

Adapted from: Michael A. Hitt, R. Dennis Middlemist, and Robert L. Mathis, *Effective Management* (St. Paul: West Publishing Co., 1979), p. 144, and William S. Stanton, *Fundamentals of Marketing,* 7th ed. (New York: McGraw-Hill Book Co., 1984), p. 24.

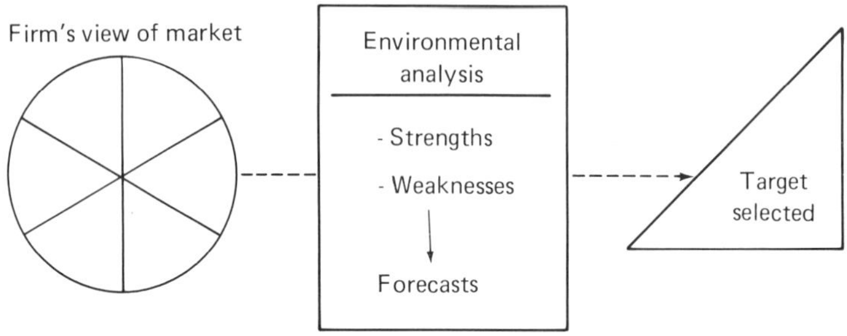

FIG. 2–3. Target selection.

some aggressive programs designed to attract high revenue and profit, individuals have been paired with equally aggressive attempts to demarket the bank to less profitable low-revenue customers. This apparently is the strategy at Citibank, which required a minimum deposit in order to transact with a teller.

Another major strategic decision which must be made is that of the *position* in the marketplace that the bank will attempt to occupy. The idea of position carries with it many perceptual and actual components. Position is the manner in which the institution and a product/service and its competitors are viewed by its customers. The idea of positioning is a hallmark of the marketing-oriented firm, because many goods are actually differentiated more by perception than by actual functional differences. Thus it is vital that an appropriate perceptual position be developed to differentiate a product and to position it in keeping with a selected target market. Firms also have a position in the competitive marketplace which may be viewed in more macro- or industry-oriented concepts. Most markets have a competitive structure featuring a market leader, one or two other important competitors, and a number of much smaller, often less profitable competitors fighting for what is left.

Once the target market is selected, the bank's or SBU's environment and the desired marketplace position form the basis for the development of the marketing mix mentioned at the first of the chapter. Marketing-mix decisions can be categorized under product/service components, promotion components relevant to a particular offering, pricing or rate decisions, and distribution decisions (Figure 2–4). Again it is obvious that the marketing-mix components are interrelated and must be considered as a package, although we shall devote a separate chapter to each.

The strategic marketing process is basically a detailed approach to the development of a plan for achieving a sustainable competitive advantage. There is considerable debate, however, as to whether this

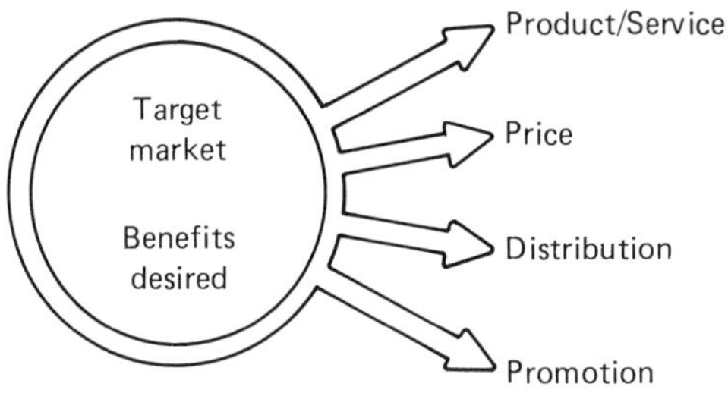

FIG. 2–4. Marketing mix.

should be a formal process bound by the tools we shall introduce in this chapter, or a more intuitive process emphasizing creative thinking. Our position is that strategic marketing planning involves the creative application of strategic planning tools to develop the necessary product/market fit, and achieving a differential advantage for the bank.

In our previous general presentation of the strategic marketing approach, we have been implicitly assuming that strategic marketing is part of the resource-allocation process for a multiproduct/multiservice and multimarket bank. That is, that the financial institution has limited financial, managerial, and personnel resources and that the strategic marketing approach is a method of analyzing and planning in the environment in which the firm wishes to apply these scarce resources. A number of formal models have been developed to provide basic guidance in resource allocation at the firm level.[6] These formal models are in wide use in many major firms, but their use does not appear to have spread to an overwhelming majority of banks.

One approach which has gained considerable use during the past several decades is the market-share/market-growth grid approach, generally referred to as the Boston Consulting Group approach. This approach will be discussed in detail in Chapter 4.

Market Strategies and Growth

There are four basic strategies which may be considered by a financial institution seeking sustained growth. These are shown in Figure 2–5. These four strategies are the combination of activities which seek growth in present versus new markets, and current versus new products/services.

When examining the combinations of these two major dimensions, the four market strategies become readily apparent. The combination of current markets and current products/services yield a *market-penetration* strategy, while the introduction of new products or services in the cur-

PRODUCT \ MARKET	Continue	New
Continue	Increase penetration	Market development
New	Product development	Diversification

FIG. 2–5. Growth strategies.

rent marketplace is termed *product differentiation.* If a new market with current product/service offerings is to be addressed, the strategy is *market development. Diversification* is when new products/services are offered in new markets. These strategies will be discussed in greater depth in Chapter 6.

MARKETING AND WARFARE

One of the more interesting approaches in the development of marketing strategy has been the use of application of military ideology to the development of strategy and competition.[8] Two major principles have been suggested as the most important for both marketing and the conduct of war: (1) force and (2) the strength of a good defense (see Table 2–4). These concepts may be applied directly to today's business environment. First, in warfare it is generally accepted that to win a war or a battle, overwhelming force of arms in men or weapons should be applied. In banking these elements of force are financial resources and the bank's marketing efforts. Consider what has happened in the micro or personal computer market with the entry of the IBM Corporation into this marketplace. IBM's tremendous resources and its accepted position as the leader in the computer industry allowed it to gain more than 50 percent of the market for personal computers in only about two years. This market share was gained at the expense of many small competitors, as well as from such midsized competitors as Apple®. None of the competitors could even attempt to match the financial resources or the appeal of giant IBM. This, of course, is exactly the strategy that many smaller banks fear as the nation's larger money center banks attempt to expand their operations through interstate banking.

The second major concept is that of the strength of a sound defense. In other words, it is much easier to defend than attack. A firm

TABLE 2–4 Concepts of War and Marketing Strategy

1. Use overwhelming force to attack.
2. It is easier to defend than to attack.

with a sound marketing position is not easily dislodged by an attacker. The defender can be expected to know the marketplace and be able to respond effectively. Also, the defender already has an established position in the marketplace while the attacker does not. In general, today's banking market leaders can be expected to continue their domination. Only when competitors with vastly superior resources enter the fray will a sound defense be overcome. Defense usually means matching new products/services, prices, or distribution initiatives. A sound defense does not mean that competitive threats are ignored, but rather that they are met and overcome through aggressive action.

Unless one has overwhelming strength, the best strategy for gaining ground in such an environment is to use a flanking attack. The flanking strategy calls for the attacker to move into uncontested areas of the marketplace. The techniques of market-opportunity analysis and product/firm positioning are specifically designed to allow the firm to select target markets in such attractive areas and then design appropriate marketing approaches to capture this new battlefield. An excellent example of this technique in consumer marketing has been the strategy of Miller Beer. Before the application of a strong marketing orientation, Miller was decidedly an also-ran in the beer industry. Their research indicated that a significant market existed for a new type of beer that would have a lighter taste and lower calories. The key to implementation was that this new product had to be positioned as a true beer product for the core middle-class male market. With no initial competition in this market, Miller was able to outflank Budweiser and establish a formidable new position in the beer market with their Miller Lite product.

IMPLEMENTING STRATEGIC MARKETING PLANNING IN THE BANKING ORGANIZATION

Based on this introduction to the basic elements of strategic marketing planning and the tools of strategic planning, the next step is to integrate this strategic marketing orientation into the existing bank organization. We have already suggested the idea of the SBU as the key unit of analysis. However, products and services within the SBU must be analyzed separately, and marketing mixes must be developed for each target market. Further, strategic analysis will often be conducted at the bank level to provide coordination across multiple SBUs, divisions, or departments and a multitude of product/service offerings and markets.

As the level of analysis advances within the firm, the question of where the strategic marketing planning process should begin must be answered. The question of whether a top-down or bottom-up approach is best cannot be answered in a general sense. Each approach has advantages and disadvantages. Planning by the top individuals with responsibility for the unit of analysis provides a broad overview by individuals who should have the most knowledge concerning both the internal and the external environment. Further, one may simply contend that planning is what senior managers are hired and paid to do.

Proponents of a bottom-up approach take a somewhat different view. They contend that building on the knowledge of the individuals with direct contact with the marketing and firm environment provides a much better basis for planning. The individuals who will carry out the activities of the marketing plan should be in the best position to plan for their own area with guidance rather than direction from the top. In the 1970s, the top-down approach generally prevailed at the highest levels of many American corporations. Corporate-level planning groups were established which often simply passed down plans to the SBUs. This trend, however, appears to be reversing and, while corporate planning is always required, most marketing planning is being conducted at the SBU level or even at the product/service organization level within the constraints of overall company objectives.

After the question of who will be responsible for developing the strategic marketing plan and its implementation, the question of appropriate time frame must be answered. Plans may be developed for long-range planning, intermediate, and short-term activities. For most firms, long-range planning involves plans for five or ten years in the future, while short-term operational plans are for one year or less and are frequently more operational in nature. Actually, the idea of a strategic planning process provides a basis for integrating the long-range and short-term processes. Strategic planning is done in response to the environment and how it may be changing rather than any arbitrary period. The firm's strategic plan should look into the future as far as possible, but should be examined whenever either internal or external conditions change.

Writing in *Marketing Management, Analysis, Planning and Control,* Philip Kotler contends that the strategic marketing process actually involves at least eight different plans, including the overall corporate plan, the divisional plan, product line, product and brand plans, geographical market plans, specific product/market plans, and necessary functional plans for such things as advertising (see Table 2–5). Profes-

TABLE 2–5 Marketing Planning Hierarchy

Bank plan
Divisional/(SBU) plan
Product line plan
Geographical market plan
Specific product/market plans
Functional plans
a. Advertising
b. Sales
c. Product research & development
d. Distribution

Adapted from: Philip Kotler, *Marketing Planning*, 5th ed. (Englewood Cliffs, N.J.: Prentice-Hall, Inc., 1984), p. 280, used with permission.

sor Kotler suggests that the strategic marketing plan should be the keystone from which the above and other business plans emerge.[9]

SUMMARY

Throughout this chapter we have attempted to provide an overview of the strategic marketing process that will be covered in detail in the following chapters. It is important to remember that the basic concepts of strategic marketing can be stated simply: analysis of the environment, target market selection, and marketing mix determination and implementation. Of course, the driving factors are the needs and wants of the marketplace and the goals of the firm. Unfortunately, few banking organizations other than the industry leaders appear to have a formal marketing plan or, more importantly, to use a strategic marketing planning approach to the development of a growing and more profitable institution.

Two ideas need to be emphasized in any organization engaging in strategic marketing and beginning to use the tools of strategic planning. First, the tools are just tools; they cannot take the place of sound managerial judgment, no matter how complex or quantitative. Firms that have attempted to rely on the quantitative aspects of strategic planning and have ignored managerial skills and inputs generally have not achieved the best results. Second is the quote attributed to Dwight D. Eisenhower: "Plans are nothing: planning is everything." Managers frequently get so wrapped up in the details of planning and the rush to develop a plan for management that having a plan takes precedence over the content.

Planning is an ongoing, evolving process that should direct the bank toward its goals in a changing and perilous environment. In the next chapters we shall examine this process for the development of an effective bank marketing strategy.

Footnotes

[1]Peter Drucker, *Management: Tasks, Responsibilities, Practices* (New York: Harper and Row Publishers, 1974), pp. 121–129.

[2]This discussion is drawn from Benton E. Gup, *Guide to Strategic Planning* (New York: McGraw-Hill Book Company, 1980). Used with permission of the publishers.

[3]For an in-depth approach to the topic from a general viewpoint, see: Subhash C. Jain, *Marketing, Planning and Strategy* (Cincinnati: Southwestern Publishers, 1981); or Derek F. Abel and John S. Hammond, *Strategic Marketing Planning* (Englewood Cliffs, N.J.: Prentice-Hall, Inc., 1979).

[4]For a discussion of the SBU concept, see Bruce D. Henderson, *Henderson on Corporate Strategy* (Cambridge: Abt Books, 1979).

[5]John A. Weber, *Growth Opportunity Analysis* (Reston, VA.: Reston Publishing Company, Inc., 1976).

[6]For a discussion of formal models, see Howard W. Fox, "The Frontiers of Strategic Planning Intuition on Formal Models," *Management Review* (April 1981), pp. 8–14 and Robin Wensley, "Strategic Marketing: Betas Boxes or Basics," *Journal of Marketing,* Vol. 45 (Summer 1981), pp. 173–182.

[7]H. Igor Ansoff, "Strategies for Diversification," *Harvard Business Review* (September–October 1957), pp. 113–124.

[8]The marketing warfare concept is discussed in Philip Kotler and Ravi Singh, "Marketing Warfare in the 1980's," *Journal of Business Strategy,* Vol. 1 (Winter 1981) pp. 30–41.

[9]Philip Kotler, *Marketing Management, Analysis, Planning and Control* (Englewood Cliffs, N.J.: Prentice-Hall, Inc., 1984), p. 280.

3

marketing opportunity analysis

INTRODUCTION

The success of any business enterprise depends on that enterprise's ability to adapt to the change that is taking place in its relevant environment. This is a lesson that is demonstrated time after time when seemingly invulnerable companies are shaken from their lofty positions. What separates strong growth organizations from those that are mired in stagnation or destined for demise is an ability to comprehend environmental change and then to react in such a manner as to take advantage of this change.

Some systems analysts have gone so far as to postulate:

> In an information environment, those systems that process information most effectively are the ones most likely to be "selected for" survival.[1]

In this chapter we will first examine the difference between environmental opportunities and threats and then analyze the nature of the macroenvironment in which banking institutions operate. The chapter concludes with identifying a number of related tools for making sense out of the changing environment.

ENVIRONMENTAL THREATS VS. OPPORTUNITIES

A major fact about the environment is that it is constantly changing. Once organizational objectives have been formulated and agreed upon, the next step is to formulate plans by which those objectives can be accomplished within the context of the changing environment. Typically, most firms gather large amounts of data, both formally and informally, and try to understand how these changes will impact the firm.

One of the first steps in this process is to analyze this data in terms of whether the changes or forces constitute a threat or an opportunity to the firm.

> *An environmental threat will be considered as a challenge posed by an unfavorable trend or specific disturbance in the environment that would lead, in the absence of purposeful marketing action, to the stagnation or demise of a company, product or service.*[2]

Two components of a threat allow us to categorize the threat as major or minor. The first is the extent of the damage to the organization that the threat could cause if it were to become a reality. The second is the probability that the threat will be realized. Major threats then would be those changes or forces with significant potential negative impact on the bank that have a high likelihood of occurring. Minor threats, conversely, would include those that have a limited negative impact on bank operations and a low probability of occurrence. No company is free from environmental threats. The greater the number of threats facing a bank at any given time, the greater that bank's vulnerability. This points out the importance of and need for environmental monitoring.

> *Bank marketing opportunities are attractive arenas of relevant marketing action in which a particular company is likely to enjoy a differential advantage.*[3]

In a similar fashion to threats, marketing opportunities are a function of the dollar potential that such an opportunity represents to the bank and the probability that the bank will have some success if it addresses the opportunity.

One aspect of an environmental opportunity is the existence of specific, identifiable success requirements that must be satisfied in order for the organization to take advantage of the opportunity. The strategic marketing planner must identify these success requirements and match them with the distinctive competencies of his or her bank. A bank's distinctive competences are those resources, activities, or capabilities that the bank has or can do very well. They are, in other words, the strengths of the bank. When the distinctive competences of a bank match up with the success requirements of a given opportunity, the bank is in a posture to achieve a differential advantage. This difference provides the bank with an advantage over competition (Figure 3–1).

Consider the following example: A regional bank is considering expanding its services to take advantage of an increasingly large segment of the market which has purchased home computers. Banking by computer is a service that the strategic marketing planner believes to be an extremely profitable market. Initial studies indicate the following demographic profile for potential users of computer banking services:

- High income
- Highly educated
- Working wives
- White collar
- 1.5 children under 18
- 35–40 years old
- Multiple users of bank products
- Heavily concerned about convenience
- Technology oriented

The strategic marketing planner in considering reaching this segment has developed the following list of success requirements:

- Trained computer personnel
- Computer equipment capable of handling off-hour transactions
- Phone lines to accommodate transactions
- Promotional capability of reaching these people
- Software capabilities to handle multiple product transactions

The strategic planner now considers the distinctive competencies of his or her bank. These include:

- Strong personal service
- Innovative marketing operations
- Well-developed electronic transfer systems
- Strong, innovative image

On the basis of the bank's distinctive competencies, the strategic planner concludes that the bank has distinctive competencies in marketing promotion, personnel, and the communication system. The

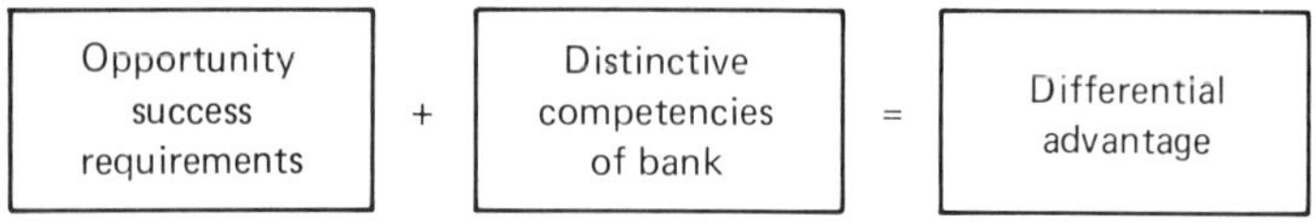

FIG. 3–1. Components of a differential advantage.

other factors of equipment and software can be acquired. Thus, in the opinion of the strategic marketing planner a differential advantage in computer banking can be achieved.

For many banks, early identification of environmental threats and competent planning and the execution of those plans can turn a threat into an opportunity. On the other hand, for those banks that ignore or inaccurately read the environmental changes, the unidentified threats can seriously retard the bank's growth and impinge upon its likelihood for survival.

ENVIRONMENTAL MONITORING

Environmental monitoring is *the activity of processing environmental information.* Strategic marketing planning must begin with an identification of the likely changes in the environment for several years into the future. This is no easy task but one which can be made somewhat less problematic with a better understanding of the relevant environment and its nature. Figure 3–2 depicts the different environments with which the strategic marketing planner and the organization must cope. Rather than viewing the environment as one amorphous field of forces, Figure 3–2 identifies the following individual but interactive environments: the technological environment, the legal/political environment, the social/cultural environment, the economic environment, the competitive environment, and the natural environment. Each of these environments is characterized as being outside of the ability of a single firm or individual to control. It is these two facts that make environmental monitoring such a problematic exercise for the strategic marketing planner. *Environmental monitoring, then, is a process by which the strategic marketing planner attempts to reduce the risk and uncertainty confronting his/her planning activities.*

What does the strategic marketing planner look for in each of the different environments? Table 3–1 divides the individual environments into specific but nonexhaustive dimensions which comprise the greater overall environment. Some or all of these dimensions will be relevant to the strategic marketing planner, depending upon the industry in

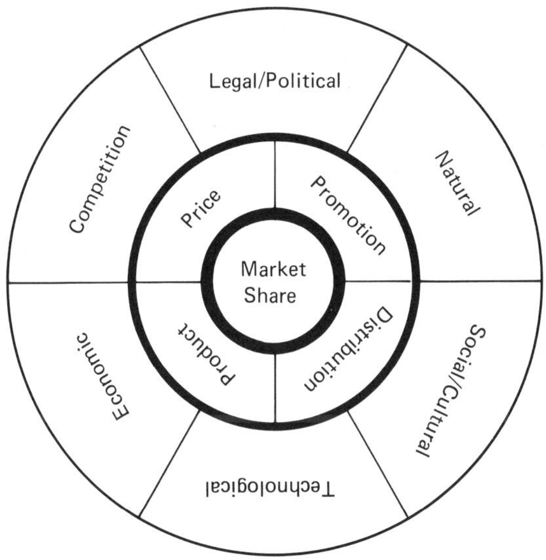

Adapted from; E. Jerome McCarthy and William D. Perreault, Jr., Basic Marketing, 8th ed. (Homewood, Illinois: Richard D. Irwin, 1984), p. 110.

FIG. 3–2. Uncontrollable environments affecting strategic market planning.

which (s)he operates. At this point it may be useful to examine some of these dimensions in terms of their potential and actual impact upon the banking industry.

Technological Environment

Some of the dimensions of the technological environment that have and will continue to have an impact on the banking industry are new inventions and innovations that will allow both bankers and consumers to more efficiently handle their money. Strategic planners in the banking industry must ask themselves, "What new inventions and innovations will evolve and how can we incorporate them into the banking business?"

The marketing planner should be concerned not only with the development of the innovation but also with its rate of diffusion. In other words, how quickly and readily will bankers be able to employ the new innovation into their normal repertoire of activities? The marketing planner must be concerned with how (s)he can make this adjustment easier and more commodious for the consumer.

The computer represents an interesting example of a technological impact on the banking industry. George Vojta, chief financial officer at

TABLE 3–1 Macroenvironmental Dimensions Impacting the Banking Industry

Technological Dimensions	*Social/Cultural Dimensions*	*Economic Dimensions*	*Legal Political Dimensions*	*Natural Dimensions*	*Competitive Dimensions*
Inventions	Value changes	Inflation	Legislation	Shortages: finite supply	Intensity of competition
Innovations	Demographic changes	Growth/recession	Bills introduced/pending	Allocation of resources	Number of competitors
Rate of diffusion	Changes in expectations	Interest rates	Regulation	Concern about environmental degradation	Size of competitors
Patents	Changing lifestyles	Use of controls	Agencies		Demand for products
Research and development	Social issues and groups	Monetary and fiscal policy	Rule-making process		Market share of competitors
		Dollar value and balance of payments	Enforcement procedures		Strength and weakness of competitors
		Discretionary income	Court cases		
		Industry growth	Intercompany		
			Government-initiated		
			Interpretations		
			Federal, state, & local		

Philbro-Solomon, Inc., sees technological change in information processing affecting the banking industry in three ways: (1) The size and potential for growth for an individual bank has increased. (2) It has expanded a bank's capacity to compete in the marketplace. (3) It is determining cost dynamics.[4]

These effects are readily seen in the strategies of a California money center, Western Community Money Center, a subsidiary of Community Financial Corporation. While not qualifying as a bank but rather chartered as a so-called thrift and loan, Western has put information technology to good use. At Western Community:

> There are no tellers, all transactions are conducted on ATMS, and customer representatives act as an on-premise sales force that sells check access accounts, passbook accounts, money market funds and other services. Owing to its small offices, cost controls and fully computerized operations, Western Community is able to offer interest rates to depositors that are higher by one percentage point than competitors', an advantage that is stressed in competitive advertising. This pricing strategy has been instrumental in the growth of this institution from deposits of $7.4 million in December 1981, its first full year, to $48.3 million at the end of 1982.[5]

The massive rate of technological change facing both the banking industry and the consumer is full of both opportunities and threats. Obsolescence of physical structures, communication systems, organizational structures, and product and service offerings are realities that the banking industry is facing and will continue to face in the future. How individual banks face these changes in technology will have a significant impact not only on the revenue side of their operations but, perhaps equally significant, on the cost side. Of course, both will manifest themselves where it most counts, on the bottom line.

Cultural/Social Environment

One of the more difficult environments to deal with is the cultural/social environment. In the last ten to twenty years the changes in this environment have been significant and, to some firms, extremely harmful.

One of the more notable changes has been in the demographic dimension of this environment (Table 3–2). We have seen and will continue to see, according to some experts, a worldwide explosion in population growth. A doubling of the world's population is currently

TABLE 3–2 Changing Demographic Patterns

Birth Rates per 1000 16.2 (1980)
Trend: Increasing

Median Age 30 (1980)
Trend: Increasing
Major increases are found in the
25–44 age bracket (29.7%)
65 and over (24.5%)

New Family Households
Single adult households account for about 20% of all households.
Trend: Increasing

Residence Location
General trend: From urban to suburban with a trickling back to urban by disenchanted suburbanites.

Income
Median household income $22,500 (1980).
Trend: Increasing.

Condensed from: E.J. McCarthy and W.D. Perreault, *Basic Marketing*, 8th ed. (Homewood, Ill.: Richard D. Irwin, 1984), pp. 167–191, used with permission.

taking place every 33 years. Contrary to this worldwide trend is a slowdown in the birth rate of the United States. This is accompanied by a general aging of the U.S. population, a shrinking of the size of the American family, a postponing of marriage, higher divorce rate, and more working wives. Add to this a rise in what are called "nonfamily households," a better-educated populace, and an America on the move, and one gets a feel for the nature of the change affecting America today.

Demographic changes can have a significant impact upon the way in which a bank does business. Product changes must reflect the changing needs of a graying America. As the population increases in age, family sizes shrink, and working wives become the rule rather than the exception, new investment products and services must be developed to accommodate the increase in the discretionary incomes Americans enjoy. New distribution methods have to evolve to account for the changing lifestyle and living patterns caused by movements to the suburbs in some locations and the reverse trend in others. Promotional messages have changed to reach new audiences, the working wife, for example. Finally, a trend in upscale banking with increased services and amenities is seen as some banks react to the rising affluence of certain market segments.

A related changing dimension of this environment is seen in the changing value structure of Americans. Table 3–3 isolates some of these changes. In general, Americans have become more focused on the self, more concerned with their immediate gratification, more willing to enjoy the easy life, less formal, and more willing to embrace a more secular orientation.

These changing values manifest themselves in consumer relationships with themselves, with others, with society in general, and with institutions. A decline in the trust of large institutions, banks, for example, which has been reinforced by increased bank closings, newspaper references to Black Tuesday, rumors of the potential collapse of banking investments, frauds or illegalities such as the laundering of huge amounts of cash linked to drug traffickers have marked consumer attitudes toward banking. Add to this the frustration of generally rising interest rates which have foreclosed many from the opportunity of owning their own home, and one can readily see potential threats to the banking industry as a whole. These threats will pose challenges to banks to identify new ways in which to rebuild or reinforce consumer confidence in banking and their product/service offerings. Banks will have to find new ways to insure that their messages do not unintentionally mislead the consumer and the banking industry. Finally, banks will have to woo a number of different publics to convince them of their reliability, good intentions, and importance in the daily operation of the economy. These are all potential marketing threats/opportunities resulting from social/cultural changes challenging the strategic marketing planner.

Economic Environment

An examination of the various economic dimensions in Table 3–1 shows a number of factors with which bankers are perhaps most familiar. Such dimensions as interest rates, inflation, balance of payments, and discretionary income are all very familiar to bankers.

An overall assessment of the changing nature of the economic environment over the last ten to fifteen years would indicate several changes which, for the most part, promise to continue. These changes include a slowdown in the growth of real income, continued inflationary pressure, actual increases in the rate of inflation, a changing pattern in the structure and relationship of debt and savings, and perhaps most notably from a marketing perspective, changing consumer expenditure/savings patterns.

All of these changes represent varying intensities of threat and opportunity for different banks. Continued inflationary pressure can impact consumer perceptions with respect to economic stability and can be translated into different patterns of activity. For example, inflation can result in consumers' seeking new ways to save money. Insur-

TABLE 3–3 Changing American Value Structures: Five Major Social Trends and Their Implications for Consumer Behavior

1. Psychology of affluence trends

The first group are traceable to the effects of "psychology of affluence." That is, they manifest themselves among consumers who feel sufficiently free from economic insecurity to seek the fulfillment of other needs.

Trend toward physical self-enhancement, spending more time, effort and money on improving one's physical appearance; the things people do to enhance their looks.

Trend toward personalization, expressing one's individuality through products, possessions and new life-styles. The need to be "a little bit different" from other people.

Trend toward physical health and well-being, the level of concern with one's health, diet and what people do to take better care of themselves.

Trend toward new forms of materialism, the new symbols and extent of deemphasis on money and material possessions.

Trend toward personal creativity, the growing conviction that being "creative" is not confined to the artist. Each man can be creative in his own way, as expressed through a wide variety of activities, hobbies and new uses of leisure time.

Trend toward meaningful work, the spread of the demand for work that is challenging and meaningful over and above how well it pays.

2. Antifunctionalism trends

A second group of trends underscores a major new force in American life—the quest for excitement, sensation, stimulation, and meaning to counteract the practical and mundane routines of everyday life. There is a reaction among certain groups in the population against the drabness of modern life, giving rise to a many-faceted hunger that reaches beyond the practical.

Trend toward the "new romanticism," the desire to restore romance, mystery and adventure to modern life.

Trend toward novelty and change, the search for constant change, novelty, new experience, reaction against sameness and habit.

Trend toward beauty to one's daily surroundings, the stress on beauty in the home and the things people do and buy to achieve it.

Trend toward sensuousness, placing greater emphasis on a total sensory experience—touching, feeling, smelling, and psychedelic phenomena. A moving away from the purely linear, logical and visual.

Trend toward mysticism, the search for new modes of spiritual experience and beliefs, as typified by the growing interest in astrology.

Trend toward introspection, an enhanced need for self-understanding and life experiences in contrast to automatic conformity to external pressures and expectations.

3. Reaction against complexity trends

A third and important group of trends cluster around the theme of reaction against the complexity of modern life. We find more and more people changing their habits and life styles in reaction to crowded conditions, complicated products, unresponsive institutions, restrictive regulations and information overloads.

Trend toward life simplification, the turning away from complicated products, services and ways of life.

Trend toward return to nature, rejection of the artificial, the "chemical," the man-made improvements on nature; the adoption of more "natural" ways of dressing, eating and living.

Trend toward increased ethnicity, finding new satisfactions and identifications in foods, dress, customs and life styles of various ethnic groups such as Black,

TABLE 3–3 Continued

Italian, Irish, Polish, Jewish, German.

Trend toward increased community involvement, increasing affiliation with local, community and neighborhood activities. Greater involvement in local groups.

Trend toward greater reliance on technology versus tradition, distrust of tradition and reputation that is based on age and experience, due to the swift tempo of change. Greater confidence in science and technology.

Trend away from bigness, the departure from the belief that "big" necessarily means "good," beginning to manifest itself with respect to "big" brands, "big" stores.

4. Trends that move away from puritan values

The fourth group of trends measure the penetration of certain new values at the expense of the traditional puritanical values.

Trend toward pleasure for its own sake, putting pleasure before duty; changing life styles and what that means for product usage and communication.

Trend toward blurring of the sexes, moving away from traditional distinctions between men and women and the role each should play in marriage, work and other walks of life.

Trend toward living in the present, straying from traditional beliefs in planning, saving, and living for the future.

Trend toward more liberal sexual attitudes, the relaxation of sexual prohibitions and the devaluation of "virtue" in the traditional sense, among women.

Trend toward acceptance of stimulants and drugs, greater acceptance of artificial agents (legal and illegal) for mood change, stimulation and relaxation as opposed to the view that these should be accomplished by strength of character alone.

Trend toward relaxation of self-improvement standards, the inclination to stop working as hard at self-improvement; letting yourself be whatever you are.

Trend toward individual religions, rejection of institutionalized religions and the substitution of more personalized forms of religious experience, characterized by the emergence of numerous small and more intimate religious sects and cults.

5. Trends related to child-centeredness

Children born into the child-centered homes of the 40s and 50s are now in their twenties and teens. Although the consequences of this orientation are difficult to isolate, research indicates that a few important personality characteristics and values associated with them can be identified. These provide the source for the final group of trends—trends which have a direct impact on marketing as well as on other facets of modern life.

Trend toward greater tolerance of chaos and disorder, less need for schedules, routines, plans, regular shopping and purchasing, tolerance of less order and cleanliness in the home, less regular eating and entertaining patterns.

Trend toward challenge to authority, less automatic acceptance of the authority and "correctness" of public figures, institutions, and established brands.

Trend toward rejection of hypocrisy, less acceptance of sham, exaggeration, indirection, and misleading language.

Trend toward female careerism, belief that homemaking is not sufficient as the sole source of fulfillment and that more challenging and productive work for the woman is needed.

Trend toward familism, renewed faith in the belief that the essential life satisfactions stem from activities centering on the immediate family unit rather than on "outside" sources such as work and community affairs.

Source: Reprinted from *The Marketing News,* 4:7, May 1971, and 4:8, first of June 1971, published by the American Marketing Association.

ance companies have capitalized on this change and have developed new insurance products different from traditional offerings. These new products are designed to pay higher rates on the savings portion while providing the traditional insurance function. Non-bank competition can successfully win over traditional banking customers, and many banks will face increasing threats in some or all of their markets. Banks will have to respond with new products and services that can compete with their newfound rivals for consumer savings. Some banks have found it profitable to do away with their consumer services and instead concentrate on commercial accounts. Others have instituted a policy whereby only consumers with accounts greater than a certain dollar amount will be serviced by tellers. All others will have to use machines to effect their banking transactions.

One area where banks have responded well is reacting to consumer willingness to borrow and their need for new housing. Rising interest rates have precluded many Americans from realizing their dream of owning their own home. Long considered an American "right," many Americans have been forced to live in apartments until some time in the future when interest rates become affordable. Many banks, through creative and imaginative thinking, have devised new loan programs which allow consumers to buy into the housing market earlier. Such loan programs as adjustable rate mortgages, graduated payment mortgages, GEMS, (Graduated Equity Mortgages) and the like are beginning to dominate the more traditional fixed-rate loan types.

A potential threat posed by such new and, in some cases, nontraditional loan programs is the lack of understanding many consumers have with respect to how these programs really work and what they will mean to them two or three years in the future. Many consumers concentrate only on the fact that they can now obtain their loan and obtain it at what appears to be a very good rate. They discount, for example, the effects of a rate acceleration on their cash flow in the future. What could be a good deal now may turn into a nightmare later as the consumer, incapable of meeting payments, is forced to give up his or her home and dream. The potential villain in this situation is the bank that made the loan and may now have to foreclose. Further, this situation represents the kind which can invite outside scrutiny by consumer watchdogs who can make and have made issues of this type *causes célèbres* at the expense of the bank. The strategic marketing planner must anticipate not only the changing dimensions of a given environment but also the positive and negative implications of these changes on different publics. Consider the California coalition which has filed a complaint seeking to restructure California's bank laws. The basis for the action is found in the deregulation which has freed state banks to concentrate on the wealthy, high-balance, and profitable segments at the expense of less wealthy and less profitable market segments. To date no action has been taken, but the negative publicity raised by such accusations is definitely not in the best interests of the banking industry.

Competitive Environment

As in all other environments, the structure and nature of competition are in perpetual change. This is markedly noticeable in the banking industry, which in recent years has exhibited a revolutionary capacity for change. How strategic marketing planners in the banking industry respond to this changing competitive environment will greatly determine the probability of survival for individual banks.

Consider the assessment of the changing competitive environment facing bankers made by Philip M. Durbrow, vice president and senior associate of Landor Associates, a marketing firm based in San Francisco:

> Independent bankers face challenges from two sources today: large banking institutions and such "new financial supermarkets" as Shearson/American Express. Alone, no independent can hope to match the giants' special skills, equipment, facilities, or promotion budgets to compete on anything like an equal basis.[6]

Competition for bank customers in a number of different product/service markets is coming from nontraditional quarters as well. A general tendency toward diversification among American industry is resulting in potentially significant challenges for the banking industry. One notable new competitor is the mammoth retail institution, Sears & Roebuck. Their acquisition of Dean Witter poses some significant challenges to certain product lines such as money market accounts, checking accounts, and discount brokerage services offered by banks. The competitive advantage may even be in Sears's corner. Their understanding of marketing, specifically distribution, may put competitors in the bank industry at a disadvantage. Sears has forged its aggressive marketing skills in the heat of retail competition, something that banks have been relatively sheltered from in the past. Other retailers watching Sears's success and a general trend toward deregulation of the banking industry, whether legislated or *de facto,* promises to bring other nontraditional competition into the arena. Already K-Mart and JC Penney have entered the industry. K-Mart has begun selling certificates of deposit and money market funds accounts in three of their stores in Florida.

As if the threat of new competition were not enough, deregulation and changes in state banking laws promise an increase in the intensity of extant competition as the larger banks plot interstate acquisitions and buyouts.

Consider the aggressive marketing activities of Citicorp, which is using "industrial banks" to extend its reach into Utah, Nebraska, Minnesota, Kansas, and Colorado. Other large holding companies competing in this way include Manufacturers Hanover Corp. and BankAmerica Corporation.

The future of middle-size to smaller banks will remain in the balance and will depend on how they react to the changing nature of competition in this changing industry. Who will be the competition, how they will compete, and where they will compete are just a few of the general questions strategic marketing planners must begin to contemplate.

Natural Environment

While many strategic marketing planners in the banking industry may tend to discount the impact that changes in the natural environment can have on their own operations, to do so is a failure to recognize the relationships that exist among and between the various environments. For example, one of the major contributions to the rising inflation rate we experienced in the early 1970s was from the resource shortage in the oil industry. Rising oil costs have driven up the cost of living and have forced consumers to seek new savings and investment opportunities that can keep pace with this rising cost of living.

Another area where some banks have found themselves capable of capitalizing on a change in the natural environment is in the public's growing concern over scarce resources and pollution. By aligning themselves on the side of environmental preservation, some banks have been able to promote a good guy image which promises to pay dividends far into the future.

Although the natural environment and consequent changes in it may have less direct impact on the banking industry than, say, the steel or oil industries, repercussions from these types of environmental changes can pose both thorny challenges and promising opportunities for strategic marketing planners in the banking industry.

Legal/Political Environment

One of the more topical and immediate environmental changes that is taking place and promises to impact the banking industry in a number of significant ways are the changes occurring in the legal/political environment. This complex environment is affected by two major sources of change, those laws and regulations promulgated at the federal level and those at the state level. Both categories of laws and regulations exert a major influence on the banking industry and define the parameters within which the strategic marketing planner must work.

Some of the more notable federal laws and regulations are shown in Table 3–4. This legislation encompasses a wide range of banking activity, defining the way in which banks can compete, with whom

TABLE 3–4 Some Notable Bank Legislation Affecting Bank Marketing

1. McFadden Act of 1927 (as modified in 1933)	Allowed national banks to add branches outside home office city, subject to restrictions as to location imposed by the law of the state on state banks.
2. Banking Act of 1933 (Glass-Steagall Act)	Prohibited banks from paying interest on demand deposits and required banks to divest themselves of many underwriting activities.
3. Securities Exchange Act of 1934 (amended)	Empowered Federal Reserve System. Board of Governors to set initial margin requirements.
4. Bank Holding Company Act of 1956	Attempted to control the process by which bank holding companies acquire additional bankers and engage in nonbanking activities.
5. Bank Merger Act of 1960	Established special procedures and criteria to govern bank mergers.
6. Amended BHC (Bank Holding Company) 1966	Placed more emphasis on the competitive effects criterion for allowance of a merger.
7. Interest Rate Act of 1966	Set maximum interest rates banks and savings and loans could pay on savings deposits.
8. Federal Consumer Credit Protection Act	Required lenders to disclose credit terms in standardized ways.
9. Amended Bank Holding Company Act of 1956	Closed the OBHC (One Bank Holding Company) loopholes.
10. Consumer Leasing Act of 1976	Requires lenders to disclose additional information to potential consumer leasees.
11. Equal Credit Opportunity Act of 1977	Prohibits discrimination in the granting of credit and contains certain consumer-protection provisions.
12. International Banking Act of 1978.	Set comprehensive rules for foreign bankers operating in the U.S.

they can compete, and even which legislation bears upon the internal operations of the bank, setting margin requirements, interest levels, types of products, and so on. Probably no other industry has been as strongly regulated as the banking industry.

After 40 years of regulation the trend today is toward reducing regulation, with deregulation not an impossibility. What this will mean for the overall industry and the individual banks that comprise it is still unknown. What is predictable, however, is that deregulation, even in a less complete form than some proponents argue, will require significant adjustments on the part of the bank. Moreover, if consumer response to deregulation is negative, the banking industry can expect to see a relatively quick reverse of this trend.

The challenge to the strategic marketing planner in the banking industry, as well as in any other industry, is to keep abreast of changes in this important environment and, if possible, anticipate changing legislation and regulation. The strategic marketing planner cannot intelligently plan without a comprehensive and strong knowledge of the major laws and regulations affecting the scope of his or her actions. This task is made even more complex when one considers the additional regulation existing at the state level.

AN INTERACTING SCENARIO

Earlier we emphasized that these individual environments were interacting in nature. This interaction poses an even greater challenge to the strategic marketing planner to identify and trace the effect of a change in one environment throughout other environments. While a change in one environment may not appear to pose a threat, it is the interaction with other environments that can cause a number of problems. Consider an earlier example.

The early 1970s was a time when Americans felt the impact of rising gasoline prices. At first consideration these rising prices posed no threat to the banking industry. Consumers continued to buy gasoline, albeit in lesser quantities than before, but high levels of consumption continued as Americans realized their individual dependence on the automobile. As gasoline began to take up more and more of the personal incomes of consumers, it also began to increase the costs of production of virtually all industrial and consumer products. These increased costs were translated into higher prices, which in turn fueled the inflationary increase in the economic sector. Moreover, higher gas prices pressured many consumers to sell their older, less fuel-efficient cars, and buy new higher mileage cars. Demand for new car loans increased. But as prices spiraled higher and higher, consumers began to buy less and instead sought better returns for their scarcer dollars. Interest rates began to creep up as more consumers, companies, and the government vied for credit. Producers began to produce less, factory capacity increased, unemployment began to climb, and income dropped. Consumers were purchasing less and the scenario was complete. Newspapers even made it official by proclaiming that the United States was indeed in a recession.

Consumers changed certain consumption values, most notably those manifesting themselves in conservation of gasoline. Government reinforced this change by promulgating a federal speed limit of 55 miles per hour. Builders were precluded from building because of the high interest rates, which at one point reached about twenty percent. The economy turned to the banks for help out of this economic and social malaise. The banking industry responded with new loan programs and policies designed to help builders and homeowners. Government and regulators created a new Individual Retirement Account through which individuals could save on a tax-sheltered basis. The number of ways in which big, medium, and small banks were affected by these turns of events was significant, as were the different ways in which individual banks responded to them. Thus, a change in the natural environment caused ramifications which were felt throughout all other environments and ultimately impacted even the banking industry. The interrelatedness of these different environments means that no industry is immune to environmental change. Even those industries which were felt to be recession-proof felt the impact of change. That this interrelatedness will grow even greater is a strong probability. Moreover, the change felt in one environment is likely to spread even more quickly and with greater impact as our world becomes even more tightly connected.

ANALYTICAL TOOLS FOR ENVIRONMENTAL MONITORING

As indicated earlier, the task facing the strategic marketing planner with respect to environmental monitoring is extremely complex. While perfect prediction of environmental change is quite impossible, the goal is to understand how potential changes will either positively or negatively impact the organization. Several tools or frameworks exist to help make this difficult task somewhat easier. It should be understood that these are only tools; the imagination and insight of the planner using them is ultimately that which determines how "good" the prediction is.

Vulnerability Analysis

A related tool for assessing environmental impact on the operations of an organization is vulnerability analysis. While more of a qualitative framework, vulnerability analysis attempts to identify the nature of the threats to the organization posed by an individual environmental change. An example of vulnerability analysis is shown in Table 3–5. The analysis lists relevant environmental dimensions and the threats these dimensions pose. For example, this strategic planner feels that value changes in the form of frustration with large institutions is manifesting itself in a lack of consumer confidence in banking in general. Similarly, the recently discovered gas reserves represent a strong positive impact on various aspects of banking operations. To the extent that the bank becomes dependent upon this gas money, it becomes extremely vulnerable to the depletion of these gas reserves. On the other hand, the planner feels that in this case the growing elderly market represents no threat to the bank.

TABLE 3–5 Hypothetical Impact Matrix

TRENDS	*Demand Deposits*	*Time Deposits*	*Trust Accounts*	*Home Mortgage*	*IRA Accounts*	*TOTALS* +	–
Increased competition from large northeastern banks	−3	−3	0	0	−3	0	9
Growing elderly demographic segment	+4	+1	+4	−3	−2	9	5
Regional outmigration	−2	−2	−1	−3	−1	0	9
EVENTS							
Establishment of credit union	−2	−2	0	−1	0	0	5
Natural gas discovery	0	+2	+4	0	+3	9	0
Repeal of McFadden Act	−2	−2	0	0	−3	0	7
CONSTITUENTS' DEMANDS							
Lower interest rates	0	0	0	−2	0		
Boycott of XYZ Company	−3	−3	0	0	0	0	6
TOTALS +	4	3	8	0	3		
–	12	12	1	9	9		

Adapted from: Benton E. Gup, *Guide to Strategic Planning* (New York: McGraw-Hill, 1980), pp. 47–62.

The purpose of vulnerability analysis is to identify those environmental dimensions which pose a threat to the bank's operations before the threat becomes critical. While perhaps not as sophisticated as other assessment frameworks, vulnerability analysis represents a good place to start the monitoring procedure. Its major advantage is that it forces the planner to consider changing environmental forces and their potentially harmful effect upon the bank. In doing so, threats to the successful operation of the bank can be detected early so that strategic responses can be made in time to deflect any of the harmful effects of the change.

Impact Matrices

As we indicated before in our discussion of threats and opportunities, there are two components which determine the severity or the potential of either a threat or an opportunity. These are the degree of impact that the potential threat or opportunity has on the firm and the probability of its occurrence. Impact matrices utilize these two components to determine the consequence of a potential environmental change on a firm. Figure 3–3 shows how these two components can be incorporated into a framework for analyzing environmental impact.

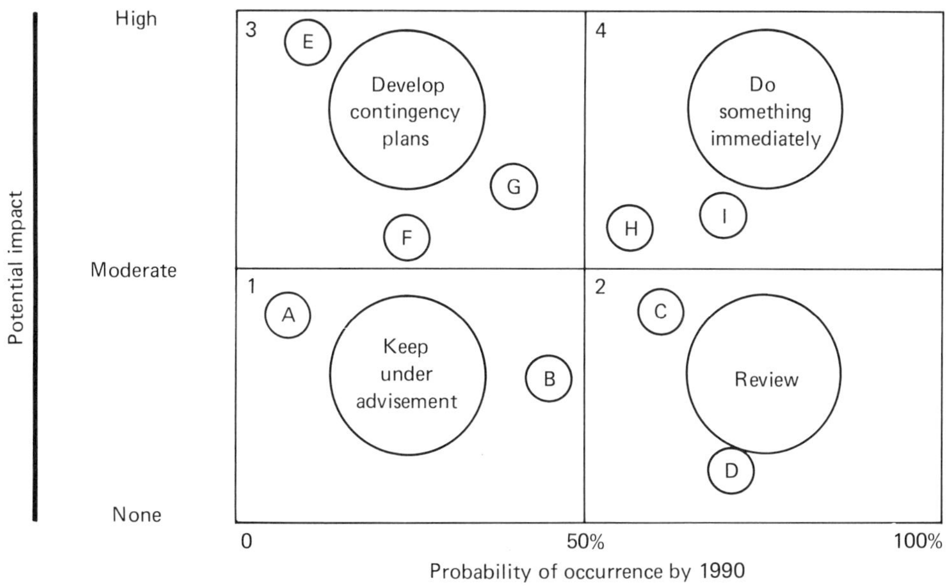

Adapted from: Benton E. Gup, Guide to Strategic Planning (New York: McGraw-Hill, 1980), pp. 47-62.

FIG. 3–3. Environmental impact matrix.

The vertical axis breaks the potential impact component down into two ranges: none to moderate and moderate to catastrophic. These are subjective designations that can reflect the values of either the planner or the bank or both. The horizontal axis represents the probability of the potential impact occurring. Again, in many instances this may involve a subjective estimate on the part of the planner. The juxtaposition of these two components permits the separation of the matrix into four quadrants: those impacts that promise to have zero to moderate impact on the firm and have a lower probability of occurring, those with zero to moderate impact potential and a higher probability of occurrence, those impacts with moderate to catastrophic potential and a lower probability of happening, and those impacts with moderate to catastrophic potential and a higher probability of taking place. By mapping onto this matrix potential environmental changes (designated by the small lettered circles) the planner now has a way to prioritize strategic planning to deal with the different types of anticipated changes. Quadrant 1, the low impact/low probability quadrant into which changes A and B have been mapped, suggests a "monitor the development" posture on the part of the planner. A and B represent the types of environmental change that if they move in either direction will call for a more actionable and vigilant posture.

Quadrant 2, the low impact/high probability quadrant, suggests a "review" posture. Changes like C and D represent those types of changes which might potentiate their impact on the bank, calling for a more actionable stance on the part of management.

Quadrant 3, high impact/low probability, represents those types of changes that if they were to occur would have heavy impacts on the bank. At present, while the potential impact is judged to be great, they have a relatively low probability of occurring and consequently merit a "contingency planning" status. Should changes E and F increase in probability, contingency plans should already be in place on which to act.

Finally, Quadrant 4, the high impact/high probability quadrant, is indicative of those changes which require immediate action. They may have resulted from changes increasing in probability or impact, in which case they should be somewhat anticipated, or they may be new changes which have just developed. The former situation is more likely if the organization has an ongoing policy and procedure for environmental monitoring.

The impact matrix provides a framework for sorting out different environmental changes and recognizes that not all changes are of consequence to the bank. Once sorted out, the strategic marketing planner can examine each of the anticipated changes and develop necessary policies, procedures, and plans for coping with either the threats or opportunities that they represent.

Table 3–6 represents a somewhat more sophisticated impact matrix in that it provides a framework for assessing specific environmental impacts on the company's product/service mix. External factors are arrayed on the vertical axis and are categorized as to whether they are trends, one-time events, or demands of different constituents that the bank must pay attention to. For example, trends may include the proliferation of home computers or increasing competition from nonbanks. Events might include legislation which would change the way banks do business, such as the repeal of the McFadden Act. Demands of constituents may include the obvious demands of stockholders in the bank as well as other interested parties, such as the community in which the bank is located.

Across the top of the matrix are arrayed different products/services that comprise the bank's product/service mix. These would include time deposits, demand deposits, IRAs, trust accounts, correspondent accounts, and the like. With this framework, the strategic marketing planner can now score the impact of individual trends, events, or demands on the different products/services that the bank offers. Scores can range from +5 to −5. A score of +5 indicates a strong positive impact on an individual product/service (an opportunity), while a −5 indicates a strong negative impact (a threat). A score of zero (0) indicates no impact at all. The numbers in between +5 and −5 represent varying degrees of positive and negative impact. By adding up the numbers in each of the cells horizontally, the planner can then assess

TABLE 3–6 Vulnerability of Demand For Personal Trust Accounts by Year 1990

Environmental Factors	*Threats*
Value Changes	Consumer loss of confidence in banking institutions
Resource Discovery of natural gas	Depletion of resources
Competition No competitors	Entry of new competition
Legal Changing regulations concerning trust accounting procedures	Change in exemption rules
Customer Growing size of elderly market	No threat

Adapted from: Benton E. Gup, *Guide to Strategic Planning* (New York: McGraw-Hill, 1980), pp. 47–62.

the overall impact of a given trend, event, or demand across all product/service offerings. Again, if positive numbers outweigh the negative totals, the trend, event, or demand represents an overall opportunity. If, on balance, the totals are negative, the impact is a potential threat.

In a similar fashion, by adding the numbers vertically, the strategic marketing planner can assess the overall anticipated environmental changes on an individual product/service offering. Perhaps of greatest importance to the planner is the ability to identify and assess the impact of various trends, events, and demands on individual and specific product/service offerings. This can be done by examining the cell corresponding to a given environmental change and specific product/service offering.

A brief example may prove beneficial in further explicating the matrix. Consider the impact matrix in Table 3–5. The strategic marketing planner of this bank has identified several trends, events, and demands which may impact the bank's product/service offerings in different ways. Across the top of the matrix are the different product/service offerings which may be affected. The strategic marketing planner has assessed the degree and type of impact that each trend, event, and demand may have upon each of the product/service offerings. These assessments are shown in the different cells of the matrix. The planner feels that the increased competition from large northeastern money centers will have a significant negative impact on demand deposits, time deposits, and the number of IRA accounts handled by his or her bank. This increased competition, however, should have no impact on trust business or mortgage loans. On the other hand, the possible opening of a credit union at the local university promises to have a somewhat negative impact on demand deposits, time deposits, and, to a lesser extent, on home mortgage loans. No impact is anticipated on trust accounts or IRAs. This analysis is made for all trends, events, and constituent demands. On balance, then, it would appear that the anticipated environmental changes pose a threat to demand deposits (12 negative to 4 positive), time deposits (12 negative to 3 positive), home mortgages (9 negative to 0 positive), and IRA accounts (9 negative to 3 positive). The only product/service offering of the bank that appears unthreatened by these environmental changes and indeed seems to be facing a significant opportunity is the trust account business (1 negative to 8 positive).

Upon further analysis, the planner discovers that certain trends, events, and demands pose greater opportunity than threat. For example, the growing elderly demographic segment appears to have a significant positive impact on both demand accounts and time accounts. Such an assessment may reflect the need for the elderly to remain more liquid in their holdings. In addition, the growing elderly segment has greater need for trust services as estate planning becomes more important to them. This accounts for the relatively high positive impact assessment (4). Notice, however, that the strategic marketing planner feels that this demographic trend poses a threat to the home mortgage business as well as IRAs. Of course, these assessments reflect the subjectivity of the individual planner and focus on the relevant trends, events, and constituent demands facing an individual bank.

The value of such an analysis is found in the practice of identifying dimensions in the changing environments that can have an impact, both positive and negative, on the bank. In addition, it forces the planner to assess the degree to which such changes may impact the operations of the bank. Finally, such an analysis can offer insights into possible responses to these different changes. To the extent that the planner or planning committee is capable of anticipating these changes, strategic responses to them can be more reasoned and effective.

Environmental Forecasts

The aforementioned frameworks are useful tools for analyzing changing environmental conditions. The specificity of these assessments can be increased through the use of several different forecasting techniques. The use of these techniques is governed by such factors as the length of the forecast, the nature and amount of data that are required to use the technique, the amount of dollar resources the organization chooses to spend on making the forecast, and the sophistication of the forecaster and the user of the forecasts. Table 3–7 lists and briefly explains some of the more frequently used forecasting techniques. As

TABLE 3–7 Forecasting Methods

Jury of Executive Opinion

This method consists of combining and averaging top executives' views concerning the item to be forecast. Generally, the company brings together executives from areas such as sales, production, finance, purchasing, and staff operations in order to get the benefit of broad experience and opinion. Often staff groups supply background information to the members of the executive group. This approach has the advantages that forecasts can be provided easily and quickly without elaborate statistics and that a range of management viewpoints can be considered. Also, it requires fewer data than mathematical techniques do.

Time Series Analysis

Several different methods belong in this category. The most common are exponential smoothing methods and moving average methods. The general approach is to identify a pattern representing a combination of trend, seasonal,

TABLE 3–7 Continued

and cyclical factors based on historical data for that variable. That pattern is then smoothed to eliminate the effect of random fluctuations and extrapolated into the future to provide a forecast.

Regression Analysis

Regression analysis assumes that the variable to be forecast (the dependent variable) can be predicted on the basis of the value of one or more independent variables. For example, if company sales were the variable to be forecast, they might be dependent on time, the economy, or sales of major customer industries. Regression analysis is a statistical technique that fits the specified model to the historical data available. One of its major attractions is that, as independent variables take on new values, the dependent variable will also change. Thus it goes beyond simple time series extrapolations and bases a forecast on a causal relationship.

Econometric Models

This approach to forecasting uses a system of simultaneous regression equations that take into account the interaction between various segments of the economy and/or areas of corporate activity. Often, companies use the results of national or regional econometric models as a major portion of a corporate econometric model. While such models are useful in forecasting, their major use tends to be in answering "What if?" questions. These models allow management to investigate the impact of various changes in the environment and in major segments of the company's business on the performance and sales of the company.

Customer Expectations

Like the method of sales force composite and the jury of executive opinion, this technique seeks to combine managerial judgments in arriving at forecasts. However, rather than using judgments from those strictly within the company, this method seeks to use customers' expectations of their needs and requirements as the basis for forecasting. This is often done through selected surveys administered by a corporate staff group, or it may be done by the sales force gathering information from selected customers. While it has the advantage of recognizing changes in customer expectations at a fairly early date, this technique is difficult to use in markets where customers are numerous or not easily identified. Much of the forecasting done by market research groups is based on variations of the customer expectation approach.

Box-Jenkins Method

This technique is a highly sophisticated approach to time series forecasting. It seeks to identify patterns in the historical values of a time series and then to extrapolate those patterns into the future. It has the advantage of being able to handle a wide range of time series patterns and to provide statistics indicating the level of accuracy that can be expected in a given situation. However, it is extremely complex and somewhat difficult to understand.

Steven C. Wheelwright and Darrel G. Clarke, "Corporate Forecasting Promise and Reality," *Harvard Business Review*, November-December (1976), p. 52.

can be seen, these techniques vary in complexity. The user should be governed by considerations of accuracy. All of the techniques are predicated on the assumption that what has happened in the past will continue to occur in the future. Accordingly, massive shifts in environmental factors cannot, in any likelihood, be predicted. However, assuming relatively stable environmental conditions, the use of one or more of these techniques may benefit the planner by removing some of the subjectivity from assessment of environmental change and by providing a level of specificity to the assessment that otherwise might be lacking.

SUMMARY

This chapter has focused on the importance and need for environmental monitoring. Successful organizations exhibit an ability to adjust to change. In an environment characterized by constant change, such as that facing the banking industry, identifying change and its potential impact on the bank will comprise a major portion of the strategic planning activity. In making these assessments the strategic marketing planner must identify those changes, assess their impact on banking operations, and develop plans to adapt the bank to those changes, both positive and negative. As we mentioned at the outset of this chapter, this is a particularly difficult task. Several tools have been identified to help the marketing planner. However, the ingenuity and creativity of the planners are the driving forces behind the use of these tools and the ongoing process of environmental monitoring.

Footnotes

[1]Noel McGinnis, "Networking: A Way to Manage our Changing World," *The Futurist* (June 1984), p. 9.

[2]Philip Kotler, *Marketing Management* (Englewood Cliffs, N.J.: Prentice-Hall, Inc., 1980), p. 99.

[3]Ibid., p. 99.

[4]George J. Vojta, "New Competition and Its Implications for Banking," *The Magazine of Bank Administration,* Vol. 9, No. 7 (1983), p. 36.

[5]Steven Mintz, "Banking on Marketing," *Sales and Marketing Management* (June 6, 1983), p. 48.

[6]Philip M. Durbrow, "Marketing Alliances: The Key to Community Bank Survival," *ABA Banking Journal,* Vol. 25, No. 5 (1983), p. 216.

4

target market selection

INTRODUCTION

One of the more recent additions to the strategic weaponry of the marketing planner is the concept and practice of market segmentation. Market segmentation begins by focusing not only on the product/service offering, but on the unsatisfied need and want opportunities that exist in the marketplace. Accordingly, it is an important aspect of the marketing concept discussed in Chapter 1. This chapter will focus on the idea and practice of market segmentation, the requirements for effective segmentation, and a number of different segmentation approaches that have achieved potential application within the banking industry.

MARKET SEGMENTATION

> *Market segmentation is the recognition that a market is composed of different buyers who have different responses to marketing offerings. No one approach to the market will satisfy all buyers. Each segment represents a somewhat different opportunity for the organization. In its most fundamental form, market segmentation recognizes that a company or its product/service offering cannot be all things to everyone.*[1]

The idea behind the use of market segmentation is that each segment is more homogeneous with respect to certain important marketing characteristics than is the overall market. The homogeneity of each segment allows for a better understanding of the wants and needs and general responses to existent and potential competitive marketing offerings.

The astute strategic marketing planner realizes that the most effective approach to the marketplace lies in analyzing the different wants and needs of the diverse market segments and then designing a marketing mix that will, as closely as possible, satisfy those wants and needs. This approach is at the heart of a sound marketing strategy. The success of most product/service offerings hinges upon identifying the right segment(s) and then targeting the marketing program to reach this segment(s).

This recognition of differing opportunities and the growing importance of segmentation to the banking industry is conveyed in the following:

> Like Citibank, most financial organizations are services that target particular consumer groups. Bankers are no "longer looking at the mass customer base," says Chase Manhattan's John Groesbeck, retail ad manager, who learned advertising at BBDO, Inc. and other ad agencies over 10 years, producing ads for such packaged-goods marketers as Sterling Drug and R. J. Reynold's Hawaiian Punch. Instead, he says, bankers are beginning to assess the "different potential and different needs" within that customer base, and are finding certain groups more profitable.[2]

SEGMENTATION STRATEGIES

There are, of course, a number of variations on this basic segmentation theme. These variations or segmentation strategies are diagramatically presented in Figure 4–1. One variation is a market aggregation strategy. This is shown in Figure 4–1(a). The nature of the demand for some product/service offerings is such that more finely tuned segmentation strategies are not necessary. Either the market is undifferentiated in its response patterns, or the nature of the product/service offering is such that it elicits no variance in response. While few product/service offerings fall into this category, some, like clothespins, do.

Another approach is to focus on one single segment [Figure 4–1(b)]. A market, keep in mind, is composed of people with a willingness and an ability to buy. While the ability-to-buy criterion is easily satisfied, people's willingness to buy may be influenced by a number of product or product-related features. Accordingly, many market seg-

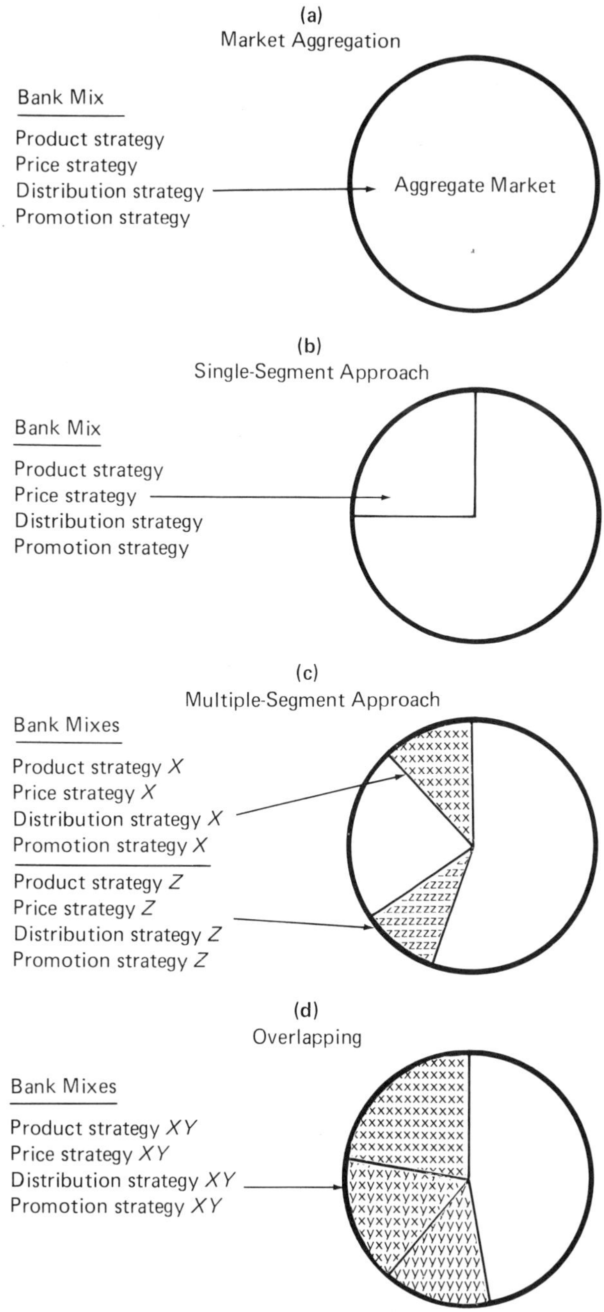

FIG. 4–1. Segmentation strategies. (a) Market aggregation; (b) single-segment approach; (c) multiple-segment approach; (d) overlapping.

ments may exist. The firm faces the decision as to which segment it will attempt to satisfy. Kentucky Fried Chicken operates in the fast-food market. Several product/service offerings are possible and many exist. Kentucky Fried Chicken, after attempting to compete in several different markets—ribs, for example—has chosen to retrench and focus on one single market. This strategy is conveyed in their campaign theme, "We do chicken right."

Some firms see the different opportunities in different segments and choose to offer product/service variations to more than one market segment [Figure 4–1(c)]. Such a multiple segmentation strategy has been extremely successful for some firms. Procter and Gamble, for example, markets a number of brands of laundry detergent. Their philosophy is to occupy effectively as many market segments in the detergent market as possible. This approach has been very successful for P&G.

Finally, some firms see overlapping opportunities existing in two different markets [Figure 4–1(d)]. By developing a product/service offering that can combine the want- and need-satisfying capabilities of two segments into one, a combining strategy is possible. Aqua-fresh toothpaste represents such a strategic approach in the toothpaste market. Aqua-fresh combines a decay prevention benefit with a clean-breath, white-teeth benefit feature. Such an approach has proven very effective and has resulted in an increase in market share for Aqua-fresh at the expense of Crest and some of the other toothpastes.

BENEFITS OF SEGMENTATION

Why should a firm, or for that matter, a bank practice market segmentation? Table 4–1 offers several answers to this question.

Remember that an overall market is typically composed of different segments, each of which represents different opportunities. Given a situation of unlimited resources, a bank may choose to compete in each segment. However, the likelihood that a bank has the resources to do this is low. Consequently, the strategic marketing planner must decide which segment(s) offer(s) the best opportunity to the bank. *In other words, market segmentation allows the strategic marketing planner to prioritize segments, and consequently opportunities, to achieve a differential advantage in the marketplace.*

TABLE 4–1 Benefits of Segmentation
Prioritize opportunities
Spot opportunities
Fine-tune product/service offerings
Fine-tune budgets

Second, a segmentation approach allows the strategic marketing planner a better vantage point for spotting opportunities and comparing them. Unsatisfied wants and needs represent opportunities. *A segmentation approach allows the strategic marketing planner a closer view of a smaller market aggregate and allows the planner to be in a better position to spot opportunities.*

Third, once the opportunities have been identified, *a segmentation strategy provides an orientation whereby product/service offerings can be fine-tuned to satisfy the wants and needs of the segment.* By "fine-tuned" we mean that products can be developed to match more closely consumer needs, usage patterns, and lifestyles. These wants and needs are typically more homogeneous in a market segment than they are in an overall market made up of numerous segments. Consequently, market segmentation provides a higher level of resolution for developing the necessary components of the marketing mix which will be targeted to that segment.

Finally, the budgeting task which supports the marketing effort in a particular segment can be more clearly identified and monitored. Allocation of resources can be done more effectively to accomplish specific goals.

REQUIREMENTS FOR EFFECTIVE SEGMENTATION

As the reader will soon find out, and as anyone who has been involved in the segmenting of markets will attest, there are many ways to segment a market. However, not all ways represent effective segmentation approaches. To be useful to the strategic marketing planner, segments must be measurable, accessible, substantial, and defensible (Table 4–2).

First, segments must be measurable. *Measurability* refers to the degree to which both the size of the segment and the purchasing power of the segment can be measured. Certain variables may be very effective in aggregating individuals into market segments, but, if the strategic market planner cannot measure this aggregation or the resulting purchasing power of the segment, no accurate assessment of its profitability can be made. A segment which would be intuitively attractive yet not possible to measure would be the market segment composed of "liberated women." While liberated women may actually exhibit certain similar beliefs and values which are translated in some types of bank-

TABLE 4–2 Requirements for Effective Segmentation

Measurability
Accessibility
Substantiality
Defensibility

ing behavior and preferences, it is impossible to measure the size of this market. Liberated women cannot readily be identified. A more realistic approach, and one which captures much of this psychological dimension, is the segment composed of working women.

Accessibility refers to the degree to which the segments can be effectively reached and served. This is an extremely important consideration in segmenting markets. Once the market segment has been delineated, the strategic planner has to consider whether or not the product/service can be distributed to this segment and if it can be communicated with. The segment that is not accessible by distribution and communication channels is of little value to the bank. Segmentation variables should be chosen on the basis of their ability to provide a segmentation approach which allows acessibility.

Substantiality represents the degree to which the resulting segments are large enough to be profitable. While the trend is to greater and greater segmentation, the danger is that these finely tuned segments will not be profitable enough for marketing effort. Of course, substantiality is relative. Smaller banks, for example, may find certain segments profitable, while some of their larger competitors may be foreclosed from competing in the same segments because of the lower profitability.

One last criterion to consider when segmenting markets is the *defensibility* of the segment. It is a well-known economic fact that profitability will attract competition. The question arises as to whether or not the bank that cultivated the segment in the first place can defend the segment, or will it lose market share and investment to larger and more capable competitors? Defensibility depends upon the resources necessary to manage a segment and the willingness of bank management to embrace the marketing concept. Profitable segments represent the single most valuable asset to any organization and must be defended against competitive intrusion, which, in a highly competitive arena such as the banking industry, is inevitable.

BASES FOR SEGMENTING BANK MARKETS

Before we identify and discuss some of the more tried and true segmentation approaches, it is important to note that segmentation is a creative process—creative, in that it involves a search for those variables which produce the most effective bases for dividing up an aggregate heterogeneous market into smaller, more homogeneous segments.

Figure 4–2 depicts some of the more often used marketing-oriented segmentation variables. In this section we review the different bases, both customer- and situation-related variables.

Customer-Related Variables

Customer-related segmentation variables are composed of two subsets of variables. These are demographic variables and psychographic variables. Both of these subsets of variables have found effective use in strategic marketing planning.

Demographic Variables. Demographic segmentation represents the most often used segmentation approach in marketing. Two reasons seem to explain this high reliance on demographic variables. First, consumer wants and product/service usage rates are associated with demographic groupings. Second, demographic variables are perhaps the most easily operationalized in a segmentation approach.

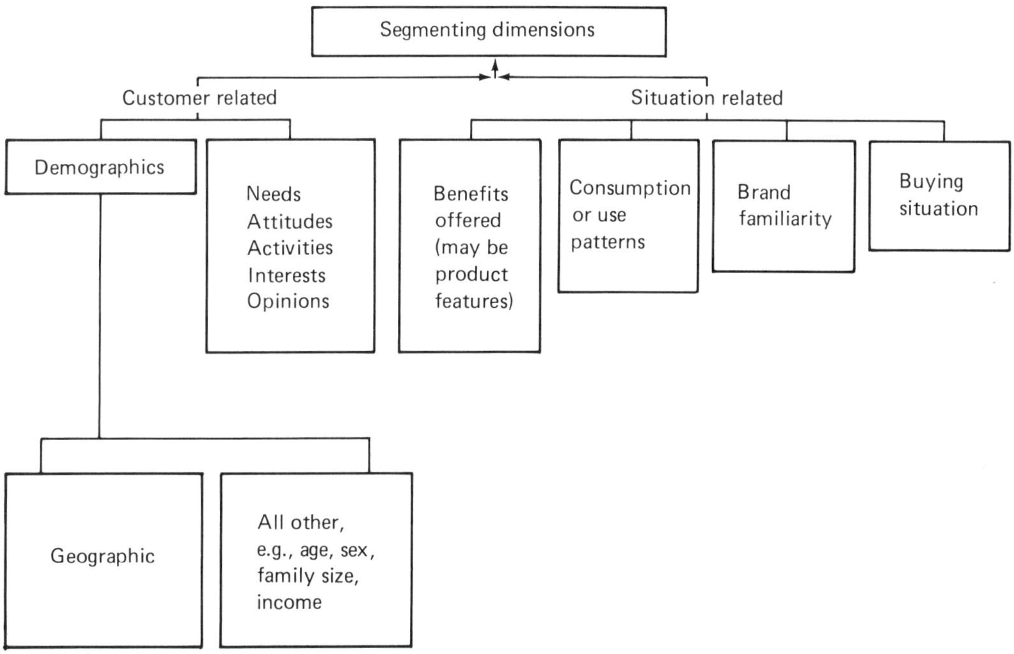

E. Jerome McCarthy, Andrew A. Brogowicz, and John F. Grashof, Teacher's Manual for use with Basic Marketing (Homewood, Illinois: Richard D. Irwin, Inc., 1978).

FIG. 4–2. Bases for market segmentation.

Table 4–3 shows the most commonly used demographic variables. Banks have found certain demographic variables particularly useful in segmenting the market for various services. For example, such variables as age, income, education, family life cycle, and sex have been effective segmenters of such markets as the savings market, the mortgage loan market, and the market for trust services. Once segmented into more homogeneous aggregates, each segment can be studied as to the best way of developing a product/service offering more closely suited to the needs and wants of that segment. Moreover, the strategic planner has also provided a way of better understanding what vehicles to use in communicating to these segments.

Demographic segmentation has proven quite useful in the banking industry. Banking services have traditionally been linked to an individual's age, which in turn is linked to his or her income and stage in the family life cycle.

For example, in a study conducted by one of the authors, it was found that heavy users of ATMs (Automated Teller Machines) were typically younger (below 30), were more highly educated, tended to hold white-collar jobs, had lower family incomes (in part explainable

TABLE 4–3 Demographic Segmenters

Demographic	
Age	Infant; under 6; 6–11; 12–17; 18–24; 25–34; 35–49; 50–64; 65 and over
Sex	Male, female
Family size	1–2, 3–4, 5+
Family life cycle	Young, single; young, married, no children; young, married, youngest child under 6; young, married, youngest child 6 or over; older, married, with children; older, married, no children under 18; older, single; other
Income	Under \$5000; \$5000–\$7999; \$8000–\$9999; \$10,000–\$14,999; \$15,000–\$24,999; \$25,000 and over
Occupation	Professional and technical; managers, officials, and proprietors; clerical; sales; craftsmen, foremen; operatives; farmers; retired; students; housewives; unemployed
Education	Grade school or less; some high school; graduated from high school; some college; college graduate
Religion	Catholic; protestant; Jewish; other
Race	White; Negro; oriental; other
Nationality	American, British, French, German, etc.
Social class	Lower-lower; upper-lower; lower-middle; upper-middle; lower-upper; upper-upper

Adapted from: Philip Kotler, *Marketing Management* (Englewood Cliffs, N.J.: Prentice-Hall, Inc., 1980), p. 198.

by their single marital status), were highly mobile, and rented their homes. Light users, on the other hand, tended to be older, to have less education, to have higher incomes (most were married with working wives), to have low mobility, and to own their own homes. While results may vary from market to market, demographic differences in product use can generally be found.

Another example is income. Affluent customers generate the most profits, and to reach them, banks are assembling standard bank products, such as checking accounts, savings accounts, money market accounts, credit card services, and others into financial service packages. Provident National Bank, Philadelphia, for instance, has a Circle of Green program, an "integrated financial management account for the *upscale customer*" (italics added).

On the other hand, low-income segments should not be ignored. The low-income market is significant; some estimates put it around 50 percent of all households that account for about one-third of annual savings. Retailers have found this group to be extremely profitable, and there is no reason why some banks may not specialize by targeting this market.

Changing demographic profiles in some markets, however, suggest that the use of demographics alone may be providing the strategic planner with only part of the picture. Increasing affluence, a blurring of social class delineations, and a host of psychographic variables threaten to make reliance solely on demographic variables dangerous. For example, one observer of retail banking agrees that personal trust bankers must seek out the other affluent segment, one he refers to as the "new money" segment. This "new money" segment differs significantly from the "old money" segment in several key psychographic variables, yet represents a lucrative potential market for the marketing of personal trust services. These psychographic differences between "new money" and "old money" may provide a basis for segmenting trust markets.

The danger arises in that the competition may better understand segment structures in the marketplace and may be better able to respond to the wants and needs of these structures. This is particularly true when one considers that implicit in the use of demographic variables is a functional view of the product/service offering. In other words, demographic variables may obscure some more deep-seated motivating factor that can positively influence a bank's approach to a particular market.

Regardless of the potency of other segmentation variables, demographics will remain exceptionally important for one major reason. All media are sold on the basis of demographic breakdowns. Publishers and producers all describe their audiences in terms of demographic variables. Consequently, strategic marketing planners in the banking industry, in order to know how to reach and communicate with specific market segments, must also know about the demographic composition of the segment. This permits a matching of individuals with an ability and a willingness to buy with a bank that has a product/service offering to tell them about.

Psychographic Variables. A more recent addition to the practice of segmentation is the use of psychographic variables. Typically, we refer to needs, attitudes, and life-style variables (activities, interests, and opinions, also called AIO variables) as comprising the category of psychographic variables.

While demographic segmentation can describe what the market looks like, psychographic segmentation can peer into these segments and provide the strategic marketing planner with a more intimate and personal view of the consumers who comprise the market. To see the higher level of resolution a psychographic profile of a market segment offers the strategic marketing planner, consider the results of a study shown in Table 4–4. This is a life-style study conducted by the Schlitz Brewing Company. It focuses on the life-style characteristics of heavy drinkers of beer. Notice how the life-style characteristics vary between heavy beer drinkers, nondrinkers, and light drinkers of beer. Notice too the profile of the heavy beer drinker that the strategic marketing planner is capable of developing from this analysis. According to the research, the male heavy consumer of beer is self-indulgent, enjoys himself, and is willing to take risks. He rejects responsibility and is impulsive. He is a sports nut who has a physical orientation. He tends to reject old-fashioned social institutions and moral guidelines. Finally, he has a very masculine view.

This analysis enabled Schlitz to develop their, "You Only Go Round Once—You've Got To Grab All The Gusto You Can" campaign. Such a segmentation approach provides the basis for a better understanding of the market segment. It provides a higher resolution picture of the segment than does the more typical demographic analysis. Lifestyle segmentation provides a platform for designing communication messages that actually speak to the segment in terms that the segment can understand. This extra communication capability is one of the strong points of psychographic segmentation.

One bank which recognizes the value of psychographics is the Citizens Bank of Windsor, Missouri. Their branch located in Tightwad, Missouri, has been officially renamed the "Tightwad Bank" in an effort to appeal to those penny-pinching segments both locally and nationally.

TABLE 4-4 Psychographic Profile of Male Beer Drinkers

Male Beer Drinkers	*Percentage of Agreement*		
	Nonusers	*Light Users*	*Heavy Users*
He is self-indulgent, enjoys himself, and likes risks			
I like to play poker	18	37	41
I like to take chances	27	32	44
I would rather spend a quiet evening at home than go out to a party	67	53	44
If I had my way, I would own a convertible	7	11	15
I smoke too much	29	40	42
If I had to choose I would rather have a color TV than a new refrigerator	25	33	38
He rejects responsibility and is a bit impulsive			
I like to work on community projects	24	18	14
I have helped collect money for the Red Cross or United Way	41	32	24
I'm not very good at saving money	20	29	38
I find myself checking prices, even for small items	51	42	40
He likes sports and has a physical orientation			
I would like to be a pro football player	10	15	21
I like bowling	32	36	42
I usually read the sports page	47	48	59
I would do better than average in a fist fight	17	26	32
I like war stories	33	37	45
He rejects old-fashioned institutions and moral guidelines			
I go to church regularly	57	37	31
Movies should be censored	67	46	43
I have old-fashioned tastes and habits	69	56	48
There is too much emphasis on sex today	71	59	53
. . . and has a very masculine view			
Beer is a real man's drink	9	16	44
Playboy is one of my favorite magazines	11	21	28
I am a girl watcher	33	47	54
Men should not do the dishes	18	26	38
Men are smarter than women	22	27	31

Reprinted from: Joseph T. Plummer, "Life-Style and Advertising: Case Studies," in Fred C. Allvine, ed., *Combined Proceedings 1971 Spring and Fall Conferences*, American Marketing Association (Chicago: American Marketing Association, 1971), p. 294.

Situation-Related Variables

As the name implies, these variables were derived from the recognition that different situations may provide a basis for segmenting markets. Indeed, some of these variables have proved very powerful, especially when used in conjunction with customer-related variables. Situation-related variables typically produce the following types of segmentation approaches: benefit, usage, brand familiarity, and buying situation.

Benefit Variables. As we have mentioned before, a product is a bundle of benefits. Consumers buy products for the benefits that the products are capable of rendering, and benefit segmentation recognizes that certain segments of the overall market buy products for certain benefits. By understanding what benefits a segment wants from a product/service offering, the strategic marketing planner can develop a marketing mix that is capable of providing these benefits.

Perhaps the best example of benefit segmentation is provided by a study of the toothpaste market as presented in Table 4–5. Four different segments have been identified—the sensory segment, the sociables, the worriers, and the independent segment. Each segment buys particular brands of toothpaste to provide specific benefits. For example, the "sensory" segment buys toothpastes which provide flavor, the "sociables" buy toothpaste that promises bright teeth, the "worriers" want tooth decay prevention, and the "independents" look for price benefits. Several other behavioral and product attributes of the different segments are also shown.

These benefits may become the central theme in promotional campaigns. Consider advertisements for toothpastes aimed at the sociable segment. Typically these ads concentrate on one theme, fresh breath

TABLE 4–5 Benefit Segments of Toothpaste Market

Segment Name	*The Sensory Segment*	*The Sociables*	*The Worriers*	*The Independent Segment*
Principal benefit sought	Flavor, product appearance	Brightness of teeth	Decay prevention	Price
Demographic strengths	Children	Teens, young people	Large families	Men
Special behavioral characteristics	Users of spearmint flavored toothpaste	Smokers	Heavy users	Heavy users
Brands favored	Colgate, Stripe	Macleans Plus White Ultra Brite	Crest	Sale brands
Personality characteristics	High self-involvement	High sociability	Hypochondriasis	Autonomy
Life-style characteristics	Hedonist	Active	Conservative	Value-oriented

Adapted from: Russell I. Haley, "Benefit Segmentation: A Decision Oriented Research Tool," *Journal of Marketing*, Vol. 32, No. 33, pp. 30–35.

and white teeth. Not one mention of decay prevention is made in these commercials. The reason is that this segment is primarily concerned with the former attributes at the expense of the latter.

Some bank marketers have become aware of benefit segmentation and are beginning to realize that people desire a number of benefits from their association with a bank. In a study conducted by one of the authors a number of benefit segments emerged. These are shown in Table 4–6. Within the particular market studied the research uncovered "status seekers," "traditionalists," a convenience segment, and the "shoppers." Rough percentage estimates of each segment are shown, as are the banks preferred and related demographic and psychographic characteristics. Customers may seek prestige, security, convenience, and deals. On the basis of the dimensions of these segments, the banks in the study could develop marketing mixes to reach and attract like customers. Finally, some want all these attributes from their bank. This has led some bank marketers to establish personal banking centers with such names as "Group One," "The President's Club," the "Circle

TABLE 4–6 Market Segmentation Based on Banking Benefits Sought

Segment Name	*Status Seekers*	*Traditionalists*	*Convenience*	*Shopper*
Principal benefits(s) sought	Prestige Recognition Modern bank Easy credit	Full service Good reputation Investment-oriented Loans	Full service Convenience stressed (hours, location) Friendly service	High interest in savings Low-interest loans
Banks(s) preferred	Bank 1	Banks 2 & 4	Bank 3	Bank 5
Related demographic characteristics	Young Upwardly mobile High discretionary income Renter White collar	Long time in area Middle-aged Family White/nonwhite-collar Home owner Average to high level of income with low discretionary income	Broad cross section No real differences	Older than average Home owner Wealthier than average
Related life-style characteristics	Credit-oriented Risk taker Hedonic	Saver Future-oriented Value-oriented	Same as "traditionalist" Active	Careful Cautious Prudent
Approximate size of segment	20%	35%	30%	15%

of Green," "Money Power," or "Select Banking Group." These special services that provide high customer service with a high degree of prestige are aimed at what is often called the upscale segment. The multidimensional nature of most bank's product/service offerings presents splendid opportunity for segmenting markets on a benefit basis. Such an approach begins with an understanding that a product or service contains much more than its basic functional characteristics.

Consumption or Usage Patterns. An interesting phenomenon has been discovered with respect to users of most consumer products. Certain common demographic, psychographic, and media preferences have been associated with heavy users of products. Just as with the case of heavy beer drinkers cited earlier, many heavy users of bank products have distinctive characteristics in common. This means that many markets can be segmented according to whether consumers are light, medium, or heavy users of a product/service offering. Notice that while the principal segmentation variable is usage, these categorizations have little strategic meaning unless these are developed in terms of their demographic and psychographic profiles as well as other meaningful marketing variables.

Usage patterns for banking products/services offer rich insights into who these individuals are. Consider the results of a study conducted by one of the authors. Customers of a bank were broken down into whether they were light, medium, or heavy users of different services that the bank offered. In some cases, service usage did not show significant differences. However, in other service offerings some interesting profiles were developed. For example, this study indicated that heavy users of checking accounts were also big buyers of certificates of deposit and big buyers of individual retirement accounts. On the other hand, this segment was a low purchaser of installment loans and credit in general and constituted one of the most profitable segments that the bank had targeted. Demographically, this latter segment was the same segment described earlier—older, less educated, higher incomes, etc. This analysis enabled the bank to develop a special banking package aimed at this particular segment. Again, markets will more than likely vary with respect to their composition and responses. However, usage patterns still tend to be robust segmenters, especially when coupled with other segmentation and descriptive variables.

A variant on the usage variable is seen in a study reported by Taylor and Bergiel.[3] The researchers found two distinct banking segments: the segment that used only one financial institution and that which used multiple institutions. Analysis showed that these two segments differed in product usages and demographics. Accordingly, media choices and product packages could be fine-tuned to reach these two segments.

Product Familiarity. This segmenting dimension does not appear to be as powerful as some of the others mentioned. It is included primarily for completeness but may prove useful under certain market conditions. The idea behind using product familiarity is that loyal and familiar customers can be profiled and these profiles can be extended to noncustomers in the hope of being able to increase market share by attracting similar noncustomers. Thus bankers would focus on their most loyal customers, develop demographic and/or psychographic profiles, and target similar "types" for marketing effort. The upscale customer, because of his or her high profitability, would be a candidate for such an approach.

Buying Situation. One final segmenting variable is that employing user status. Banks have traditionally utilized segmentation approaches which recognize the consumer market and the commercial market. The problem is that these segments are too broad in most markets to be of value in targeting efforts. As initial delineators they are very valuable, since responses to bank product/service offerings are likely to vary depending on whether the customer is a consumer or a business. Secondary analyses of these markets based on usage rates, benefits, and/or some of the other segmentation variables mentioned earlier can provide a very potent basis for a strong segmentation policy.

SEGMENTATION DEVICES

There are a number of different devices available to the strategic marketing planner for segmenting markets. These devices vary in sophistication from the relatively simple user-friendly approach to the more complicated computer-based statistical algorithms. In this section we will take a brief look at a couple of the more usable devices, beginning with a simple segmentation approach.

User-Friendly Segmentation

There are seven steps in this segmentation approach (Table 4–7). What makes user-friendly segmentation most attractive is its ease of understanding and its low cost relative to the other devices.

TABLE 4–7 User-Friendly Segmentation

1. Select market area to be considered.
2. List all banking needs of customers (consumer and commercial).
3. Group needs by demographic characteristics.
4. Remove common dimensions.
5. Name each segment.
6. Summarize what is known about each segment.
7. Link each segment to "uncommon dimensions" identified in step 4.

Adapted from: E. Jerome McCarthy and William D. Perreault, Jr., *Basic Marketing*, 8th ed. (Homewood, Illinois: Richard D. Irwin, 1984, pp. 260–264.

This approach begins by selecting the market area to be considered. For most small- or medium-size banks this will be the surrounding geographic area which the bank serves. Depending on state banking laws with respect to holding companies, branch banking, and multiple bank ownership, the geographic areas can be either constrained or expansive.

The second step is to make a list of all the banking needs that customers (either consumer or commercial) may have. This need list may vary by geographic market area. This is important to keep in mind. Banking needs of a New Yorker, for example, will probably vary from those of customers in Ohio. Be sure also to include potential customers because, while they may not be present users of your services, they may be future users if you can satisfy their banking needs.

The third step is to group these needs by demographic characteristics. The relevant demographics to use are listed in Figure 4–2 in an earlier section of this chapter. Such variables as income, age, sex, and stage of the family life cycle may provide insight into possible segmenting dimensions.

Once this is done, remove all of the common dimensions, because these are not determinant dimensions. In other words, those demographic characteristics that are common to all or most of the needs do not offer a segmenting basis, because all potential segments possess those characteristics. The common dimensions are called *qualifying dimensions* and may provide backup information on the ultimate segmenting dimensions.

Fifth, tentatively name each segment. Naming the segment will bring it back to the customer base that you are trying to segment.

Sixth, determine and summarize what is known about each of the segments that you have identified. At this time you may want to add additional dimensions to your list. Moreover, this process may lead to splitting some of the original segments into smaller segments, providing a higher level of resolution.

Finally, link each segment to the qualifying variables identified in step four and any customer-related variables such as other product/service offerings that the segment uses. This will allow for the development of packages and cross-selling strategies in addition to the development of promotional programs to reach them. Also, the linkage to other customer-related variables such as services already used may provide guidelines for pricing individual and bundled services.

An example will show how "user-friendly segmentation" can produce actionable segments. The marketing manager for a medium-sized bank with 33 branches in 20 different locations was considering a new branch in a new location. The new market area differed from the ones the bank had previously entered. Whereas the established branches tended to be primarily rural, the new branch was to be located in an urban market.

The marketing manager, on the basis of his or her personal experience, "brain-stormed" the following list of banking needs of potential customers (step 2).

BANKING NEEDS

- Financial security
- Convenience
- Quick, friendly service
- Low loan rates
- Hassle-free loan process
- Personal service
- Investment counseling
- Retirement advice
- Credit availability
- Ample parking
- High interest savings instruments
- Prestige service

Using a life-cycle/demographic approach, the manager grouped these needs into the following initial segments (step 3).

- *A young, single* banking customer would want a bank which would provide financial security for his or her money, convenience, quick, friendly service, credit, convenient hours, prestige service, and ample parking.

- *A family with teenage children* would have banking needs such as financial security for their money, convenience, low loan rates for their prospective college students, retirement advice, credit availability, high interest savings investments, ample parking, and convenient hours.
- *A retired couple* would be looking for a bank which could provide financial security for their money, personal service, retirement advice, investment counseling, convenience, and ample parking.

The marketing manager reviewed common needs (step 4) of ample parking, convenience, convenient hours, and financial security for customers' money.

This allowed the marketing manager to tentatively name each of the segments (step 5) and to summarize what was known about each segment (step 6).

In addition, each segment was linked to banking products that satisfied the banking needs identified in step 2. This is shown in Table 4–8.

On the basis of this analysis the marketing manager identified four basic segments. By consulting census data it was determined that singles constituted about 10 percent of the market, loan seekers about 15 percent, full-nesters, and empty-nesters, about 40 percent. This is indicative of a maturing market where full-nesters and empty-nesters account for about 75 percent of potential banking customers. Consequently, the bank's product mix emphasized student loans, IRAs, NOW accounts, money market funds, retirement counseling, and user-friendly service with a strong personal touch.

Clustering Programs

Most market research in the development of market segments will utilize one or more of a number of computer-based clustering techniques. Although an in-depth discussion of the numeric analysis involved is beyond the scope of this book, it is possible to examine the application of this technology to bank marketing. Each of the techniques has the ability of putting people, objects, and products into different groups according to common dimensions. For this reason, clustering techniques are particularly well suited to market segmentation problems.

An example of a quick clustering application will illustrate the use of clustering techniques in general to the problem of market segmenta-

TABLE 4–8 User-Friendly Segments

Segment Name	*People Characteristics*	*Product/Need Characteristics*
Swingers	Young, single, high discretionary income, image conscious, renter, job-centered, new to area (10% of market)	Quick service Prestige service Credit card
Loan seekers	Newly married, young, family oriented, wife works, renter but looking to buy, saver (15% of market)	Investment advice Mortgage loans Personal loans NOW accounts Money market funds
Full-nesters	Married couple, teenage children, own home, not much discretionary income (35% of market)	IRAs Personal loans Student loans Credit cards NOW accounts Money market funds
Empty-nesters	Older, no children, retired or close to retirement, home owner, long-time resident, good discretionary income (40% of market)	Retirement counseling Personal service Check cashing Check depositing Convenient

tion. In a study of attitudes toward banks in a metropolitan area the following steps were followed:

1. Each attitude response for each bank was correlated with other attitude responses for other banks in the study. The correlation matrix is shown in Table 4–9. This matrix indicates the similarity in attitude perceptions of the different banks.
2. Underlining the highest entry in each column indicates the bank which is most highly related to the other bank.
3. Choose the highest underlined value in the table. In this case it would be .64. This corresponds to bank 2 and bank 8. These two banks form the first cluster.
4. Now read across row 2 and row 8. If another bank in these rows is underlined (bank 10, row 2), include that bank in the first cluster. Notice that no other bank is underlined in row 8, so cluster 1 is defined.
5. This procedure is repeated after banks 2, 8, and 10 are omitted. When all the banks are classified, the clustering procedure is

TABLE 4–9 Correlations among Bank Images in Terms of General Attitude

	Bank I	*Bank II*	*Bank III*	*Bank IV*	*Bank V*	*Bank VI*	*Bank VII*	*Bank VIII*	*Bank IX*	*Bank X*	*Bank XI*
Bank 1	–	.006	.358	.382	.325	.289	.262	.108	.368	.178	.404
Bank 2	.006	–	.157	.157	.088	.134	.161	.130	.640	.184	.200
Bank 3	.358	.157	–	.337	.375	.343	.340	.057	.322	.256	.336
Bank 4	.382	.088	.337	–	.430	.452	.326	.053	.357	.266	.337
Bank 5	.325	.134	.375	.430	–	.445	.484	.170	.432	.325	.281
Bank 6	.289	.161	.343	.452	.445	–	.358	.119	.454	.177	.322
Bank 7	.262	.130	.340	.326	.484	.358	–	.110	.393	.300	.230
Bank 8	.108	.640	.057	.053	.170	.119	.110	–	.349	.301	.180
Bank 9	.368	.184	.322	.357	.432	.454	.393	.349	–	.238	.307
Bank 10	.178	.360	.256	.266	.325	.177	.300	.201	.238	–	.208
Bank 11	.404	.200	.336	.337	.281	.322	.230	.180	.307	.208	–

Adapted from: Joseph M. Kaman, "Quick Clustering," *Journal of Marketing Research* (May 1970), p. 200.

finished. By carrying out this procedure the following clusters will be formed:

CLUSTER I Bank 2, Bank 8, Bank 10
CLUSTER II Bank 5, Bank 7, Bank 3
CLUSTER III Bank 6, Bank 9, Bank 4
CLUSTER IV Bank 1, Bank 11

The researcher then interpreted the cluster in the following manner:

- Cluster I consists of the small, limited-service banks.
- Clusters II and III are composed of medium-sized banks, fuller-service banks.
- Cluster IV consists of the full-service leaders.[4]

An additional value of the clustering technique is that after the clusters have been formed they can be studied in terms of other related factors. For example, clusters of bank customers can be examined with respect to their relevant demographic composition and usage patterns. This can provide valuable segmentation information to the strategic marketing planner.

Discriminant Analysis

Another technique which has the ability to group things is discriminant analysis. This procedure begins with groups, heavy users versus light users, for example, and then identifies the different variables that can statistically differentiate the two groups.

A study designed to identify differences between heavy users of ATMs and nonusers of ATMs produced the results shown in Table 4–10.[5] A feature of discriminant analysis is that the relative dis-

TABLE 4–10 Analysis of Discriminant Analysis

	Standardized Discriminant Coefficient	
	User	*Nonuser*
Dwelling value		
Home or rent	.02306	.01037
Age	.00337	.01396
Total family monthly income	−.00999	.03659
Check only at this bank	47.75320	33.51255
Check and save at this bank	42.41445	38.51111
Save only at this bank	16.63940	39.57430
Check at other bank	50.29208	24.43076

criminating importance of the variable is indicated by the standardized discriminant coefficients. In this study, four variables accounted for the major portions of the discrimination. These were checking account (only at this bank), savings account (only at this bank), checking and savings accounts (only at this bank), and checking accounts (only at other banks). When these discriminant coefficients are translated into actual percentages, the following discriminating profile emerges:

	User	*Non User*
Checking Account (only at this bank)	51%	25%
Savings Account (only at this bank)	0%	18%
Checking & Savings (only at this bank)	49%	23%
Checking Account (only at other banks)	5%	14%

In addition, the demographic profile shown in Table 4–11 was produced.

Discriminant analysis does not necessarily have to be confined to a two-group analysis. Multiple discriminant analysis can operate on a number of different groups. Problems of interpretation increase as the number of groups increases.

Other techniques such as factor analysis and multidimensional scaling are useful in segmentation analyses. All of the techniques identified here are relatively sophisticated techniques requiring knowledgeable researchers and equally knowledgeable users of the research. Studies of this sort can vary significantly in price but, while somewhat expensive, may be important investments in the development of strategic marketing plans.

TABLE 4–11 Demographic Profile of ATM Users

Heavy Users	*Light Users*
Younger (−30)	Older (+50)
More highly educated	Less education
White collar	Higher incomes
Lower family income	Married—working wives
Often single	Low mobility
Highly mobile	Home owners
Renter	

SUMMARY

This chapter has examined the concept of market segmentation and has discussed several different approaches that banks can use to segment markets. *The process of segmentation is a highly creative one.* There is no one right way to segment a market. The only correct way is the one that works. The actual process of segmentation may take a number of attempts before an effective and workable approach is discovered. It is a process that is at the very heart of the marketing concept, because it is the most effective way to understand the wants and needs of the market, the hallmark of a successful marketing program.

Footnotes

[1]Philip Kotler, *Marketing Management,* 3rd ed. (Englewood Cliffs, N.J.: Prentice-Hall, Inc., 1976), p. 57.

[2]Steven Mintz, "Banking on Marketing," *Sales and Marketing Management,* Vol. 130, No. 10 (1983), p. 43.

[3]Ronald D. Taylor and Blaise J. Bergiel, "Financial Services: Implications for Marketing Segmentation," *Mississippi Business Review,* Vol. XLVI, No. 5 (1984), pp. 3–7.

[4]Adapted from Joseph M. Kamon, "Quick Clustering," *Journal of Marketing Research* (May, 1970), p. 200.

[5]Albert A. Pool, "Application of Discriminant Analysis in Formulation of Promotional Strategy for Cash-Dispensing Machines," *Journal of Bank Research* (Spring 1974), pp. 13–19.

5

positioning strategies

INTRODUCTION

Positioning refers to the perceptual relationship of a firm and its products/services to its competitors. The purpose of positioning is to perceptually differentiate the firm and its products/services from competition. First popularized by advertising executives Al Ries and Jack Trout, positioning has been used extensively in the consumer goods market to provide a unique marketing appeal for products that are generally viewed as homogeneous. According to Ries and Trout, positioning is not what you do to the product/service, but what you do to the mind of the consumer.[1] If the product has "add-on" value, it increases the perceptual opportunity to provide a means of differentiation. Of course, this difference must be perceived if the product/service is to be differentiated.

The initial product positioning concept has led to the development of positioning as a vital aspect of strategic planning both at the firm level as well as the product/service level. The firm's position in the marketplace provides a consistent basis from which management may evaluate its goals and differential advantage with the various targeted segments in the market.

In this chapter we will examine positioning as a means of differentiation for the bank and its products and services. The concept of positioning will be applied as a strategic planning tool through which the bank may seek out and exploit market "niches." The idea of a positioning strategy, in which the firm defines the overall marketing strategy around a consistent approach to the market, will be developed.

The use of positioning in developing marketing strategy requires that the bank marketer know how the firm is perceived in the marketplace. This knowledge of the firm's current position and its competitors' strategies may be used for (1) maintaining a position, (2) combating competitors, or (3) addressing unfilled marketing positions. Before examining the mechanics of positioning, an understanding of how a firm may use a positioning approach to develop strategy is necessary.

STRATEGIC ORIENTATION AND POSITIONING

In a recent *Bank Marketing* article, Nelson Valverde, formerly with the World Bank and now manager of Valverde and Co., proposed a two-by-two positioning scheme bounded by the "extent of the product line" and "value added."[2] The product line variable is defined as the number of product/service offerings. "Value added" is determined by the ". . . amount of additional benefits perceived by the customer beyond the intrinsic cost of the product and for which he/she is willing to pay extra." Combinations of these two variables offer the bank the four possible strategies indicated in Figure 5–1.

Valverde suggests that these approaches may be used as a basis for developing a strategic position. For example, the bank offering high value-added products/services and a narrow product line should emphasize its uniqueness, quality, and personal service. He calls this positioning strategy a *mink* strategy with Morgan Guaranty Trust as an example of a bank using the strategy. Narrow product-line/low value-added strategies (termed *mule* strategies), such as that of the money-market funds, emphasize the value and low price of their products/services. Wide product lines and low value-added strategies (*horse* strategies) also emphasize low price and economies. But unlike the mule strategy, the horse strategy calls for the bank to differentiate itself from its competitors on both the range and thus the convenience of its offerings. Banks such as Prudential, with its multitude of financial services and high efficiency, is an example of a firm using such a strategy. The bank attempting a high value-added and a wide product-line strategy is positioning itself as a *lion* in the industry. This strategy calls for the bank to seek a leadership image in the industry, to offer personal service, and a "powerful affluent presentation." Valverde points

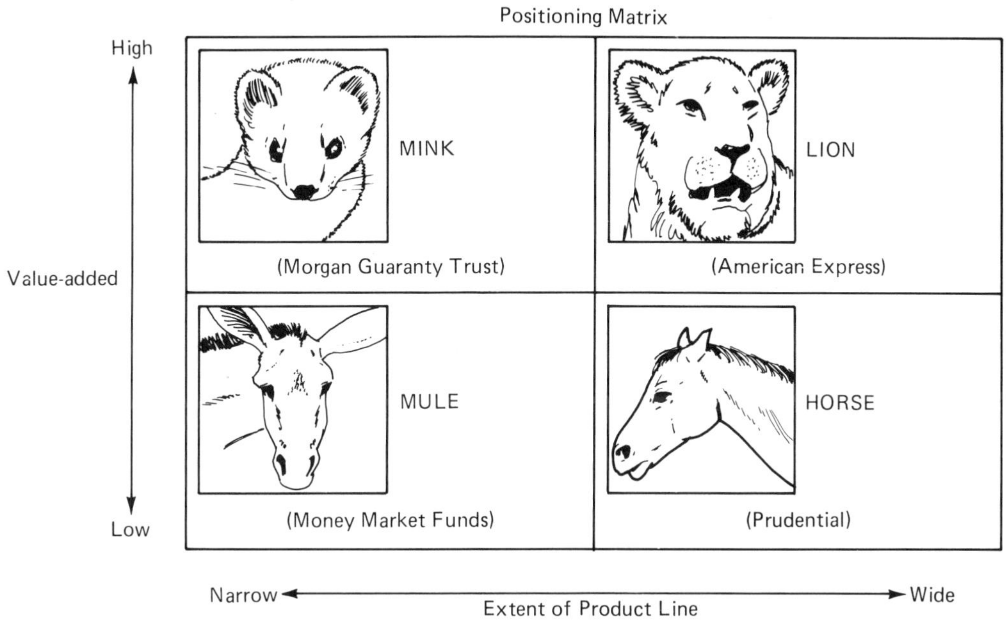

Implications of the Positioning Matrix

Strategy	Key Factors for Success
MINK (Narrow line/high value-added)	Exclusive, speciality image Unique or high-quality products High price/high margin Personal service/advice Expensive presentation
LION (Wide line/high value-added)	Leader, "class" image Creative marketing High price/high margin Personal service Powerful, affluent presentation
MULE (Narrow line/low value-added)	Value conscious, consistent image Speciality mass marketing Lower price/lower margin Nonpersonal or self-service Nondifferentiated, identical presentation
HORSE (Wide line/low value-added)	"Good buy," convenient image High volume, economies of scale Low price/low margin Low or self-service Efficiency of operations presentation

Source: Nelson Valderde, "Developing Profitable Strategies that Don't Box You in," Bank Marketing, June 1983, p. 10. Used with permission.

FIG. 5–1. The four strategies map.

to firms such as American Express, whose aggressive position exemplifies this strategy.

The trend in the financial industry as a whole appears to be toward wider product lines, a legacy of full-service banking that has dominated the industry. Citibank, American Express, and Sears are examples of national firms that have expanded services and distribution and are becoming aggressive competitors in many regional and local markets. So-called "thrifts" now offer commercial and consumer loans as well as credit card and trust services. Many regional and local banks are also expanding their product lines into traditionally nonbank areas with the addition of insurance and real estate services.

The four-strategies-positioning approach can and should be applied to positioning efforts by regional and local banks as well as national financial leaders. It is important for bank marketers to realize that customers have a perception of their bank and its products/services, and that it is marketing's task to shape and control that perception as a consistent part of the bank's strategy.

Market Leadership and Positioning

An inherent part of the framework of strategic positioning is the idea of a hierarchy of competitors in the marketplace. Most markets have a "market leader," the dominant bank in the relevant marketplace. The market leader generally will possess the greatest proportion of market share in the relevant market, and is typically the first bank the consumer thinks of when considering the product/service. Using the four strategies framework, the market leader will typically offer high levels of added value and thus high-price and high-margin products/services. Customers are generally willing to accept the market leader's products/services as being worth more even if the products are no better than those of the competition.

Many strategic planners may find it odd that the market leader may not necessarily be an innovator in product/service. The market leader will attempt to stay dominant in the areas in which it competes, but in order to protect its position will not enter a market until it is sure it can capture the leadership role. When the market leader moves into a market or brings out a new product/service, it attempts to do so with enough force to capture and maintain its leadership. As you might have already surmised, the market leader's high margins and large market share generally produce the greatest profits in the marketplace.

The task facing competitive banks in the marketplace is to decide whether to position themselves as challengers to the leader or as specialists in market "niches" which are too small to be attractive to the leader and the challengers. The challenger's role in marketing is frequently exciting but seldom as profitable as that of the leader. In order to challenge the leader, small, less dominant banks must resort to relatively expensive promotional efforts, offer lower prices, and ensure that they offer more value in the exchange than the leader. In effect, most challengers become price competitors unless they can position their product/service as offering unique advantages over the leader. Banks which neither challenge the leader with differentiated products nor seek out uncontested market positions may find themselves perceived as low-cost, low-value banks who inevitably must offer their products at lower relative prices to attract customers.

For many banks the solution to this dilemma is to use the positioning techniques presented in latter sections of this chapter to examine the marketplace, themselves, and their competitors and to find market segments in which they may become the dominant bank, the market leader in a "niche." This, of course, requires careful research and the development and execution of an effective marketing strategy. The bank must not only find a segment in which it can excel but also must be willing to assume the role of the leader in that segment.

The computer industry offers excellent examples of positioning strategies and how firms have used their position to respond effectively to changing market conditions. Without question the market leader in the overall computer industry is IBM. IBM emphasizes the quality of its machines, the fact that it is number one in the industry, its service, and so on. The industry, however, is actually composed of several segments generally defined in terms of the size or power of the computing equipment involved. IBM's real dominance has historically been in the mid-size business market, which stresses service and reliability. While many competitors have withdrawn from the market for mid-size computers, others have found very profitable niches in producing either very large or very small computers.

The case of the micro/personal computer market shows what can happen when the market leader decides to move into a new market in force. Apple pioneered this segment and is credited with being the first to mass produce so-called personal microcomputers. As the demand for personal computers grew and market forecasts indicated that much of the growth in the product category would be in this segment of the market, IBM began its development program. Their product was not necessarily technologically superior to the competition, but had the advantage of carrying the leader's name. It was an IBM, just like the computers in businesses all over the world. In less than two years, IBM garnered a leadership position in the personal computer marketplace, forcing Apple to seek a competitive position as a more "user-friendly" alternative and forcing the other competitors to simply follow IBM's lead as low cost but less attractive alternatives.

As one can see, positioning requires that the firm apply the concepts of market segmentation to the fullest if one is to be successful. Today's less regulated banking environment makes the positioning decision(s) of the bank a vital part of marketing strategy if new-bank and nonbank competitors are to be met.

To position the bank and its products/services effectively, resource strengths that can be differentiated from competitors must be identified and strategies developed to employ these resources to provide "unique customer value and generate profits." Writing in the *Bankers Magazine*, Colin L. Jones calls knowing one's market position "the fifth commandment in bank marketing." According to Jones, the five commandments are (1) know thyself, (2) know thy customers, (3) know thy competitors, (4) know thy market, and (5) realize the importance of being different. This fifth commandment is to position your firm in a unique place in the market.[3] Before we explore the application of positioning further, we need to examine the importance of the knowledge the firm will gain through the application of the first four commandments.

Most bank managers do not really know their bank! Unfortunately, most bank managers do not really know their bank from a marketing perspective, the perspective used by customers. In the past, they have never really had to. Internal analysis of the strengths and weaknesses of the firm's personnel, its product/service offerings, prices, and distribution are first steps. Realistic analysis of the capital requirements of the bank and its resources are also necessary. An external market research approach must next be used to determine customer perceptions. The consumer's reality may differ radically from the reality viewed by those inside the organization. Bank image research and the various perceptual mapping approaches presented later in this chapter will provide consumer insight into the firm and its product/service offering.

Customers and Their Needs

As previously discussed, part of "knowing your customers" is understanding the demographic and the psychographic makeup of the bank's customers. Demographic characteristics include sex, race, education, and age, as well as socioeconomic factors such as income and employment characteristics. The psychographic profile of your customer base refers to the orientation of the bank's customers in terms of their values, personalities, and life-styles. Effective analysis of the characteristics of the bank's customers, however, is not simplistic and will require study at the product/service level and careful examination of the range of customers.

The strategic marketing planner needs to look at several different ways of analyzing such data in order to gain as complete a picture as possible of the bank's customers. As can be seen in Table 5–1, the size of the firm will determine to a great extent what type of services a business firm will seek from the bank and whether the business will prefer in-state to out-of-state banks.

Competition in the Financial Marketplace

Defining the extent of competition in the financial marketplace poses one of the more difficult problems for the bank marketer. The range of new products/services has increased tremendously during the past decade. Many so-called nonbanks are transacting in what were previously strictly regulated bank products/services. Deregulation has fostered a tremendous increase in competition, as major banks and other financial institutions enter national, regional, and local competition. Many banks, which previously defined their competition as the several other local banks (not even S & Ls) offering similar services in the marketplace for total bank services, must reconsider their perceptions of competition. Credit unions and savings and loan organizations must now be viewed as close competitors for many bank services/products. As many banks venture into historically nonbank product/service areas, such as real estate, discount brokerage, and insurance, the bank will find itself facing an entirely new and frequently unknown group of competitors.

Today, a number of sources of information concerning the financial performance of the competitors identified for a particular product/service are available. Private firms, such as the highly regarded Alex Sheshunoff, Inc., regulatory examiners reports, National Bank Surveillance FDIC reports, etc., provide useful data to compare your performance in key areas with your competition. Information on nonbank competitors is frequently available through firms filing with the Securities and Exchange Commission and national and state regulatory agencies.

A list of 23 criteria which should be considered in the evaluation of a bank's performance are shown in Table 5–2. Dr. William F. Ford of the Wells Fargo bank, formerly director of research and planning for the American Bankers Association, contends that "high-performance" banks will outperform their competition not in just one or two of the areas, but that the factors are interrelated and linked to bank marketing and assets at the broadest level. Such criteria must be carefully evaluated for each bank. We should note, for example, that the 100 high-performance banks examined in Dr. Ford's study enjoyed a 31.5 percent advantage overall in deposit growth when compared to all banks

TABLE 5–1 Banking Services Utilized by Smaller Firms

In-State Banks			*Out-of-State Banks*		
Rank		*% of Smaller Firms Utilizing These Services*	*Rank*		*% of Smaller Firms Utilizing These Services*
1	Demand deposits	97	1	Demand deposits	11
2	Line of credit	82	2	Term loans	9
3	Term loans	56	3	Deposits transfers	9
4	Lockbox	47	4	Line of credit	8
5	Time deposit	41			
6	Trust services	41		No other significant use of out-of-state banks by small businesses.	
7	Money-market services	38			
8	Deposit transfer	33			
9	Coin and currency	33			
10	Revolving loans	23			

Banking Services Utilized by Larger Firms

In-State Banks			*Out-of-State Banks*		
Rank		*% of Larger Firms Utilizing These Services*	*Rank*		*% of Larger Firms Utilizing These Services*
1	Demand deposits	89	1	Demand deposits	50
2	Line of credit	75	2	Line of credit	40
3	Money-market service	57	3	Deposit transfer	30
4	Investment advice	56	4	International banking	28
5	Deposit transfer	53	5	Coin and currency	22
6	Term loans	50	6	Money-market services	22
7	Coin and currency	43	7	Term loans	22
8	Time deposits	39	8	Investment advice	21
9	Trust services	32	9	Stock transfer agent	18
10	Stock transfer agent	25	10	Time deposits	18

Source: B.J. Campsey, L.C. Pettit, R.F. DeMong, and Benton E. Gup, "Surviving Money Center Competition," *Bank Marketing*, Vol. 165 (July-August 1982), p. 49. Used with permission.

in the United States for the years examined. The "high-performance" banks, however, paid out less interest on total deposits but paid more interest on time and savings deposits than other banks.[4] Again, management should collect and carefully evaluate such data for its own bank and relevant competitors.

TABLE 5–2 Evaluation Criteria for Bank Performance

Profitability measures
1. Net income/average equity
2. Return on earnings assets
3. Net interest income/earning assets

Expense control measures
4. Operating expense/earning assets
5. Overhead/earning assets
6. Interest on deposits/all deposits
7. Interest on deposits/time & savings

Employee utilization measures
8. Net income/employees
9. Payroll expense/employees
10. Assets/employees

Asset management
11. Gross loans/all deposits
12. Cash & treasuries/DDA (Deceased Deposit Accounts)

Revenue enhancement
13. Loan income/gross loans
14. Securities income/securities
15. Muni income (tax adjusted)/munis (Muni = Municipal bonds)

Credit quality control measures
16. Loan loss provision/earning assets
17. Gross chargeoffs/loans

Leverage and loss coverage
18. Equity/assets
19. Loan loss coverage ratio
20. Reserve/loans

Growth measures
21. Asset growth
22. Deposit growth
23. Equity growth

Source: William F. Ford, "Using High Performance Data to Plan Your Bank's Future," *Banking*, Vol. 70 (October 1978), p. 40. Used with permission.

WHAT IS THE RELEVANT MARKET FOR A PRODUCT/SERVICE?

In the past it was quite reasonable to expect that the bank manager would have extensive knowledge of the financial marketplace in which the bank conducted business. Today's competitive environment presents new challenges, new markets, new products/services, and new ways of reaching these markets. One of the first things the bank marketer must do is to determine the market "structures" that must be addressed in the financial marketplace. If the marketplace is to be examined from the customer's viewpoint, then the structure of the marketplace should be examined in terms of products/services which the consumer accepts as substitutes within a given usage situation; in other words, an analysis of the products/services that the customer sees as providing the same benefits. Competition is defined in terms of product/service offerings rather than the firms offering the products/services. In a recent study of bank service usage Srivastava, Alpert, and Shocker found that many financial services overlap in terms of their usage in the marketplace and that many bank products/services are competing with each other.

Figure 5–2 shows the financial services market structure determined for 24 financial services. Each of the six clusters of services determined in the study may be viewed as a submarket of substitutable services. The arrows indicate the situations with which use of the services in the group or cluster is most strongly associated. The authors of the study interpret the findings as indicating that "each cluster may be viewed as a submarket. Thus bank credit cards, credit card account checks, and debit cards are competitive with retail credit cards and retail installment loans in out-of-town settings, and with travel and entertainment credit cards and travelers checks in out-of-town nonretail settings."[5] A summary of the market structures and their interpretation is provided in Figure 5–3.

As we have indicated previously, followers must inevitably select less profitable strategies while the leader in a specific market is generally the most profitable of the competitors in a specific target market. For a number of years, most experts thought that to operate at a profit and generate a high return on assets, the firm must command a major share of a market in broadly defined terms. There is considerable evidence today that smaller firms can be very profitable through the use of market segmentation and positioning. They generally still have a small share of the broadly defined market, but are in fact leaders with a major share of a unique segment of the total market. While these smaller firms may frequently be forced to offer superior performance and services than the leader's in the broadly defined market, their specialization can lead to lower operating costs.[6]

It is interesting to note that in today's marketplace for financial services, the medium-sized banks are considered most vulnerable. Banks with assets between $300 million and $1 billion averaged only about 65 percent of the growth rate of the rest of the industry between 1973 and 1980.[7] These "full-service" banks are unable to provide full financial services, while facing competition from both national money-center institutions and local savings and loan and other nonbank financial firms. Banks of this size appear to resist what they perceive to be the limitations of addressing a selected target, and of positioning themselves as

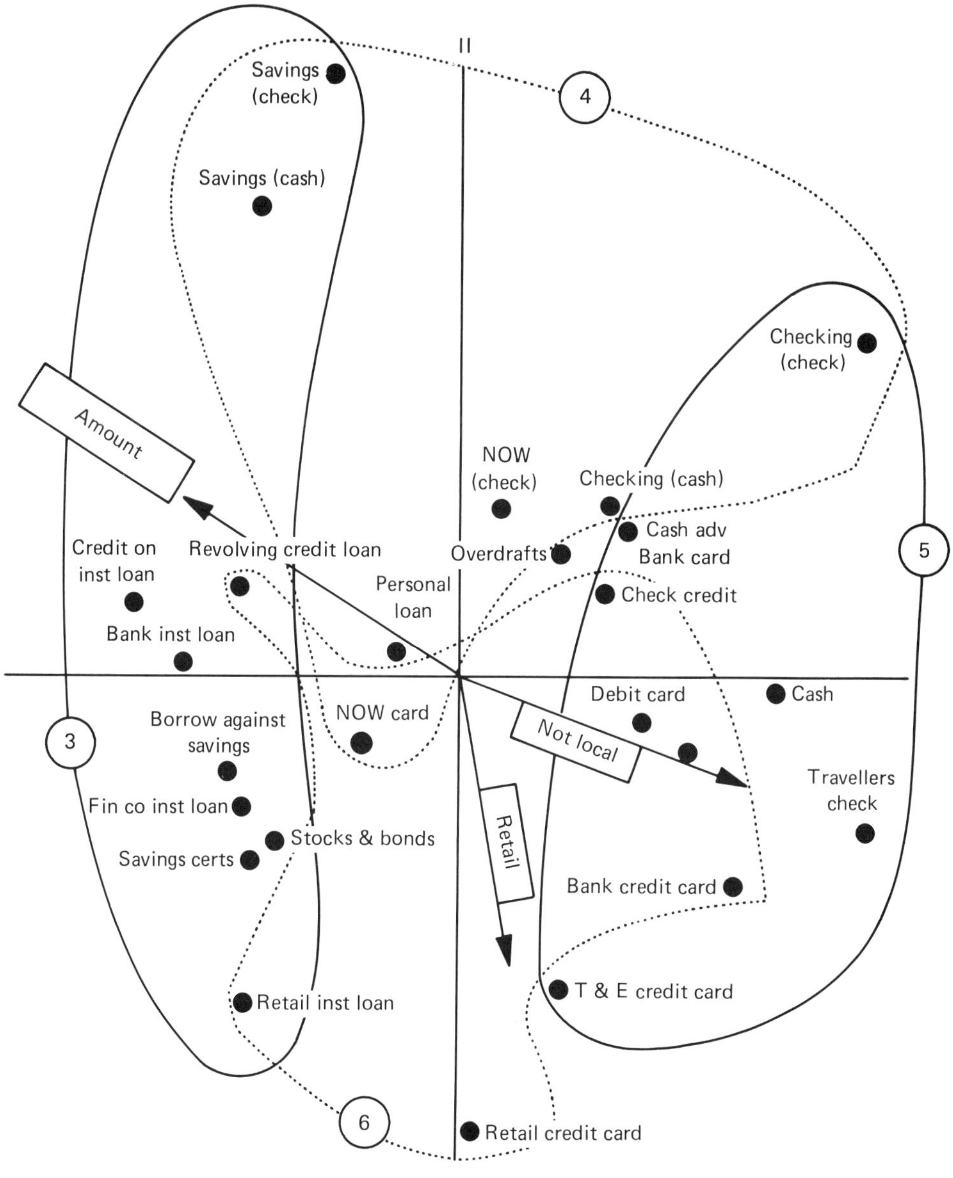

Source: Rajendra K. Srivanstava, Mark I. Alpert, and Allan D. Shocker, "A Customer-Oriented Approach for Determining Market Structures," Journal of Marketing, Vol. 48 (Spring 1984), p. 41. Used with permission.

FIG. 5–2. Financial services market structure (overlapping clusters).

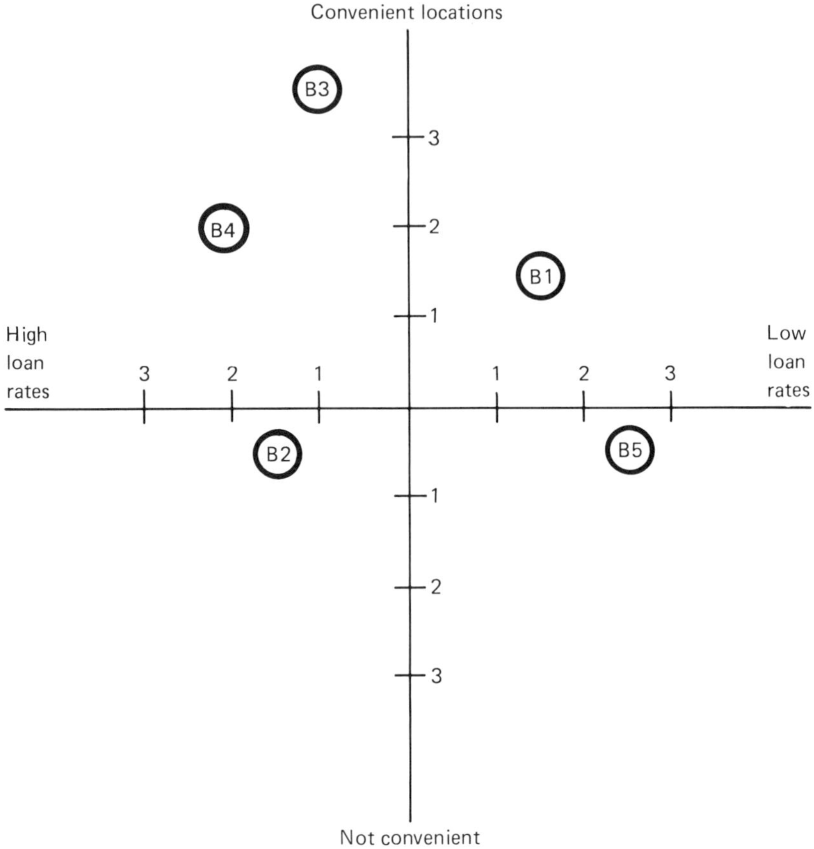

FIG. 5–3. Perceptual map for five competing banks using two attributes.

uniquely suited for that market. Positioning, however, is a multilevel concept which may be applied at the bank level and at the product/service level. Positioning does not limit a bank's ability to market its products/services, but rather it is simply realizing that a bank cannot adequately satisfy the needs of all portions of the marketplace, and that each bank and its products/services provide a unique mix of benefits for the customer.

POSITIONING SERVICES AND PRODUCTS

So far the discussion of positioning has been at the industry level, and generally from the point of view of the bank's concept of what it wants to be in the marketplace. The key to strategic positioning, however, is an understanding of how the bank is perceived in relation to its competition along those factors that underlie consumers' decisions about the product/service. This type of analysis is an application of attitude and image research, commonly called *perceptual mapping*. The perceptual map is a graphic representation of the perceived characteristics from which demand for products/services are produced.[8]

A Simple Mapping Approach

Several quantitative methodologies, from the very simple to the complex, may be used to develop perceptual maps for use in positioning. However, as Table 5–4 indicates, the first requirement is to determine the relevant product/service characteristics used by customers in a par-

TABLE 5–3 Interpretation of Financial Service Market Clusters

	Groupings for 24 Financial Services						
Order of Entry	1	2	3	4	5	6	*Interpretation of Clusters (in order of entry)*
Rank by Weight	1	4	2	5	3	6	
Cluster Weight	64	43	56	35	50	31	
Cash on hand		X			X		(1) Products likely to be used when large amounts are required (local use).
Checking (cash)		X		X			
Checking (check)		X		X	X		
Debit card		X			X	X	(2) Products likely to be used when low/medium amounts are required in retail settings.
Savings (cash)	X		X	X			
Savings (check)	X		X	X			
NOW account (check)	X			X			(3) Products likely to be used when large amounts are required in retail settings (local use).
NOW account (cash card)	X			X		X	
Savings certificate	X		X				
Stocks and bonds	X		X				
Borrow against savings	X		X				
Travelers check		X			X		(4) Products likely to be used when low/medium amounts are required in nonretail settings (local use).
Cash advance—bank card		X		X	X		
Overdraft—checking		X		X			
Check credit—bank card		X			X	X	
Bank credit card		X			X	X	(5) Products likely to be used when low/medium amounts are required in out-of-town settings.
T&E credit card		X			X		
Retail credit card		X				X	
Personal loan—relative	X			X			
Bank installment loan	X		X				(6) Products likely to be used when medium amounts are required in retail settings while out of town.
Finance co. installment loan	X		X				
Credit union installment loan	X		X				
Retail installment loan		X	X			X	
Revolving credit loan	X		X			X	

Source: Rajendra K. Srivanstava, Mark I. Alpert, and Allan D. Shocker, "A Customer-Oriented Approach for Determining Market Structures," *Journal of Marketing*, Vol. 48 (Spring 1984), p. 41. Used with permission.

TABLE 5–4 Steps in Positioning

1. What is to be analyzed
   a. Product/services
   b. Competition (firms)
2. Identify decision criteria of customers
3. Determine group whose perceptions are to be examined
4. Select mapping methodology
5. Develop data collection instrument
6. Apply mapping techniques
7. Analyze market positions
8. Determine strategy
   a. Solidify and hold position
   b. Reposition

ticular market segment in selecting a source for the financial product service being positioned. Fortunately, there are a number of published studies of bank selection which may be used as a basis for developing the perceptual criteria underlying bank and product/service selection. The criteria used in four published studies of bank selection, image, or positioning are shown in Table 5–5. It is important to realize that these criteria can vary radically from market to market.

As can be seen, a variety of perceptual characteristics are thought to underlie the consumer's overall perception of the competition in the marketplace and product/service use decisions. The relevant set of criteria will vary depending on the competing banks or other financial institutions in a particular market, current economic conditions, and other factors. Managerial evaluation and a sound knowledge of market and competitive factors must be applied to develop an initial set of perceptual-decision criteria on which to base the perceptual mapping. One should note that in each study an effort was made to examine variables including distribution, pricing, promotion, and product/service-related factors. One should also note that the reputation of the bank and its recommendation by current customers were most important in differentiating between the banks studied. This general-image factor is very similar to the idea of the image-halo effect enjoyed by the market leader and is also an indication of the importance of word-of-mouth communication, as we will discuss in a later chapter.

A two-attribute map for several competing banks and a savings and loan is shown in Figure 5–3. This perceptual map was derived from consumer responses to questions concerning the convenience of the locations and the cost of loans of each of the institutions, as shown in Table 5–6.

TABLE 5–5 Bank Attributes Frequently Used in Positioning

Free checking service	Recommendation by friends
Drive-in service	Reputation
Bank statement service	Availability of credit
Mail service	Service charges on checking accounts
Competent teller service	Overdraft privileges on checking accounts
Competitive interest rates	"Full-service" offering
Bank hours	Parking
Friendly, helpful personnel	Hours of operation
Convenient location	Interest payments on savings accounts
Lines	Special services for youths
Best savings rates	Special services for women
Interest in me as a customer	New account premiums or gifts
First with new services	A large, growing bank
Offers a greater variety of financial services	A very conservative bank
Trust services	Does a lot of advertising
Bank for families and individuals	Bank's advertising is interesting
Bank for small business persons and professionals	Advertising tells me the bank wants me as a customer
Bank for medium and small businesses	Has the best bank management
Bank for large businesses	Interest in helping our city grow
Modern buildings	Makes it easy to cash checks
Efficient bank employees	Auxiliary bank services
A progressive bank	Personalized service
Speed of service	

Source: Richard M. Durand, Donald W. Eckrich, and C. Ronald Sprecher, "Bank Image an Adequate-Importance Approach," *Journal of Bank Research,* Autumn 1978, pp. 168–172. Richard H. Evans, "Bank Selections: It All Depends on the Situation," *Journal of Bank Research,* Winter 1979, pp. 242–245; Richard H. Evans, "The Validity of Service and Situational Perceptions: A Caution," *Journal of Bank Research,* Summer 1979, pp. 119–123; W. Thomas Anderson, Jr., Eli P. Cox III, and David G. Fulchner, "Bank Selection Decisions and Market Segmentation," *Journal of Marketing,* Vol. 40 (January 1976), pp. 40–45. Used with permission.

The two-dimensional presentation was generated by using the mean values of the responses to a consumer attitude survey, with the questions scaled from minus three to plus three. It should be noted that the development of such maps using simple statistics assumes that the two criteria used to develop the map are not correlated. The most important consideration is the determination that these are the most important criteria used by the consumer in evaluation of competing financial institutions.

TABLE 5–6

	Locations Are Convenient						*Locations Are Not Convenient*
Bank 1	____	____	____	____	____	____	____
Bank 2	____	____	____	____	____	____	____
	Low Interest Rates						*High Interest Rates*
Bank 1	____	____	____	____	____	____	____
Bank 2	____	____	____	____	____	____	____

As one can see from Figure 5–3, bank B3 is perceived as having convenient locations, followed by B1, while the locations of B2 and B4 are not perceived as convenient. Bank B4 is closely followed by the S & L for the lowest perceived rates, while B2 has the highest loan rates. The two-dimensional map of the mean responses, however, indicates that B1 appears to have the best combination of location and perceived rates.

Multidimensional Mapping Techniques

For most situations it is desirable to use more sophisticated analytical techniques, such as one of the many multidimensional scaling methodologies, canonical discriminant analysis, or factor analysis to produce composite representations of the perceptual positions of the firms or product/service.[9] These techniques allow analysis under more realistic conditions in which more than two attributes are evaluated. (These statistics also provide the pictorial representation of characteristics that may have related responses.) Data for these methods of analysis are collected in the same manner as that for the map in the earlier figures and through the use of similarities. Similarities input for multidimensional scaling consist of an evaluation of how similar each of the items (banks and S & Ls in our example) are to each other.

A perceptual-positioning map for the firms is shown in Figure 5–4 with the financial institutions mapped into the same perceptual space as the attributes along which they are evaluated.

This analysis indicates that several criteria are statistically related to the survey respondents' perceptions of the competing banks and the S & L. The placement of the banks in relation to each other and to the

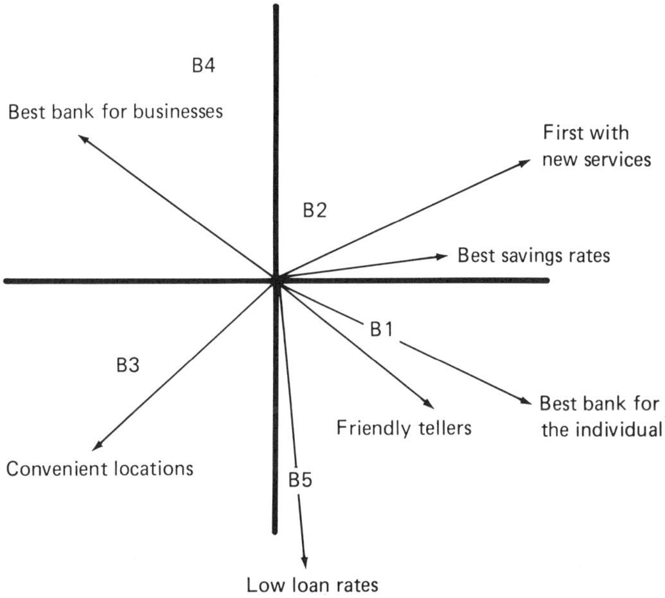

FIG. 5–4. Perceptual map of five financial competitors and attributes.

attributes provides the manager with a visual representation of the consumers' view of the marketplace. This placement is also the basis for understanding the bank's position and repositioning when desirable and necessary. The six attributes determined to be related to respondent perceptions of the bank are "friendly tellers," "first with new services," "best bank for the individual," "best bank for business," "convenient locations," and "low loan rates." Remember that the relevant criteria in the study will depend on the competitive environment the strategic planner is facing in the bank's market area. The map shows that bank 1 lies close to the "friendly teller"attribute line but is half of the length of the line from the origin to the plot. The mapping approach used in this figure places the length of the attribute position lines equal to the strength of association between the attributes and the perceptual configurations. However, this is not the case with all the techniques that may be applied to produce perceptual maps. "Best for individuals" and "first with new services" are very close together in the map. This indicates that the responses to these questions were correlated and that both would not have been included if only a simple plot, such as those shown previously, (Figure 5–3) had been used to map the perceptual positions of the firms. Bank 4 is perceived as being quite different from the other firms and as being more of a business than an individual-oriented firm. This map was generated from a random sample of possible bank customers in a market area and, as we have already discussed, within this market we expect to find several market segments with differing banking needs. Figure 5–5 presents this same perceptual map with the location of the respondents' ideal banks shown as large circles.

This step in the positioning mapping methodology was conducted by using a computer technique called *cluster analysis* to determine groups of respondents with similar "ideal" financial institutions. The mean ideal locations were then plotted onto the perceptual map. The size of the circle indicates the relative size of the market segment preferring each ideal institution.

Bank 1 lies very close to the largest ideal bank position. This was expected, as bank 1 was the dominant bank in the market area. Further, the largest ideal segment lies directly on the "friendly teller" attribute line, again indicative of this bank feature in the small town in which the study was conducted. The study was conducted as a survey of consumer, not business, banking, which resulted in the lack of an ideal group near the position of bank 4 and the business orientation. The position of bank 3 and the ideal segment B is very interesting. The bank is very close to a group that appears to desire convenient loca-

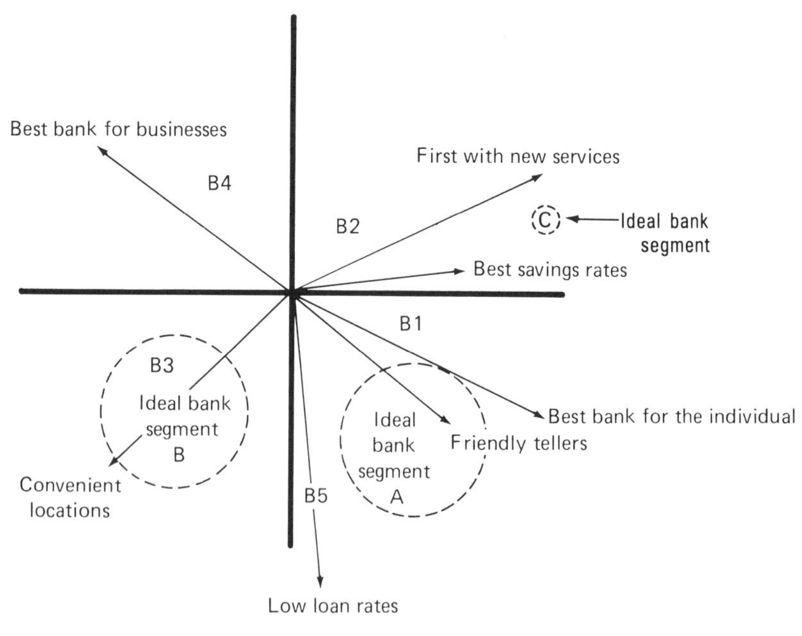

FIG. 5–5. Perceptual map of five financial competitors and attributes: ideal points.

tions above all other features. This bank had recently added a new branch and several automatic teller locations and promoted its convenience heavily in the market.

REPOSITIONING

The positioning map may be used as a basis for the development of strategies to reposition the firm within the perceptual marketplace to a more advantageous position. Bank 2, for example, lies far from either ideal position. It appears to be perceived as a very general "full-service" institution, but with high loan rates and less than convenient locations. This bank needs to develop a strategy to bring it closer to one of the two ideal groups if it is to gain in market share. Examination indicated that the bank maintained its main office in a downtown area and that its lone branch was located on a busy four-lane bypass with no turn lane. The bank's promotion had stressed its many new services and a wide variety of loan plans, but rates were never promoted. This bank had not attempted to establish a position in the marketplace and had lost share to the other more aggressive competitors during the last three years.

A repositioning strategy for bank 2 requires first the selection of a positioning strategy. In this case the selected strategy called for efforts to emphasize the bank's competitive loan rates, a new, more individual emphasis, and its friendly atmosphere. As we have already discussed, these efforts required an integrated approach with changes in loan procedures, new customer service efforts, and a strong promotional program. In this case, the management of bank 2 must ensure that the firm has the resources to challenge bank 1 for market leadership.

An alternative strategy would be to emphasize a small market niche such as that offered by ideal group C. Analysis indicated that the consumers who made up this group were younger and tended to be professionals looking for new money management services. This particular target market appears to be quite small. Management must decide if it will attempt to gain a smaller proportion of a large market or attempt to capture a major share of a smaller target.

POSITIONING AND THE MARKETING MIX

We should emphasize that the concept of positioning the firm in the marketplace relevant to its competition involves the entire marketing mix. Many financial firms have responded to competition from nonbanks and new bank products by attempting to position themselves as multiservice providers by simply changing their logos and their names. Other firms have added nonbank services without addressing the impact of these changes on their competitive position. A simple name change to some broad financial term does nothing to reposition the bank in the marketplace without the other elements of the marketing mix. Likewise, decisions to add services or to reposition should not be taken lightly, as change can cost current customers. For example, banks considering expanding to include nonbank products such as insurance and real estate as a means of positioning themselves to capture related business should consider how existing customers in these business areas might perceive such change.

SUMMARY

Overall, the position of the bank is one of the major elements in relating the bank and its strategy to the marketplace. Bank management needs to realize how it is perceived in the marketplace and to have a consistent strategy in keeping with its desired position. Positioning was presented as an industry level decision concerning the totality of the firm's orientation toward the marketplace strategy. In addition, positioning was discussed in a micro application to a specific product/service. The concept of positioning provides a framework for viewing the firm and its products/services as competitors in the marketplace.

Footnotes

[1]See Jack Trout and Al Ries, "The Positioning Era Cometh," *Advertising Age*, April 24, 1972, pp. 35–38; May 1, 1972, pp. 51–54; May 8, 1972, pp. 114–116.

[2]Nelson Valverde, "Developing Profitable Strategies That Don't Box You In," *Bank Marketing*, June 1983, pp. 1–16.

[3]These tenants of positioning are drawn from Colin L. Jones, "Know Thy Niche," *The Banker's Magazine*, Vol. 165 (July–August 1982), pp. 32–35.

[4]William F. Ford, "Using High Performance Data to Plan Your Bank's Future," *Banking*, Vol. 70 (October 1978), p. 40.

[5]Rajendra K. Srivastava, Mark I. Alpert, and Allan D. Shocker, "A Customer-Oriented Approach for Determining Market Structures," *Journal of Marketing*, Vol. 48 (Spring 1984), p. 41.

[6]For a discussion of small share firms, see: Carolyn Y. Woo and Arnold C. Cooper, "The Surprising Case for Low Market Share," *Harvard Business Review*, November–December 1982, pp. 106–113.

[7]Jones, op. cit., p. 32.

[8]For an introduction to perceptual mapping, see: William D. Neal, "Strategic Product Positioning: A Step-by-Step Guide," *Business*, May–June 1980, pp. 34–42.

[9]For a discussion of these and other multivariate techniques in positioning, see: R. Eric Reidenbach and Robert E. Pitts, "Marketing Research in the Financial Industry," working paper 84–101, Bureau of Business and Economic Research, University of Mississippi (1984).

6

product decisions

INTRODUCTION

The product/service offering is the most important element in the marketing mix. With the recent explosion of new products/services and competition, strategic marketing planners in the banking industry today face many of the same types of decisions that their counterparts in the consumer goods industries face. This chapter explores the nature of the product/service offering and then continues by examining some of the different tools available for managing the product/service mix.

THE NATURE OF A PRODUCT

As we have indicated in Chapter 1 and elsewhere, a product is something more than the mere physical entity that consumers buy and use. We shall define a product as:

> Anything that has the capacity to provide the satisfaction, use, or perhaps the profit desired by the customer.

We have intentionally defined product from a very broad perspective. We shall also use the words *product* and *service* interchangeably.

The key factor is that, regardless of the form of that which is being exchanged, our focus is the want- and need-satisfying aspects of the product/service offering.

The concept of the want- and need-satisfying aspects of the product/service offering cannot be overemphasized. All too often, marketers become overly absorbed in the form of the product/service offering only to forget that the entire rationale for the product/service offering in the first place is its want- and need-satisfying capacities. If and when a product/service offering no longer is capable of satisfying consumers' needs and wants, the product/service offering will cease to exist.

When marketers speak of the total number of products or services that they market, they are referring to their *product mix*. Product mixes are composed of *product lines* which are similar products or services, loans, DDAs, or investment counseling services, for example. These may be different versions of savings or checking accounts, for example. The *width* of the product/service mix refers to how many product lines are offered by the bank, while the *depth* of the mix refers to how many product services are offered within one line. Banks that offer student loans, mortgage loans, personal loans, and auto loans, for example, have a relatively wide loan mix. On the other hand, banks that offer GEMs, ARMs, fixed-rate mortgages, balloon notes, etc., have a relatively deep mortgage loan mix. The job of the strategic marketing planner involves managing this mix, deepening it or widening it in response to varying marketing opportunities and threats.

THE PRODUCT SYSTEM

While it is completely accurate to speak of the product/service mix, it may be more appropriate to think of the different product/service offerings as a product *system*. A system is composed of components that have several interesting properties. First, these components are interactive. Often, changes in one or more of the components will cause changes in other components. For example, individuals who have sprained an ankle often compensate by walking so that their weight is displaced on other parts (components) of their body. Such a compensatory behavior may cause additional problems for other parts of the body, such as pain in the hip, knee, or back. This is a good example of the interactions that take place between components of a system.

Another aspect of system behavior is the importance of the total system relative to the individual components. Emphasis on system management should be directed toward maximizing total system performance and not maximizing the performance of a single individual component. Stereo systems are good examples of this rule. The important consideration in developing a good stereo system is the need for balancing the individual components. It does not mean incorporating into the system a receiver of such high wattage that the speakers cannot accommodate its power.

Finally, we have the idea of *synergy*. Synergy says that the whole is often greater than the sum of the individual parts. In other words, 2+2=5. This phenomenon occurs in those systems which are properly managed.

Let's see how the system concept can be applied to the product/service offering of a bank. Bank customers go through what might be described as a financial life cycle. In Chapter 4 we found that life cycle was often an underlying dimension in demographic segmentation accounting for the different banking needs of different demographic segments. As an individual enters the banking market, (s)he enters with certain specific needs. Initially, these may include only a savings account. However, as individuals grow and mature, their banking needs change. New product/service offerings are needed to help them satisfy their financial needs and wants. The product system concept recognizes that the bank's product mix is composed of components (services) which are more or less applicable at certain times of an individual's life cycle. The bank marketer must recognize that as a customer passes through various stages of this life cycle, these product/service offerings will become more appropriate for the customer. Thus, the key is to match the changing needs of the customer with the different system components. This will mean finding the product/service offerings within the product system that will satisfy both present and future banking needs of the customer. This is a key to the personal banker approach, which is gaining acceptance in the banking industry.

The concept goes beyond the idea of cross-selling products. Cross selling has received a lot of attention and necessarily so. In many banks, however, cross selling has not been able to transcend departmental barriers. The product system concept says that the different departments within a bank must operate together in such a fashion that the total wants and needs of an individual customer can be satisfied within that one bank.

If a savings account or a certificate of deposit, for example, is incapable of satisfying a customer's investment needs, then a customer service representative must be willing and able to direct that individual to someone in the trust department. What this means is that while the customer does not stay in a particular department and the department does not make a sale, the customer stays within the bank and the whole bank profits.

The product system concept requires several considerations on the part of the strategic marketing planner. First, it is incumbent upon him or her to make sure that all employees in the bank are aware of the different product/service offerings of the whole bank. When new product/service offerings are made available, all personnel must be made aware of them. Each employee does not need full in-depth knowledge, but simply an understanding of what the product is and which department will handle the product. Second, the philosophy behind the product system concept must be communicated with every department, management making sure that all involved understand the rationale for such an approach. This communication must accentuate the importance of the total performance of the bank and not the optimization of any one single department. Reward systems should be established for those employees who embrace this approach. Finally, when the strategic marketing planner finds that too many present customers are leaving the bank in search of other product/service offerings at other banks, (s)he should see an indication that the product system may need additional components. Increasing the width or depth of the system may be advisable at this time. Of course, it might signal other problems such as noncompetitive offerings. This again, would indicate that some adjustment in the mix is advisable. Recognizing the systemic nature of the bank's product/service mix can lead to greater consumer satisfaction, increased market share, and greater profitability.

TYPICAL BANKING PRODUCTS

For a long time, banks were limited in the types of products/services they were allowed to provide their customers. Deregulation and the establishment of the DIDC (Depository Institutions Deregulation Committee) loosened restrictions on banks' service/product offerings, as the DIDC began to set forth the new depository products which banks could offer. As a result, banks are becoming more market-oriented. While still offering the typical demand and time deposit accounts and assortment of loans, some banks have increased the width and depth of their product mix by offering NOW accounts, Club As, senior-citizen accounts, CDs, trusts, junior savings accounts, a number of new loan products, Christmas Club accounts, discount brokerage services, plus a host of commercial accounts. Consider, for example, the California Thrift, Federal Savings & Loan which offers an election day account. This is a time deposit that expires on November 7. It is a product aimed at those who fear interest rates will rise after the election and don't want to have their money obligated beyond that date!

Many banks choose to "bundle" accounts and offer packaged accounts to different segments, although there appears to be a tendency toward "unbundling" and the offering of specific and individual fee-based services. The product/service mixes to be offered are, of course, market specific to each bank and should reflect the needs of the market(s) that the bank is serving.

The trend toward market-oriented product development will put a greater burden on the research and development efforts of each individual bank. Me-too strategies may have been sufficient in the regulated world, but the competitive environment will demand much more creativity in terms of product development. According to Jolen Festen, Bank One vice-president, "product development gets a lot of lip service. *The challenge is not to create new ideas but to implement accepted ones."* (Italics added.)[1]

Typical of the creative approach to new product/service offerings are the efforts of Fidelity National Bank in Baton Rouge, Louisiana. Fidelity has packaged a week-long tax seminar to be held in Aspen, Colorado. The seminar is directed to the upscale consumer (professional with an income of $50,000 or more) who may or may not be a Fidelity customer. Mr. Brent Bruser, vice-president of Fidelity's Metropolitan Branch, states that competition for the upscale customer is tight. The tax seminar is one way of attracting attention to Fidelity and provides an entree for selling other Fidelity products/services.

Registration for the seminar is $125, while trip expenses are $770 per person. This figure includes:

- Roundtrip airfare from Baton Rouge to Grand Junction, Colorado.
- Ground transfers to lodging
- 8 days, 7 nights lodging in The Continental Inn in Aspen
- 6 days ski rentals
- 3 days lift tickets
- 1 ski lesson on Mt. Sneaux in Baton Rouge (an indoor mountain)
- 1 ski lesson on the slopes in Aspen
- 1 lunch
- Wine and cheese parties
- NASTAR Fun Race
- Louisiana's Skier Discount Card for discounts on local Aspen services
- Tax and gratuity
- Up to 30 percent discount on ski clothing, ski gear, and accessories from a sporting goods store in Baton Rouge.

Fidelity does not expect to make money from this seminar. Rather, they use the seminar to gain access to new and in this case profitable cutomers who can be brought into the bank. Fidelity's objective is to provide comprehensive banking service to this segment.

One area in which new product development effort can be directed is in the area of services that a bank can offer which complement or augment their basic product mixes. Consider mortgage loans. In addition, banks can wholesale decorating services, special low interest loans for home decoration or improvement, appraisal services, and insurance help.

Commercial DDAs could also be a basis for new products. In spite of the many differences that might exist between the needs that an individual consumer may have and a business, both are probably concerned about their money's ability to make money for them. Consumers have money market funds and NOW accounts which earn interest on their checking. Business would probably respond favorably to a product which would provide unlimited check-writing privileges with interest being paid on the average daily balance in excess of some set account minimum balance.

THE PRODUCT LIFE CYCLE

A key concept on which most packaged goods marketers rely is the concept of the product life cycle (PLC). In essence the PLC says that a product is born, goes through various stages in its life, and then ultimately dies. From a strategic marketing perspective, the PLC provides important guidelines as to the management of the product over this lifetime.

Figure 6–1 depicts a typical product life cycle. While the number of stages may vary depending on the particular interpretation of the PLC, most marketers would probably suggest that there are four stages. These are the introductory stage, the growth stage, the maturity stage, and the decline stage. As we have indicated before, the value of the PLC lies in its ability to suggest strategic guidelines for managing a product through the different stages of its life cycle.

Introductory Stage

The introductory stage of the product's life cycle is characterized by low sales and, often, negative profits. This typically short run condition is attributable to a number of factors. First, few in the marketplace are

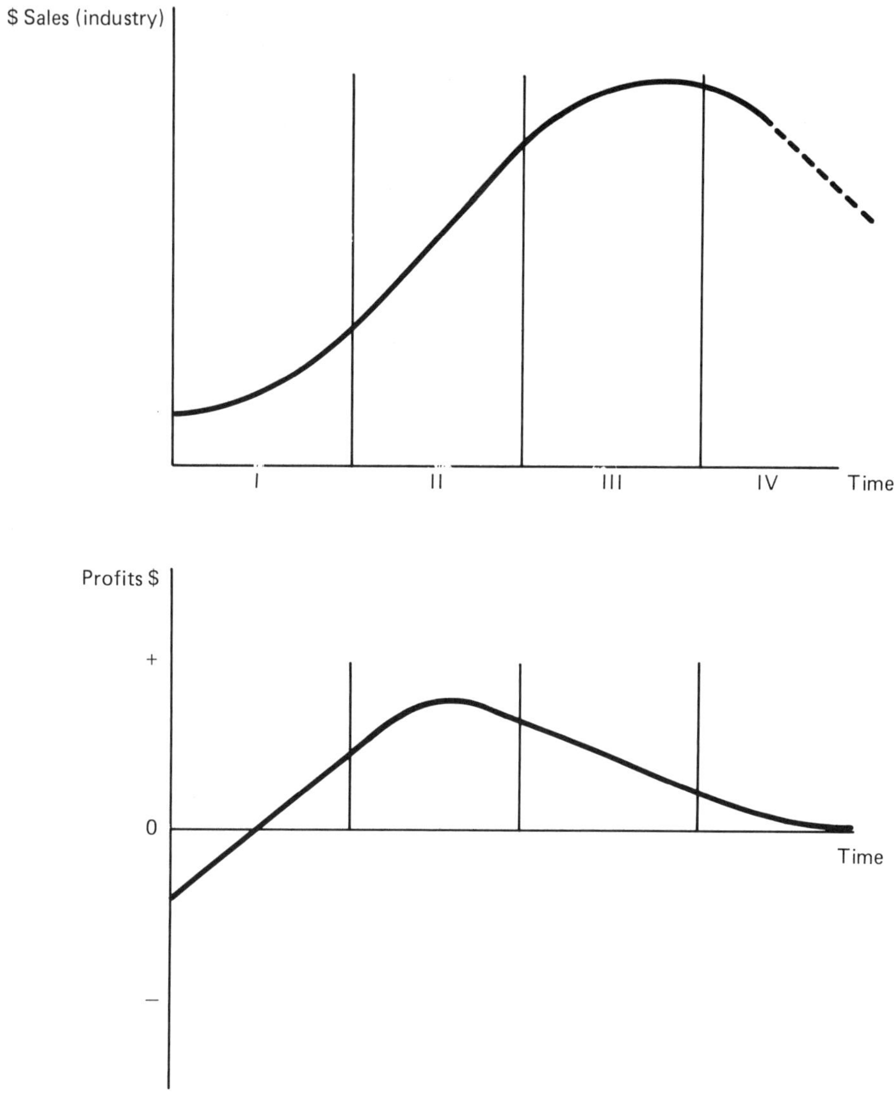

FIG. 6–1. The product life cycle (PLC).

aware of the product; consequently promotion costs are high. This newness and the high promotion costs account for both the low sales and low profitability. In addition, distribution of the product may be somewhat limited. Management may choose to distribute the product on a step-by-step basis to limit costs and risk.

The banking industry generally operates somewhat differently from consumer goods industries because for so long all new products were regulated. As a result, when regulations permitted banks to market new products, the tendency was for slightly different versions of the same product to be introduced at the same time. Price was generally fixed by mandate, as was the distribution variable in some cases. Promotion was the only truly manipulable variable, and new product introductions were traditionally fought with premiums, contests, and heavy advertising.

The tendency toward deregulation has changed this scenario somewhat. Banks are now having to rely more heavily on their own R & D departments to generate new product/service offerings which are competitive with other offerings. There is a great tendency toward "me-too" types of product introductions. That is, if one competitor in a marketplace offers a new product, most others will follow if that introduction is successful. Cash management accounts or assets management accounts are examples of new me-too products. In addition, the move toward deregulation has removed many of the restrictions on the use of the other marketing mix variables. Both price and distribution, as well as the product variable, are just that, more variable.

The Growth Stage

After the product survives the introductory stage, it passes into the growth stage. At this time competitive pressures tend to increase as other banks, for instance, see that the product has been successfully introduced. The promotional task has changed in the growth stage. Awareness gives way in importance to product identification and a "buy-mine" approach. There may be both a softening of high price entries and an increasing of price of the bargain products. Finally, the product itself may undergo certain modifications as adjustments are made to fine-tune it so that it is more responsive to market needs and wants.

When IRAs were introduced, banks began by offering only CDs with only one or two maturity choices and no fees for the accounts. As they progressed, they began to see a need for more alternatives in IRA accounts. Many banks now offer "self-directed" IRA accounts through their trust divisions or discount brokerage divisions—allowing the customer to choose his or her own investment vehicle and charging the customer fees for the various services provided.

Profits tend to turn positive in this stage as the sales of the product begin to increase at an increasing rate. Market acceptance of the product accounts for this change.

The Maturity Stage

Once the product leaves the growth stage, it enters into the maturity stage. The most salient characteristic of this stage is the slowdown in sales and profit growth rates. Products in the maturity stage pose a different kind of problem for the strategic marketing planner.

Competition, especially marginal competitors, begins to fall out. The market is reaching its limit for acceptance of the product. The strategic marketing planner must now be willing to make certain additional adjustments in the marketing mix. This may include adjusting the product form as well as the other controllable variables. Prices may continue to soften somewhat. The distribution of the product may be reduced as other rising products get more attention and are targeted for more promotional and distribution effort. Generally, a hard core market may exist at this time which precludes some organizations from ceasing to provide any marketing effort and leaving the market. As margins become thinner and thinner, an emphasis from revenue production to cost savings may be prudent. The strategic marketing planner may now turn his or her attention to marketing the product at a lower cost than before. This may mean additional cuts in promotion and distribution.

Passbook savings accounts have entered the maturity stage in many markets. To improve the profitability of these accounts, some banks are now charging service fees on accounts with balances below a certain minimum and are requiring a certain minimum amount to open a new passbook savings.

Regular checking accounts are in the maturity to decline stage in most markets. In order to keep this very basic product alive and profitable, bankers have had to set up some new fee schedules and cost savings procedures. Offering "limited activity" checking accounts is one way of keeping this basic account profitable. Check truncation is another way of keeping the costs associated with checking accounts down. Gaining public acceptance of new fee schedules and check truncation is a challenge for bank marketers.

The Decline Stage

Products in the decline stage are characterized by a strong downward drift in sales and a continual erosion of profits. The task facing the strategic marketing planner is one of harvesting or divesting the product mix of this dying product. To carry the product to the point where it is no longer profitable is foolish. While some companies may produce products which, when no longer profitable to them, can be sold to other companies who may be able to squeeze continued profitability from them, this is generally not feasible in the banking industry. However, deregulation has allowed some financial competitors to diversify into other areas. In these cases, declining profitability in diversified areas derived from dying products may signal a time for voluntary divestiture.

PROPOSITIONS ABOUT THE PLC

There are several propositions concerning the use of the PLC as a strategic guide that should be considered. First, not all products pass through the idealized S-shaped curve shown in Figure 6–1. Some products, fads for example, have life cycle curves more closely approaching inverted Vs. Introduction and growth are relatively quick, followed by an equally rapid maturity and decline.

Second, the time span associated with each of the four stages will vary. Some products may have exceptionally long growth and maturity stages while introduction may have been relatively rapid.

Third, it is important to define the level of aggregation to which the PLC is applied. The level of aggregation can be either the industry, the firm's product line, or a single product. Depending on what level of aggregation is being considered, variances in the PLC can be expected.

One of the problems with the PLC is that it is difficult to place a product in the proper stage. This makes it important to clearly distinguish the definition of market toward which the PLC is being applied. For example, a product may be in the growth stage in one market while in the maturity stage in yet another. Keeping these propositions in mind makes the PLC a useful tool for understanding the strategic implications of time and competition on the life of a product.

USING THE PRODUCT LIFE CYCLE TO MANAGE BANKING PRODUCTS

What is characteristic of banking products in general is that, depending on the market, certain banking products can be identified in a number of different PLC stages. For example, discount brokerage services for many banks are in the introductory stage. Here the task is to create awareness for the services in general, focusing, not necessarily on a specific bank's discount brokerage service, but rather the fact that banks *are now offering the service.*

Products in the growth stage may be NOW accounts, money market funds, and bank cards. Here the task is to create a selective demand by tying the product to the bank. In addition, some adjustments in the product may have to be made as competition enters. For example, minimum deposits may have to be lowered on NOW accounts and money market funds to attract new customers. Similarly, service charges on bank cards may have to be reduced. Changes of this type should keep sale of bank products in the growth stage solid.

Mature bank products would include the traditional passbook savings accounts and Christmas Club accounts. Many banks will begin to find these products losing profitability as newer and better products begin to cannibalize sales of the more mature products. To the extent that these products can be delivered at lower costs to the bank, their life may be extended. These types of products will eventually move into the decline stage (in some markets they may already be in this stage). When this occurs, the strategic planner must be prepared to prune these nonprofitable products for his or her mix. In addition, there must be new products entering the life cycle to maintain the overall sales and profitability of the bank. This is the value of the PLC—its forewarning that new products are continually needed to replace maturing and declining products. Moreover, strategic adjustments are needed as environmental changes impact the different products.

PRODUCT PORTFOLIO MANAGEMENT

One aspect of the system's concept mentioned earlier applied to bank marketing and product management decisions is found in the portfolio approach. Most bankers will be familiar with the basic concepts of portfolio management when applied to investments. Marketers have found an analogous application to the management of a firm's product mix.

Product portfolio management is most commonly associated with the Boston Consulting Group. The premise behind the product portfolio is that a product manager typically manages a number of different products which are in different stages of their life cycle. This disparity of performance calls for different types of decisions in response to differing market circumstances. What is crucial to all products regardless of the stage of their life cycle and market specific conditions is that each product/service offering will be either a *cash user* or *cash generator*. Cash flow is important because it enables the financing and manipulation of marketing variables to accomplish market share objectives and, ultimately, profit objectives.

Reliance on portfolio approaches is being catalyzed by several factors in the banking industry. These include:

- An increasing number of new products, each requiring the development of specific marketing plans to manage them through their life cycles.

- A need to prioritize products with respect to the resources which will be expended toward their management. Some products will offer better opportunities for achieving the bank's objectives than others.
- Many of the products are related. The likelihood of "cannibalization" or crippling an existent product with a new product is greater. Portfolio approaches provide the strategic market planner with a better vantage point, thereby reducing this problem.[2]

Two variables are important in motivating the BCG product portfolio. The first is market share. Typically, market share is depicted in terms of relative market share, that is, relative to the next largest competitor. Thus, individual product/service offerings can be described in terms of their relative market share. A second variable is the growth rate of the individual product/service markets. When the two variables, relative market share and market growth rate, are juxtaposed in matrix form, a market share/market growth matrix like the one in Figure 6–2 is developed.

The matrix in Figure 6–2 is divided into four quadrants. A bank's product system can be mapped onto this matrix depending upon an individual product/service offering's relative market share and market growth rate. This mapping and ultimate product/service configuration provide a number of insights into how that product/service offering can best be managed in terms of cash flow relative to the other product/service offerings comprising the bank's portfolio.

Those products with relatively small market share and little market growth are located in the lower right-hand corner. Typically, these product/service offerings are called *dogs* because of their present poor performance and bleak prospects for future growth. Christmas Club savings accounts are a good example. There are several options open to the strategic marketing planner with respect to the management of dogs. First, additional market share could be "bought" which would move the product/service to the left. The marketing manager can do this by increasing promotional effort, by reducing the price of the product/service offering, or by increasing the distribution of it, or any combination of the above. All of these options cost money, and the marketing manager has to consider the likely consequences of this approach relative to the other product/service offerings in his or her portfolio. In other words, what are the opportunity costs associated with such a strategy?

Another approach is the harvesting of the product. Harvesting involves minimal marketing effort to sustain the product while maximizing cash flow. It is a short-term strategy designed ultimately to phase out the product. A final approach to be considered in managing

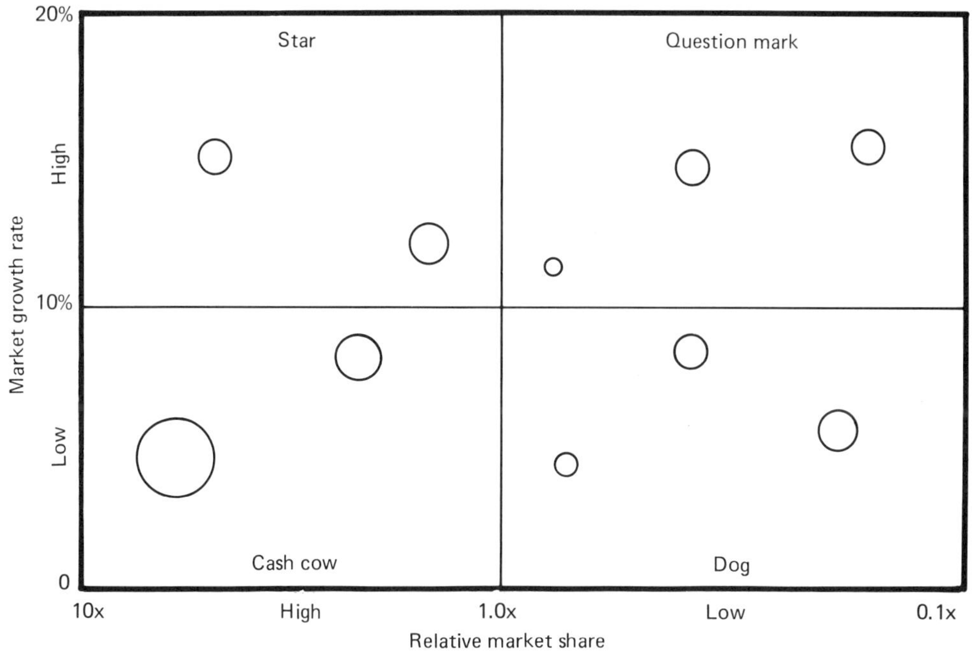

FIG. 6–2. Product portfolio matrix.

these so-called cash traps is a divesting strategy. Divesting involves the liquidation of the product/service offering because the cash can be better utilized elsewhere. This is particularly applicable to those dogs which a bank's management feels have no prospects for growth.

Question marks are those product/service offerings which are presently enjoying relatively low market share but are considered to have high growth potential. Discount brokerage services and asset management accounts fall in this quadrant for most banks. The strategic options facing the marketing planner focus on how to increase the market share of the product. Again, market share can be purchased by additional expenditures on one or more of the marketing mix variables. It is for this reason that question marks are typically cash users. If management decides to make this product/service offering a market leader, additional cash will be spent. If, however, they decide not to, the focus is then on how to harvest and ultimately divest it from the portfolio.

Stars are those product/service offerings that are enjoying relatively high market share in growth markets. They are heavy cash users because competition for market leadership requires heavy marketing expenditures. Eventually the growth of the star will slow down but, until it does, the strategic concern facing the marketing manager is the maintenance of a high share position.

Low growth/high share products are called *cash cows*. Contrary to their high growth counterparts, these product/service offerings are cash generators. This cash generation is extremely important, because it is used to finance other cash users in the bank's portfolio. The task facing the strategic marketing planner is the maintenance of high market share which, in this case, may not be as expensive as in the case of high-growth products. A declining market may allow some banks the opportunity to increase their market share rather inexpensively as other competitors, for any number of reasons, drop out of the market. As a number of competitors drop out, those remaining may experience a short-term gain in market share by default. Evenutally cash cows will become dogs, at which time a harvesting and ultimately divesting strategy will be necessary.

PROPOSITIONS CONCERNING THE BCG APPROACH

There are several propositions concerning the use of the BCG product portfolio. First, the bank marketer must keep the proper balance of cash users and cash generators in the portfolio. Too many cash users may be more problematic than too many cash generators. An imbalance of cash generators, however, may precipitate a future problem, as the bank may not be developing enough new products to meet its future growth needs. Too many cash users may indicate an overly aggressive marketing strategy. Some of these products may have to be withdrawn so that the more promising products can receive the resources necessary to market them properly.

A second proposition of the portfolio approach is that the higher the market share of the product/service offering, the greater its cash-generating ability. Moreover, marketers in the consumer goods industries have long recognized the long-term relationship between market share and long-term profitability.

Third, high-growth products tend to be cash users. Competition for market share in high-growth markets is generally the most intensive. The rewards of high share in high-growth market share are cash cows.

As time passes, product/service offerings will move throughout the matrix. It is the job of the strategic marketing planner to manage these moves rather than let time, competition, and environmental change do it for him or her. Projections of the different product/service offerings over time can be made on the matrix. This will allow the strategic marketing manager to make contingency plans depending on the specific scenario.

One complaint of the product portfolio approach is that there are other factors which are also important in the management of products. This shortcoming can be overcome by incorporating an index of factors such as market size, market growth rate, profit margins, competitive intensity, and other factors. This index could replace the market growth rate and provide the strategic planner with a more comprehensive and sophisticated analysis. Overall, the growth/share matrix is an extremely useful tool for monitoring the health of the bank's product/service mix. It recognizes, from a cash flow perspective, the interdependence of marketing decisions and accordingly allows the strategic marketing planner to deal with the entire product/service mix rather than just a single offering.

PRODUCT/MARKET STRATEGIES

Figure 6–3 identifies four different types of product/market strategies which are applicable to the banking industry in varying degrees. Market penetration, market development, product development, and diversification represent four types of strategies. Each has variations which may be more applicable and successful depending upon various factors.

Market Penetration

Market penetration strategies involve increasing the sales for an existent product in existent markets. Generally this involves an increase in marketing effort. Three variations of this market penetration strategy

	Existing products	New products
Existing markets	1. Market penetration	2. Product development
New markets	3. Market development	4. Diversification

Philip Kotler, Marketing Management, 3ed ed. (Englewood Cliffs, N. J.: Prentice-Hall, Inc., 1976), p. 49.

FIG. 6–3. Product/market strategies.

are possible. These include increasing the current rate of usage of a product, attracting competitor's customers, and attracting nonusers of the product.

Increasing the rate of usage is a strategy used by many consumer good marketers. Shampoo manufacturers advise customers to wash their hair twice. Lysol disinfectant urges mothers to take their product on summer vacations, and toothpaste producers have convinced customers to brush their teeth several times a day.

Bank marketers can use this strategic option to promote increased usage of certain services. When IRAs were first introduced, most banks concentrated on the upscale market because of their ability to make the maximum contribution. Less affluent segments who are also IRA buyers can be targeted for increasing their contributions to the IRA accounts. Not all services are conducive to this type of strategy. Consumer loans, for example, represent a product for which too much demand and marketing effort can be detrimental to the bank's profitability.

Attracting competitor's customers is another variation of a market penetration strategy. For many banking markets, especially in smaller towns, a market share equilibrium has been reached. With the possibility of deregulation of interstate banking rules, this equilibrium may be upset as the definition of bank competition is broadened significantly. Already, large banks are readying themselves for movement into certain attractive markets.

Attracting nonusers is a third strategic option. Cross-selling of a bank's products is an example of market penetration. As was mentioned earlier in Chapter 4, an effective cross selling program has the potential of making users out of nonusers for certain banking products. The trust services of a bank are a good example of a product which should respond favorably to this type of strategy.

Product Development

Product development involves increasing the bank's overall sales by developing new products or improving existing products for its current markets. Several options exist: modifying existing products, creating different quality products, developing new products.

Modifying existing products is a strategy which is followed by many banks when they offer different minimum investment levels for CDs. Jumbo CDs, which are attractive to the upscale markets, foreclose a large number of buyers from making this type of investment. Aware that other segments would be willing to buy lower-denomination CDs, many banks offer CDs of varying denominations. Adding new product features to mature products may give the old product a new look that will be attractive to existing markets. Passbook savings accounts represent such an opportunity.

Variations of different quality are another product development strategy. The Circle of Green, The President's Account, Group One, and Money Power are examples of account packages which use quality as a differentiating device. Not only does an increase in quality represent a strategic product development strategy, but so too does a less-than-premium approach. The beer industry understands that there exists a significant market that is price-oriented. By reducing the prices of their products and by marketing no-frills products many brewers have been very successful. This approach may be equally successful for banks, who may find a very functionally oriented segment. While the emphasis is on the upscale segment because of its overall profitability, less affluent segments may offer strategic opportunities for a quality differentiation approach in the opposite direction. Many discount retailers have found a very profitable niche serving this market.

New product development has been tightly controlled in the banking industry. Most banks have responded to the opportunity to offer newly approved products. Deregulation promises to open up this particular area of banking. A study conducted by the American Banking Association's Economic Advisory Committee, for example, has identified three new products which offer promise to most banks. These include real estate equity investing, insurance brokerage, and discount securities brokerage.

Market Development Strategies

Market development strategies involve the increase of marketing effort for existing products in new markets. Two variations exist: attracting new segments for established products and geographic expansion.

Attracting new segments for existing products appears to be a natural strategy once new products have been introduced and adopted by the initially targeted groups. More and more banks are turning to less affluent segments for IRAs, for example. Banks initially targeted customers who could make the maximum deposit. Once this segment had been developed, banks are finding a profitable market among those who want an IRA but can't afford the maximum deposit.

Geographic expansion has been accomplished in the past through branching, where applicable. The development of ATMs has made market development strategies available to all sizes of banks. Presently, the banking system is attempting to sort out rules and policies concerning interstate banking at the federal level. At the writing of this book, a type of *de facto* deregulation of interstate banking is taking place through limited-service banks, mergers, and acquisitions. New technology promises to provide continually new means of expansion as banks utilize computer and satellite systems to penetrate new geographic markets.

Diversification

Diversification strategies involve the marketing of new and generally unrelated products to new markets. This is a relatively risky proposition for many organizations, which is one reason why bank regulators have traditionally prevented banks from using this strategic option. Citicorp has recently petitioned the federal regulators to permit the bank, through IRA-linked insurance policies, to enter the insurance industry. While banks are permitted to sell credit-related insurance policies, such a move by Citicorp represents a new diversification move that is still under consideration by federal regulators. Many organizations find it more prudent to acquire existing organizations and thereby to acquire instantaneous competence and market share. This tends to reduce some of the risk of a new venture. Discount brokerage is an example of a permissible diversification in the banking industry. Whether or not banks will be allowed to continue to diversify and how to diversify are issues under considerable debate.

What is interesting is that many of the banking industry's competitors are becoming competitive to the banking industry through this strategic option. Consider JC Penney, Sears, and Kroger, for example. These retailers are taking advantage of an increasing trend in "one-stop shopping" and diversifying into the financial industry. Where such strategies will lead to makes for some very interesting speculation.

SUMMARY

This chapter has examined the nature of the product/service mix. In doing so, we have introduced the concept of the product life cycle and portfolio management and have identified several product strategies. The management of a bank's product/service mix in an increasingly competitive and deregulated market arena will determine the degree of success and survivability that banks will enjoy in the future. Creative and responsive banks will find the product/market matches paying strategic dividends.

Footnotes

[1]Stephen Mintz, "Banking on Marketing," *Sales and Management,* Vol. 130, No. 10 (1983), p. 48.

[2]Joseph P. Guiltinan and James H. Donnelly, Jr., "The Use of Product Portfolio Analysis in Bank Marketing Planning," *Journal of Retail Banking,* Vol. 15, No. 1 (1983), pp. 15–24.

7

product development decisions

INTRODUCTION

One facet of strategic marketing planning which will be most heavily affected by the uncertainties of competition and environmental change is product development. The importance of new product development is underscored by the trend toward the unbundling of products/services and the need to understand the costs and prices of individual product/service offerings. In order to stay ahead of, or at least to keep abreast with the massive changes in the banking industry, strategic marketing planners will have to adopt a more aggressive and innovative product development structure. Marketers in other industries know very well that long-term growth, market share, and profitability are the fruits of a prudent, yet bold, program of product innovation. Because of the importance of this topic to bank marketing, we are dedicating one chapter to discussing a framework for evaluating new product ideas.

A FRAMEWORK FOR EVALUATING NEW PRODUCT IDEAS

The framework presented in this chapter is an adaptation of the type of paradigm used by many marketers operating in both industrial and consumer goods markets. There are, of course, numerous variations of this model, and the reader is encouraged to use this particular framework as an initial starting point for developing his or her own framework which might be more applicable to the structure and organizational climate of their particular bank.

Essentially, there are five distinct yet related stages or steps in this product development model. The value of having a fairly well delineated procedure for product development is the systematic approach that such a framework offers. At each stage of the process certain decisions are required. These typically involve either returning to an earlier stage in the process, continuing on with the development process, or killing the product. The entire framework is depicted in Figure 7–1.

Stage One: Idea Generation

The first step in the product development procedure is developing candidate ideas for consideration. All employees of the bank should be encouraged to provide input into this stage. No idea should be discarded offhand because it is too outlandish. With a little additional effort, idea refinement may turn an otherwise unworkable idea into one which has great potential.

Occasional brainstorming sessions can also prove fruitful for generating new product ideas. In these sessions individuals are encouraged to examine the bank's present product/service mix, see where the mix can be broadened or deepened, examine what competition is doing, and see whether certain changes, refinements, or adaptations of a present product/service offering can be better effected.

Tellers may be extremely valuable sources of new product ideas. They represent one of the more important organizational interfaces with the market. When involved in the process, their closeness to the market may be helpful in identifying unsatisfied needs or improved ways in which customer needs could be satisfied.

These ideas should be collected for further screening. Studies by different marketers indicate that statistically it requires somewhere over 60 new product/service ideas to produce one new product. The attrition rate of new product ideas is very high in the product development process, and new products are only as good as the ideas that produce them. Once these ideas have been collected, they are ready for further screening.

Stage Two: Concept Generation

As Figure 7–1 indicates, the next stage is generating a product/service concept. A concept is something more than a mere idea but is not yet a product. It is a detailed statement of what the new product will be and do. This is an integral step in the development process. Passage from this stage to subsequent stages means that the concept is compatible with the purpose and goals of the bank. This provides a strong reinforcing basis for continued development.

In this analysis it is assumed that the idea has been generated, has been "fleshed out," and must now be evaluated in light of company objectives, strengths, resources, new product criteria, and prevailing

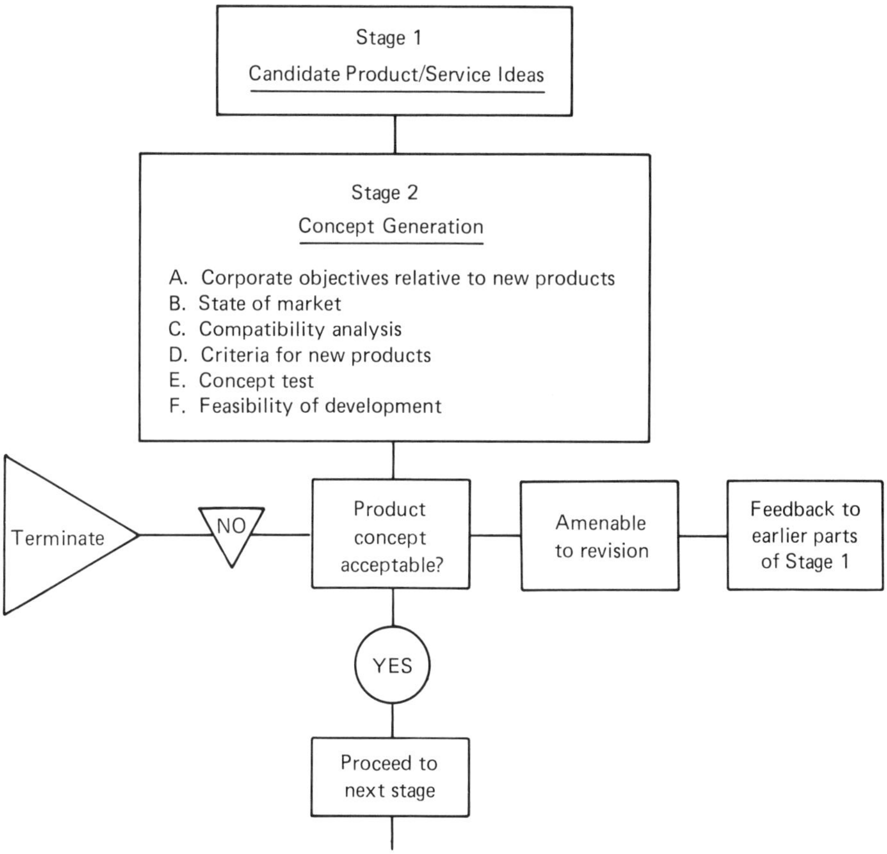

FIG. 7–1. A framework for product/service development.

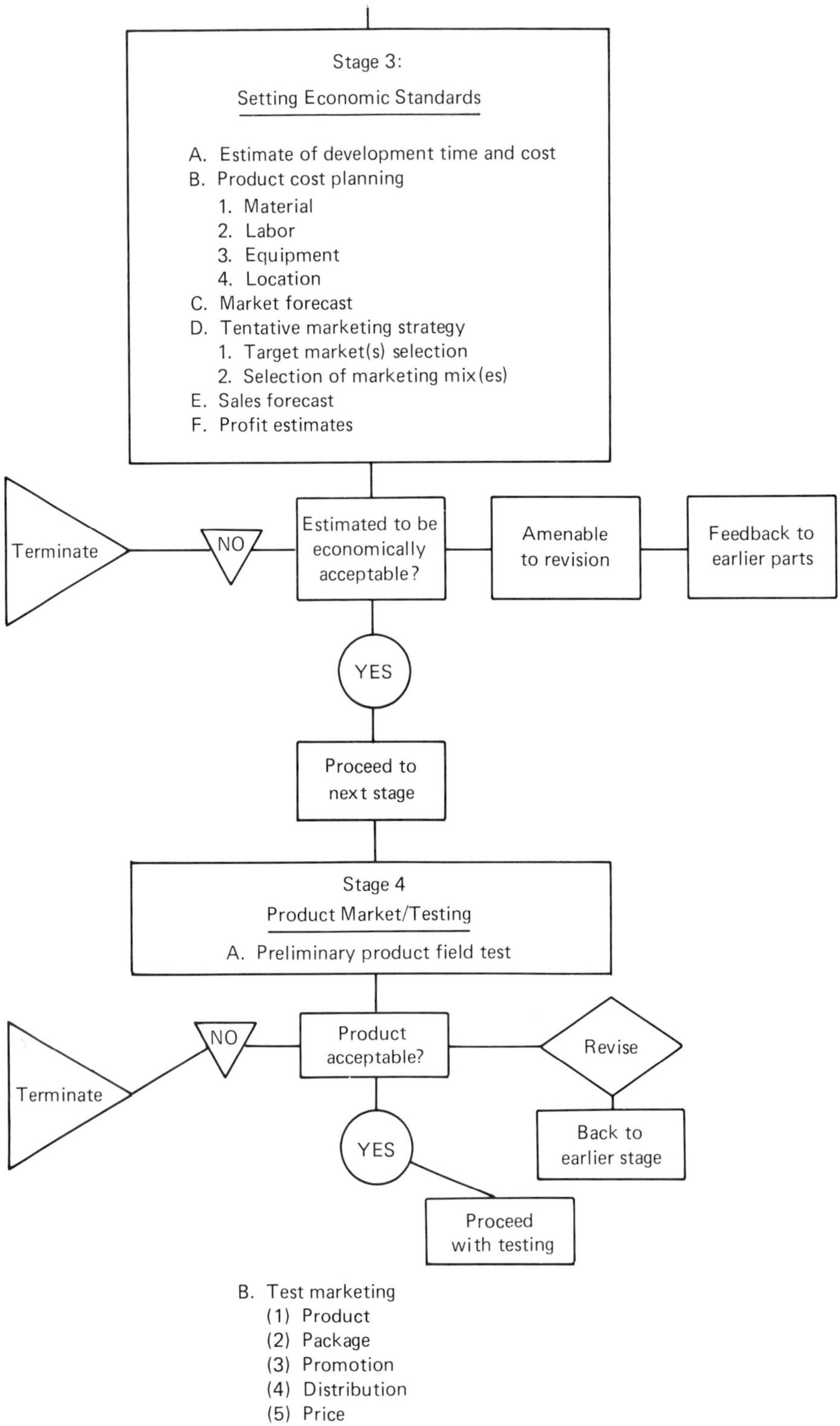

FIG. 7–1. *(continued)*

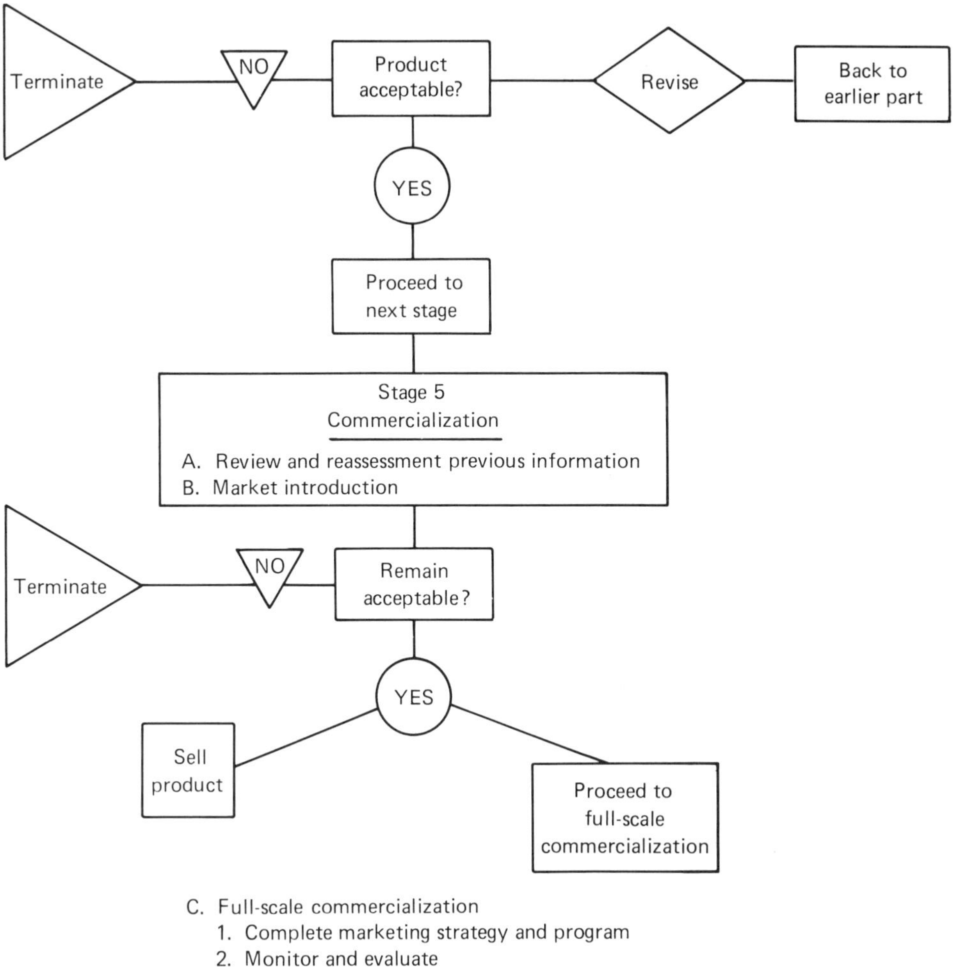

FIG. 7–1. *(continued)*

market conditions. Serious deficiencies in any of the aforementioned areas signal a potential kill point for the project, while moderate deficiencies may simply indicate the need for concept revision.

Several specific questions should be asked at this stage. These include:

1. What is the definition of the bank's business? This definition provides a directing influence for the utilization of bank resources and the meaningful evaluation of innovative opportunity.
2. Is the concept compatible with the definition of the bank's business?

3. What are the bank's objectives that bear on new product/service development? These can be examined in terms of ROI (return on investment), payback periods, and profitability.
4. Does the concept provide the potential for satisfying these objectives? The word *potential* is stressed at this point because only estimates of the above criteria can be made. At this point only those concepts which are seriously lacking in potential are sent back for revision or are killed.
5. What are the specific strengths and resources of the bank? This evaluation should be made in terms of the bank's financial strength, its technical, personnel, and management strengths, marketing capabilities, and any other factors which might impinge upon the development and delivery of new product/service offerings.
6. What are the success requirements inherent in the new product/service opportunity? Again these would include financial, technical, personnel, and management and marketing requirements.
7. Are the strengths and resources of the bank adequate to support and nurture the proposed new product? Is there a match?
8. What is the present state of the market? Has a market potential been established? Has a user breakdown been established? Have price levels been evaluated? Has competition been evaluated?
9. How does the concept stand up in the marketplace (concept testing)? Is it clearly understood? What benefits are perceived in it? What problems are perceived in it? How does it compare with competitive offerings? What improvements can be made in it? What price would the user expect to pay? Does the targeted user intend to adopt it? If so, what is the intended usage pattern? Answers to these questions are obtained by measuring targeted user reactions to the concept. These reactions are only initial assessments of the concept's potential. Serious deficiencies in concept acceptance would signal one of three courses of action: revision, continuation, or the killing of seriously deficient concepts. The concept generation stage involves a certain expense on the part of a bank. Often, this expense is not recovered because the concept does not make it past this stage. However, when the costs of full-scale commercialization of an unsuccessful concept are weighed against those spent identifying a deficient concept, the longer-term loss is minimal. Those concepts which survive this stage of the development process are passed on to the next stage.

Stage Three: Setting Economic Standards

This stage focuses on many of the considerations necessary to determine if commercialization is warranted from a revenue/cost perspective. The tasks facing the strategic marketing planner involve answering the following key questions.

A. Have estimates of the development time and cost been prepared?

B. Have production/delivery costs been determined?

C. Has a market forecast been developed?

D. Tentative Strategy Development. This step develops initial plans for the marketing mix to enable continued testing to occur.

1. Target Market(s) Selection. Have market segments with the greatest opportunity been identified as targets? Target markets selected must be consistent with objectives and resources.
2. Marketing Mix Evaluation. Has evaluation of the various combinations of marketing variables been completed? Have the tentative costs of the various combinations been established? This evaluation is necessary to establish the relationship between levels of marketing expenditures and the resultant output in the form of sales, revenue, or profit. A flexible budget matrix may be established to accomplish this analysis for each variable. A flexible budget should be developed for the alternate marketing systems that may be employed. Once an evaluation of each variable has been developed, the individual variables can be combined to form alternate marketing mix combinations. Flexible budgets can be prepared for all the marketing mix alternatives to allow selection of the most desirable mix for the target group or groups selected.
3. Marketing Mix Selection. Has a marketing mix been selected to match the characteristics of the total offering to those identified as desired by the target customers? Subsidiary questions include:
   a. Is the product/service in optimal form?
   b. Has an optimal price level been selected?
   c. Is the optimal distribution structure selected?
   d. Will the promotion program match the needs of the target customers?
   e. Have separate strategies been developed for each target market?

f. Can some strategies be combined to produce economies in marketing?

E. Have sales forecasts been developed? Market response will be dependent upon the mix chosen. The sales forecast should be established upon the principle that relative sales in the market will be in proportion to the proportion of marketing expenditures by the company as a percentage of total industry sales.

F. Have profit estimates been developed? Profit estimates are the culmination of this stage. The sales forecast and marketing cost estimates developed are coupled with cost studies to develop full profit estimates for the most consistent marketing strategies. Flexible budgeting may again be employed, particularly if costs will vary under alternative marketing conditions. These budgets will help in analyzing effects of price changes, various levels of marketing expenditures, and various competitive responses. In addition, they will aid in developing a range of outcomes which can be expected under various circumstances which might occur once commercialization is achieved. Break-even analysis should also be conducted to determine the minimum acceptance levels for profitable operation under different marketing or competitive circumstances.

Stage Four: Product/Service Testing

Here the testing gets at the only meaningful answer to the question of quality; that is, how does the market view the product? Note again that decision points are a vital and explicit part of this stage.

1. Preliminary Product Field Test. Here the strategic planner should try to answer the question of how the product/service is assessed by *the market* under experimental use. Potential customers and users would evaluate the product under prevailing marketing and use conditions. It is actual use as closely as a test can be. It is experimental use but not experimental marketing. No one is required to make an actual buying decision in the face of all the complexities that attend such a decision.

   This part of the testing is an extension of the concept test to a physical product.

2. Test Marketing. This is the most rigorous and crucial of all the tests. Here the product must stand the rigors of selling in adequate quantities under existing market conditions. Data should be gathered from a mirocosm of the total market(s) into which the product would be entered.

It can be observed from the diagram that not only the product, narrowly conceived, is being tested here; the broad conception of the product, including price, communication, and distribution, should also be tested. The test can be split further into a positioning test pitting the product against each competitive product.

Stage Five: Commercialization

This stage should begin by evaluating previous steps to determine that all factors affecting the project have been considered. Specific questions to be addressed at this stage include:

1. Have product/service delivery costs changed?
2. Has the market changed in terms of size, use, or attitude?
3. Have market circumstances caused a need for alteration of forecasts of market or sales levels?
4. Have any factors occurred which modify the profitability analysis?
5. Was the test market satisfactory?

If positive answers are obtained to the above questions, and no changes have taken place with respect to corporate objectives, then introduction appears warranted.

Market Introduction. Have market introduction plans been developed? Entrance into the market will require the establishment of many external relationships between the bank and facilitating organizations, such as distribution intermediaries, advertising agencies, investment firms, etc.

A reasonable time period for analysis of the launch results should be established. Once the necessary time has passed, the product/service offering should be reviewed to determine what adjustment, if any, is needed prior to full-scale commercialization.

Full-Scale Commercialization. Have long-term plans for satisfaction of objectives for the offering been prepared?

The marketing mix will be planned for adjustment based upon competitive response, which can vary.

Monitor and review methods need to be established to enable the bank to continuously appraise market and competitive characteristics to determine what fine adjustments to the marketing strategy may be necessary.

Table 7–1 summarizes the key questions that need answering during the different stages of the development process. In addition, sources of information are presented as are the methods for collecting this information.

TABLE 7–1 Summary of Questions to Be Answered in Product Development Process

Question	*Needed to Answer*	*Source of Data*	*Data Collection Method*
Compatibility of concept with bank objectives and resources	Goodness of fit of opportunity success requirements with distinctive competencies of bank	Bank policy statements	Management decisions
State of the market: a. Technological/political b. Legal environment c. Social/cultural d. Economics e. Competition	Conditions existing within the market so that entry may be facilitated. Market structure	Environmental monitoring process and management information	
Product positioning	Perceptual state of the market, state of competition, ability to enter, input on marketing mix decisions. Attitude toward proposed product and subsequent revisions (if necessary)	Company recorded sources, market studies of users	Secondary research, user studies, concept test
Tentative strategy	Information on levels and types of price, promotion, and distribution to accompany concept	Users, published data from census and trade	Market studies, secondary research
Technical acceptability	Information on the product's ability to deliver what it is supposed to deliver under field conditions	Field studies of targeted users	Experiments and survey
Successful product introduction	Information to determine if mix is correct for launch	Users	Experiments via test marketing survey
Success of full-scale marketing	Information on actual results relative to objectives by time frame	Internal data compared with external and internal standards	Secondary, internal

INNOVATION DIFFUSION AND ADOPTION

Two related concepts come into play in the commercialization process. The first is the concept of innovation diffusion, and the second is the adoption process. The first describes a social phenomenon; the latter, an individual process. Knowledge of these two processes can help the strategic marketing planner to plan, direct, and coordinate product/service introduction and management.

Innovation Diffusion

This is the process by which innovations become assimilated into our society over a period of time. Diffusion refers to "the spread of a new idea from its source of orientation or creation to its ultimate uses or adoption." Figure 7–2 depicts what is regarded as a generalized diffusion of new products over time.

The innovation diffusion process identifies adoptee categories based on the idea that some types of consumers are quicker to adopt new products than other consumers. The diffusion process does not take any predetermined amount of time. Some innovations will be assimilated sooner than others.

The first adopter category is composed of innovators who comprise about 2½ percent of the total adopters. These individuals have

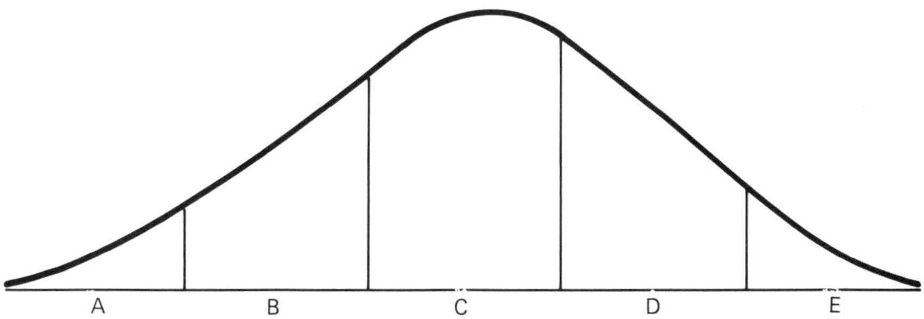

A. Innovators: 2½% of adopters
B. Early adopters: 13½% of adopters
C. Early majority: 34% of adopters
D. Late majority: 34% of adopters
E. Laggards: 16% of adopters

FIG. 7–2. Innovation diffusion: adopter categories.

certain characteristics, both demographic and psychographic, dominated by a "willingness-to-take-risks" trait. Innovators are typically the first to adopt an innovation because of the willingness to accept some risk. They are generally more cosmopolitan than individuals in other adopter categories.

The second group to adopt a product/service offering are the early adopters who comprise somewhere in the vicinity of 13½ percent of all adopters. Early adoptees are characterized by the respect accorded them, an opinion leader status, and a tendency to use discretion in the adoption decisions. Accordingly, they become role models for the next category.

The early majority account for about 34 percent of adopters. They are typified as being deliberate and willing to adopt an innovation before average consumers.

Late majority types are known for their skepticism and generally do not adopt until the innovation appears to have passed the test of time. They, like the early majority, constitute about 34 percent of all adopters.

The final adopter category is called the *laggards*. As their name implies, this is the last group to adopt an innovation. Their dominant trait is their traditional values, adopting only when the innovation becomes a part of those values. They comprise about 16 percent of all adopters.

The value of these categories lies in the ability of the strategic marketing planner to identify early adopters. The problem is that they do not easily conform to the rules of segmentation which require accessibility and measurability. However, if identified and linked to other more discernible demographic variables, they become a viable target for newly launched products.

The Adoption Process

While innovation diffusion is a social phenomenon, the adoption process is individual and describes the steps that an individual goes through in adopting an innovation. These steps are shown in Figure 7–3.

First the consumer must become aware of the new product. At this point little consumer knowledge may exist concerning the new product. Awareness stimulates an interest to learn more about the product and acts as a motivator to push the consumer into information-seeking behavior.

After information has been received, the consumer begins to evaluate this new information, assimilating the new with old information and experiences. If evaluation is positive, the consumer is urged to try the new product. Expectations are compared with actual experience.

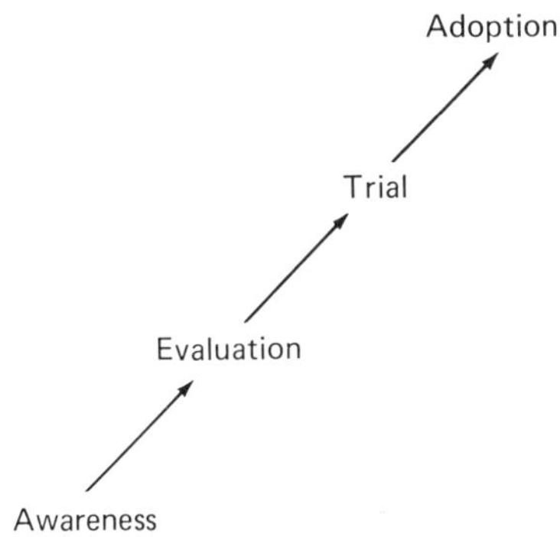

FIG. 7–3. The adoption process.

Again, a positive trial experience will generally motivate an adoption decision, all things considered.

The value of knowing about the adoption process lies in the development of communication messages and promotion strategies formulated by the bank marketer to facilitate the adoption process. The first task is attention getting and making the consumer aware of the new product/service offering. Too much information in the early stages can result in information overload and a slowing down or truncation of the adoption process. This is especially true if the information is of a technical nature, as is the case with many banking products.

As the process continues, different promotional vehicles become more important and effective. These will be discussed in greater detail in the following chapter.

SOME LESSONS ABOUT NEW PRODUCT DEVELOPMENT: CREDIT CARDS[1]

The most modern manifestation of the development of consumer-convenience credit plans is the widespread rapidly expanding bank-sponsored credit card. The history of shoppers' credit systems reveals that the concept was sufficiently simple and advantageous to have occurred to several imaginative individuals more than a quarter of a century ago. In 1938, a successful and independently sponsored plan was in operation; however, subsequent efforts to establish credit plans on a broad scale largely failed.

The major impetus of bank charge account plans began about 20 years ago when the Franklin National Bank near New York City sponsored a plan that received massive publicity within the banking community. By mid-1953, 75 commercial banks had set up the plan. However the risks associated with this new type of business and the lack of quick profits by early entrants led to a gradual withdrawal from the plan, and by the end of the year only 63 plans remained in operation. The first decade after implementation of the plan passed with modest activity followed by slow growth, but, during the last 10 years, the pace at which banks have moved into consumer-related credit has been increasingly breathless. In October 1967, bank credit-card holders owed almost $838 million, up 28 percent during the preceding six months of the year. In the same period, the number of banks offering a charge plan rose from 372 to 503. In their rush to place credit cards, many banks lost some of their dignity and learned a lesson or two in consumer credit and collection problems. But market position was established, and much of the price of learning the game has been paid. Some time will pass, however, before a full adjustment has been made.

It is useful to reflect on the position of a progressive banker who tried to analyze the potential of bank charge plans in 1953. He was hard pressed to assess the whole range of developments that might make the venture more or less attractive. He did not really understand the internal operation of the plan, even though it looked superficially similar to other bank functions. Furthermore, he did not know how merchants would respond, and he did not know what it would do to the bank's image in the eyes of the depositor and charge plan user. In short, it looked like a very chancy business. As time passed, revolving credit with its shift of charges to the consumer became common, credit-card usage in all forms of consumer credit increased sharply, computing machinery that would lower handling costs was becoming available, and some experience by other banks was accumulating. When the Bank of America demonstrated the plan's profit potential under computerized accounting procedures, the fear of getting in too late to achieve an economic volume created a near stampede in some regions. It is easy to be apathetic about innovation and change until your competition threatens to beat you to the pot of gold at the end of the rainbow.

Several general points about product innovation are illustrated by the history of the credit services offered by merchants and financial institutions. First, basically sound ideas for new products or services frequently lie dormant or develop slowly until the proper conditions appear to make them blossom. Here, sensing what the critical barriers are and how circumstances are changing is the key entrepreneurial and managerial responsibility. Second, important new products or services frequently are invented or discovered by independent operators or small firms. Seldom do these innovators reap the full fruits of their contribution. Third, established firms—often the large organizations—may have little incentive to innovate or adopt the new concept until after it is relatively well proven and/or becomes a competitive threat. Fourth, the stronger the institutions' and industries' traditions, the less likely it is that a proposal for significant change will receive a fair hearing. More often, the change is forced by circumstances external to the firm and industry.

SUMMARY

This chapter has presented a framework for developing new bank product/service offerings. While some bankers may be able to use this model as is, some because of structural, organizational, and personnel reasons may choose to adapt it to their own particular situation. That, we encourage. The value of the model is the systematic appraisal it lends to new product ideas. New product development will be of great importance for those banks seeking a leadership niche. Product line extensions and "me-too" strategies will tend to characterize the followers.

We have concluded the chapter with a brief discussion of innovation diffusion and the adopter process. These concepts can provide some valuable guidelines in the commercialization stage.

Footnotes

[1]Edgar A. Pessemier, *Product Management: Strategy and Organizations* (New York: John Wiley & Sons, 1977).

8

promotion

INTRODUCTION

Promotion is a generic term for the communication efforts of the firm which are directed toward achieving the objectives of a marketing strategy. The elements of promotion include the mass communication channels of advertising, publicity, and sales promotion, as well as the person-to-person communications of personal sales (see Table 8–1). These elements of promotion provide the firm's primary communication linkage with its target markets. In this chapter we shall discuss the theory of communication and its application in banking institutions through the elements of the promotional mix. It must be emphasized that promotion is not simply advertising but includes all the communication efforts of the firm. Further, promotion is a planned, goal-oriented effort which must be coordinated with the firm's overall goals and objectives, its desired position in the marketplace, and the other elements of the marketing mix.

TABLE 8–1 Elements of the Promotional Mix

Mass Communications	*Person-to-Person Communications*
Advertising	Personal sales
Public relations	
Sales promotion	

A MODEL OF COMMUNICATION AND ADOPTION

Each of us spends a great deal of our lives communicating with others. While promotional communications take place within a business context, they, like all communications, may be explained with a fairly simple model.[1] The communications model includes the sender and an intended receiver, a message and some channel or communication media through which this message may be transmitted, as shown in Figure 8–1. The information in the intended message is encoded into a transmittable form, transmitted through a media channel, and decoded by the intended receiver. This process can be as simple as a smile that is understood by both parties or as complex as morse code or other electronic signals transmitted through any number of telecommunication devices. The key is that both parties must be able to encode and decode the message with the same meaning and that the message channel or communication media must be able to carry the message without distortion.

As you can see from the model in Figure 8–1, communication is really a two-way, rather than just a one-way, process. For the process to be completed, the sender needs feedback that the intended message

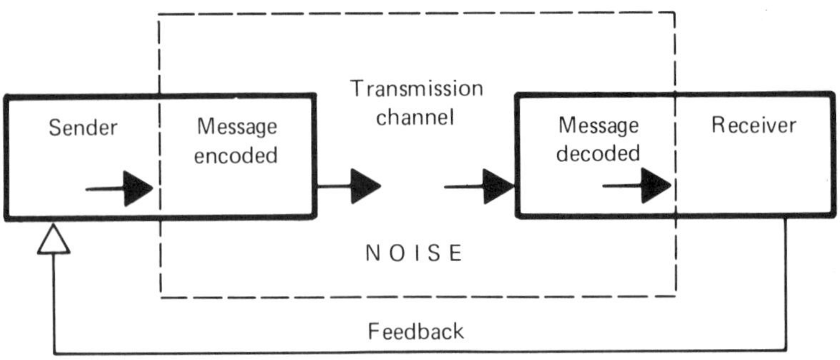

FIG. 8–1. Model of the communication process.

has been received. For example, think how difficult it would be to actually provide information to someone over the telephone if for some reason you could not hear the other person. That is what sending messages without feedback is like in marketing promotion.

It is very important to note that the model also includes noise, the basic problem in all communication systems. Noise is anything that hinders the receiver from an accurate decoding of the message. Noise may be a simple mistake, such as a misspelled word in a written communication, or as fundamental as the use of terms in the message which cannot be understood by the receiver. A good example of how noise may be controlled is the Annual Percentage Rate (APR) now used as an interest rate comparison in the banking industry. This mandated encoding of rate information was designed to provide the consumer with a way of making informed rate comparisons without the bewildering array of rate terminology which underlies the determination of interest and payment schedules for the borrower. While many would still argue that few consumers are really aware of how the APR is determined, a consistent term is now used in communications concerning interest rates.

The purpose of the communications directed toward a target market through the elements of the promotional mix is to facilitate purchase and adoption. Many communications, however, inform or entertain without really affecting purchase and adoption. The manager should understand the multistage process through which adoption takes place and the interaction of communication with this process if effective marketing communications are to be developed.

Adoption is generally viewed through five stages: awareness, interest, evaluation, trial, and adoption (as shown in Figure 8–2). In the awareness stage the potential adoptee first becomes aware that a product exists to satisfy perceived needs. The interest stage begins when the individual begins to seek information about the product; evaluation is the stage in which this newly acquired information is used to determine if the product/service will in fact satisfy customer needs. In this particular stage the product/service is put into use; if it is found satisfactory, adoption, the stage in which acceptance and repeat purchase or use is established, occurs.[2]

It is apparent that communications should be targeted toward the needs of potential customers in accordance with the stage in the purchase process. The entire makeup of the promotion mix and particular elements of the mix may be designed for particular adoption stages. For example, the mass media tools of publicity and advertising are most useful in awareness, while sales promotion may stimulate evaluation and trial.[3]

FIG. 8–2. Adoption process.

PROMOTION OBJECTIVES AND THE MARKETING MIX

Next, consider how communication may impact on the other elements of the marketing mix and what is meant by objectively based promotional planning. Just as the strategic marketing process begins with goals and objectives, the selection of communication vehicles should begin with formal consideration of communication objectives. Few banks have yet to begin major promotional campaigns that might compare to those by other industries which may spend up to 30 percent of their total revenue on promotion. Promotional expenses, however, are a significant factor in any bank if the entire communication process is considered. In general, advertising reaches more people at lower cost than personal sales efforts, but one-to-one impact and the ability to receive immediate feedback and tailor the message to the individual is lost. While the cost of sales promotions may be high, they frequently go further in stimulating behavior than advertising alone. The application of each mix component will be discussed in detail in later portions of this chapter.

HOW MUCH TO SPEND ON PROMOTION

The one thing the bank manager must remember in the determination of a promotional budget is that promotion is what produces added deposits and new loan customers for increased revenue and profitability.

In fact, it may be argued quite reasonably that much of the expenditure for promotion should actually be considered as a capital expenditure rather than an expense. This argument is based on the long-term impact of promotion on the position of the firm in the marketplace and the consumer's perception of firm and product. Promotional activities provide the means through which the bank not only communicates short-term inducements but through which the firms' image and position in the marketplace can be established. Effective communications help establish positive attributes and thus positive attitudes toward the firm. Such attitudes, generally based on the firm's communication strategy, are enduring and remain long after the particular communication is forgotten. Thus, spending money for a well-thought-out communication strategy is much like investing in other income-producing assets. While the accounting implications of capitalizing part of promotional expense may preclude the practice, the very suggestion provides a framework for the consideration of an appropriate level of expenditure. Further communication effects are in fact established as a capital asset in the form of goodwill when the actual market value of a firm is established. Remember that *goodwill* is the accounting term for the differences between the actual market value of an asset and the price paid for that asset when it is transferred. While communication-based benefits are only one component of this goodwill, they are an extremely important determinant of the firm's long-term success in the marketplace, not simply an expense of doing business.

Properly spent promotional dollars have a long-term effect and greatly impact the total enterprise. It is, however, possible to overspend for promotion. In theory there is some point after which additional expenditures produce marginally declining rather than marginally increasing returns. As Figure 8–3 shows, the promotional response function is thought to be generally S-shaped. Below some point expenditures will be inefficient and ineffective, and little or no results will be apparent. At the other end of the curve is the saturation point past which additional expenditures will have little effect. Perhaps everyone in your market area knows your bank's name, your location, and your new 24-hour automatic teller service. At this point only what is termed *reminder* advertising is necessary, and maintaining a high promotional expenditure for this service will add little. Your goal, in theory, is to spend just enough to be at the point of inflection on the promotional response curve.

In practice, difficulties in obtaining feedback and differentiating short- and long-term impacts make such economic analysis almost impossible. But it is easy to believe that many firms and entire industries may spend too much for promotion, while others never really spend enough to inform the public of what they offer. Two widely differing

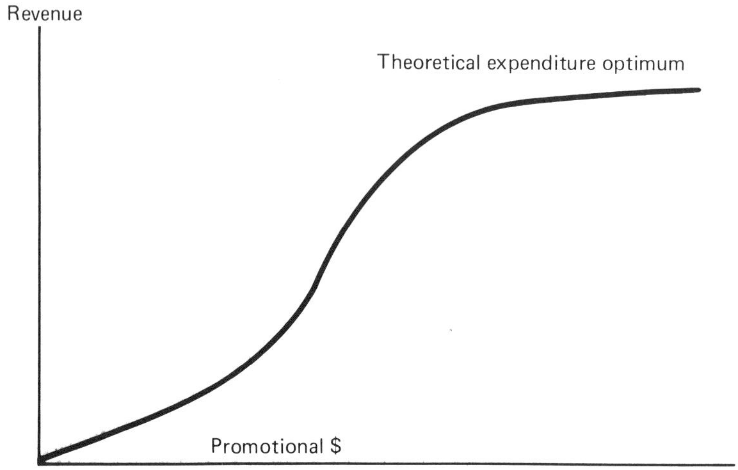

FIG. 8–3. Relationship of promotion and revenue.

studies give some indication of these two extremes. A study of the cigarette industry after the ban on television advertising indicated that the tremendous amount of promotion with a heavy emphasis on television was inefficient. Potential consumers were simply flooded with ads as each manufacturer attempted to outspend the other. The ban on television use appears to have had little negative effect on sales.[4] At the other extreme, the United States Congress passed a 15 percent tax credit to stimulate the use of home insulation, storm windows, and other energy-saving devices. During the first eighteen months of the availability of the credit, fewer than 10 percent of the taxpayers in the nation knew of the credit's existence.[5] Similar examples may be found in banking. Bank promotional expenditures have frequently been squandered on cartoon characters or other themes which have no real link to the strategic promotional objectives. Further, competing banks in a local market often spend promotional dollars simply because a competitor does rather than as part of the bank's overall strategic plan. Similarly, promotional messages do not focus on product offerings and instead make it incumbent on bank customers to discover what services a bank offers. Most commercial customers, for example, learn of products/services such as lock boxes and letters of credit out of need, rather than through the bank's promotional efforts. Such an approach puts the burden on the potential customer rather than on the respective promotional vehicle where it belongs.

Almost all firms use either one of several arbitrary allocation methods shown in Table 8–2 or an objective-task approach to set promotional expenditures. Each technique has advantages and disadvantages, but we will argue that the objective-task method is preferred.

Of the frequently used budgeting techniques, the *historical allocation* is naturally the least desirable. Generally, the manager is following historic practice for his or her bank or perhaps is following competitors. Formal consideration is not usually given to the impact of the expenditure, nor where the expenditures may fit on the promotional response function, or of the promotional objectives. Having a budget, however, is better than spending with no plan at all.

At first the *available-funds* approach may appear a very odd approach. This budgeting technique, however, is indicative of the budgeting used by many new firms or for new products. Essentially, the promotion budget is made up of all the available funds the organization has.

Typically, most firms apply some form of the *ratio of sales/revenue in budgeting* technique. Some measure of revenue or size is selected, and the promotional budget is set as a percentage of this figure. This technique has many advantages for the manager. It is easy to use and to defend. Many firms use the ratio technique as a basis for comparison and spend at about the same ratio as their competitors. While the technique provides promotional budgets which may have a relationship to some measure of the firm's size, no consideration is given to current or expected promotional goals and needs. Further, the technique implies that sales should lead promotional expenditures rather than that promotions generate sales.

The best approach to the determination of both the total promotional budget and allocation of mix expenditures is the *objective-task* approach. To use this approach, the manager must examine the objectives of the promotional component in the marketing strategy and then budget to accomplish the tasks necessary to meet these objectives. For example, if the planner wishes to introduce a new service, (s)he might decide to make sure that the majority of potential customers in the market area would see or hear of the service through advertisements during the first month of introduction. This objective leads to several task considerations for media selection and the number of exposures you consider necessary to inform the consumer. As one can see, objec-

TABLE 8–2 Promotional Expense Allocations

1. Arbitrary Allocation
   a. Historical practice
   b. Available funds
   c. Percent of sales or revenue
2. Objective—Task

tive-task is more of a bottom-up approach while the other techniques are more top-down.

EXAMINING PROMOTIONAL MIX COMPONENTS

Each of the promotional elements offer unique communication advantages. In the following section we will explore advertising, public relations, sales promotion, and personal sales as promotional tools in the marketing-oriented banking firm.

Advertising

Advertising is the most familiar mode of communication for most bank managers. Well over 20 billion dollars were spent on advertising in the United States in 1984. The dollars spent and the percentages of sales ratios for some firms are truly staggering. As Table 8–3 shows, Procter and Gamble spent more than 726 million for advertising in 1982. Of the 100 firms with the most for advertising in 1982 Noxell spent the greatest sales/advertising ratio, with 18.9 percent of its total revenue going to advertising, while giant IBM spent only .02 percent of its $34 billion. The top spending financial institution, with the exception of the large retailer Sears, in the top 100 advertising firms was American Express. American Express spent $95.5 million for advertising in 1982 to place 63 on the list. As you can see, the percentages of expenditures to sales vary greatly by industry and firm.[6]

TABLE 8–3 Leading Advertisers, 1982 (Millions of Dollars)

1. Procter & Gamble	726.4
2. Sears Roebuck & Co.	631.2
3. General Motors Corporation	549.8
4. R.J. Reynolds Industries	530.3
5. Phillip Morris, Inc.	501.7
6. General Foods Corp.	429.1
7. A T & T Co.	373.6
8. K Mart Corp.	365.3
9. Nabisco Brands	335.2
10. American Home Products Co.	324.4

Source: "100 Leaders Parry Recession with Heavy Spending," *Advertising Age,* September 1983, p. 1.

Types of Advertising. Obviously, within such a tremendous quantity of expenditure exist several classifications of advertising which may be directed at specific goals. *Institutional advertising* is designed to promote overall organizational and industry ideas, perceptions, and positioning, while *product-oriented advertising* is directed toward specific products or services.

Advertising may also be classified in accordance with its intended goals of informing, persuading, and reminding. These goals will vary with the stage of the life cycle of the product/service. *Pioneer advertising* aimed at primary demand creation is used in the earliest stages of the product's life to introduce the service concept to the public. The greatest emphasis is placed on the product's features and advantages to the target market. *Competitive advertising,* or selective demand generation advertising, is designed to emphasize broad features and to differentiate the product/service from the competition. *Reinforcement advertising* is designed specifically to reduce dissonance that a buyer may feel after the purchase by providing reassurance that the purchase was sound. Consider how such goals might shape a promotional campaign for a relatively new product such as the variable-interest-rate home mortgages which gained great popularity in the last decade. At first, pioneering advertising would be used to explain the basic advantages of such mortgages. Their affordability and availability would be emphasized with particular attention given to the initial payment advantages offered. As several banks in a market begin to offer and promote the product, total promotional/informational efforts increase and consumers have a better likelihood of learning of the product.

With most banks in the area offering the product, efforts turn from explaining the basics of the product to differentiating the bank's offerings from those of competitors. In this competitive mode, emphasis shifts from statements that show that this type of loan is better to "Our bank's loan of this type is better than others." Finally, reinforcement advertising should be used. These messages would be designed to reassure purchasers of variable-rate mortgages that they had made a sound decision when this loan was acquired. Messages could emphasize the benefits of home ownership that had already been obtained and reassure the customer that his decision was financially sound. This is rarely done in the banking industry.

Comparative advertising is a fairly recent addition to the advertising arsenal. Until the mid-1960s it was considered inappropriate to make comparisons by name between brands or firms. The competition was brand X, even though most consumers probably knew which company brand X represented. But if you don't actually name your competition, comparisons can be difficult. Comparative advertising is best when a direct comparison is made which exploits a decisive comparative advantage for the challenger. Such comparisons may also be used to position a challenger as a true alternative to existing products.[8] Comparative advertising should almost never be used by the market leader. For the leader to use such comparisons is an admission that the challenger is a true alternative and actually provides recognition and position for the challenger.

Advertising Goals and Objectives. Most marketers begin with objectives for the advertising program in terms of sales or other quantifiable measures of performance. Unfortunately, such objectives, even when further delineated to include a time frame, ignore the difficulty of relating performance through time to a particular element of the marketing strategy and the environment. To be useful as a means of planning and evaluating advertising performance, the bank's objectives need to be turned into measurable results that may be related to message and media impacts on the target market. Thus, meaningful advertising goals may include such criteria as increasing market awareness of a new service to 50 percent during a two-month period, changing existing attitudes to position an existing firm into the same perceptual position as a competitor, or exposing 70 percent of a target market to the bank's new logo. Essentially the same rules for setting promotion objectives apply as when one is setting overall strategies for marketing objectives.

Message, Media, and Creativity. The importance of detailed knowledge of the attitudes, needs, and behavior of the target market in advertising strategy and campaign implementation is vital. Knowledge of existing perceptions, attitudes, and needs leads directly to the development of effective messages, while current behavioral patterns are vital for media selection.

The Message. The effectiveness of any advertisement depends on the message communicated. This message includes the copy, the verbal part of the message, and the visual and other nonverbal components of the message. Remember that the communication should carry the receiver through the four steps of: attention, interest, decision, and action. Further, the message should be straightforward and should emphasize the communication goals and the name of the bank or the product/service being promoted. The consumer today is literally bombarded with thousands of different advertisements. In such a cluttered communication environment many marketers go to great lengths to emphasize the attention component of the communication without actually producing an effective message.

The message should be in accordance with the bank's advertising goals. One need only look at different bank ads to see the wide range of goals and equally wide variety of messages.

Media Selection. Although most consumers think of media first, the media decision actually comes only after the advertiser has already made a number of decisions. The media selection must fit the product, the target market, and, of course, the message.

The American consumer spends a great deal of time every day with one form or another of the mass media. The average female consumer spends more than 39 hours and the average male almost 35 hours each week with one of the four basic communication media. This average consumer, male or female, spends 45 percent of his or her media time watching television, 35 percent listening to the radio, 14 percent reading the newspaper, and only 5 percent of this time reading magazines.[9]

Table 8–4 provides a summary of the amount spent for advertising for the most common advertising media.

Characteristics of Media. (See Table 8–5).

Television. During the past several decades television advertising revenues have gradually increased while newspaper revenues have declined. Part of this shift is because of the increased use of television at the local level. Television offers the communication appeal of providing both visual and audio channels. Bank marketers can provide large amounts of information of symbolic and factual natures. While local production costs are not high, the users of television should always realize that their advertisements will frequently be presented along with

TABLE 8–4 Media Expenditures in 1983 (Amounts in millions of dollars)

Newspapers	$2,450
Magazines	3,421
TV	
Network	6,233
Local	4,893
Radio	
Network	131
Local	262
Outdoor	511

Source: "100 Leaders Parry Recession with High Spending," *Advertising Age*, September 8, 1983.

TABLE 8–5 Intermedia Comparison

	Broadcast Media		*Print Media*		*Other*		
Characteristic	*Radio*	*TV*	*Magazine*	*Newspaper*	*Direct Mail*	*Outdoor*	*Specialty*
Exposure (reaches large audiences)	X	X	X	X		X	
Selectivity (easy-to-reach targets)	X	X	X	X	X		X
Low production costs	X			X	X	X	X
Low cost per audience member	X	X		X		X	
Flexible closing dates	X			X	X		
Long-lasting message			X	X	X		X
Appeals to more than one sense		X					
Prestige		X	X				
Suitable for lengthy, complex messages			X	X	X		
Good reproduction quality	X	X	X		X	X	X
Message must stand alone (no editorial matter to attract)	X	X			X	X	X
Usually has full attention of audience		X	X	X	X		X
Little regulation			X	X	X		X
Data available about audience			X	X	X		
Data available about exposure			X	X	X		
Flexible format	X		X	X	X		X
Attended to at convenience of audience		X	X	X	X		X
Often many competing advertisers	X	X	X	X			

Source: William Lazer and James D. Culley, *Marketing Management Foundations and Practices* (Boston: Houghton-Mifflin Co., 1983), p. 726.

those of national advertisers. The bank marketer must make every effort to ensure the highest quality advertisement possible.

Radio. Radio advertising today offers the advantages of inexpensive, high-quality message production and very good targetability. Radio stations generally have narrowly defined music programs and thus a definitive audience. The ability to target your message and the relative low cost of radio make it extremely useful for advertisers wishing to emphasize frequency in their advertising plans. Many advertising programs are integrating television and radio by using the audio portion of the television advertisement as the basis for the radio advertisement. In this manner the visual message is thought to be reinforced by the much less expensive radio repetition.

Newspapers. Almost every adult in the country spends at least a few minutes each day with the newspaper. The bank marketer can attempt to target advertisements through the placement of the advertisement within the various sections of the newspaper. Low cost per reader (reach), low production costs, and the ability to present a great deal of information make the newspaper an ideal media for many of the bank's communication needs.

Magazines. Regional publication of national magazines has dramatically improved the usefulness of magazines as a bank communication vehicle. Unlike the newspaper's very short communication life, a magazine may provide the message for months. The regional advertisement in a national magazine may provide increased prestige by associating the bank's message with a highly respected communication vehicle. This is particularly true for regional banks.

Outdoor Advertising. Billboards and signs have long provided a primary communication medium for many banks. Careful selection may provide extremely strong reach at a low cost. A major limitation, of course, is the rapidity at which the information from most outdoor advertisements must be perceived.

Direct Mail. The strength of direct mail lies in the ability to personalize the message by using computerized word processing techniques and to focus on specific (desired) target groups. Seven steps for using direct mail in bank promotion are shown in Table 8–6. Direct mail is especially useful for cross-selling key target customers within the bank.

Ad Budgets. In the systematic development of marketing strategy the development of the promotional budget's advertising section is a major

TABLE 8–6 Seven Steps for Direct Mail Marketing

1. Begin with a small subset of customers by limiting initial mailings to 20 percent of the bank's customers. Motley suggests the bank's largest money market account customers.
2. Obtain the necessary hardware and software to allow you to sort your file of customers as necessary and then to print personalized letters.
3. Send a letter or note with usable and desirable information as well as sales material.
4. Don't use labels; obtain the equipment to type addresses directly on envelopes.
5. Use a signature machine to "personally" sign each letter.
6. Assign a "direct mail manager" with full-time responsibility to manage the data base and the message.
7. Provide a means of assigning account responsibility and use the account executive as the sender.

Source: Lawrence Motley, "Seven Steps for an Ongoing Direct Marketing System," *Bank Marketing*, July 1983, pp. 5–6.

consideration. The advertising budget is frequently called the *media strategy*. Each medium has distinct advantages and disadvantages. Before examining several of the media in detail as communication vehicles for the bank's marketing program, a means of making cost comparisons is needed. The standard for comparisons in the advertising industry is the cost-per-thousand, or CPM. While the units vary with the medium, the basic formula is as follows:

$$\text{CPM} = \frac{\text{Cost of one unit of media} \times 1000}{\text{Number of individuals reached}}$$

The basic CPM formula has a major flaw and should be modified with the replacement of the total number of households reached with the effective reach per media insertion. To do this modification, the number of households reached is reduced to reflect the number of individuals reached in the target market.

$$\text{CPM} = \frac{\text{Cost of unit of media} \times 1000}{\text{Number of individuals reached in target market}}$$

In addition to cost-per-thousand, media strategies should also include considerations of reach and frequency. Reach is a measure of the proportion of the target market to be exposed at least once to the message carried by the advertising media. Frequency measures the number of exposures per individual. While reach and frequency do not measure whether the message was received or if it had the desired effect, they are very useful tools in planning and budgeting.

An interesting concept in developing media plans is Herbert Krugman's "three-hit" theory. This theory provides an effective means of reaching the saturation point past which learning from an advertisement deteriorates. That is, by the time the individual has actually seen and attended a commercial three times, he has assimilated the message and decided if the information is useful in making a decision about the product/service.[10] Howard Kamin has applied the three-hit theory to the study of the number of exposures necessary to achieve learning. Kamin found that the marketer needs to provide 12 exposures (frequency) to maximize the probability of the consumer's receiving the message three times. He suggests that frequency levels should be set between 5 and 20 depending on the media and the target audience.[11] Over the years many different approaches have been used in attempts to set advertising budgets most effectively to reach the optimum point on the advertising response function and to select advertising mixes. Many firms have attempted to use somewhat complex market research experiments to examine the effectiveness of ads both before they are presented, and as they impact on the consumer.[12] Banks have also found that attempts to forecast sales/revenue require that the level of advertising and other promotional efforts be included as a factor in the forecasting model used.[13]

Publicity

Publicity includes all communication activities for which the bank does not pay. Publicity is extremely important to the bank both as a part of a particular promotional campaign and as a component of the bank's overall promotional and positioning strategy. As we have emphasized in other sections of this chapter, the consumer is faced with a bewildering array of advertisements and does not either attend or believe much of what (s)he is told. Publicity, because it is reported as news rather than as an advertisement, is not only more or less free to the sender, it is much more believable when received.

However, a caveat concerning the true cost of publicity is necessary. Many firms spend considerable amounts of time and money in planning and managing their publicity even though it is by definition "free."

Publicity may be classified under the broad headings of *information releases, special events* sponsored by the firm, or *participation in newsworthy activities.* Effective use of the opportunities afforded by publicity requires that the firm use every occasion for positive exposure in keeping with the marketing strategy. The effective use of public relations can be a major factor in a bank's image in the community. For example, the leading bank in the community is expected to take a position of strong civic leadership.[14]

Special events with specific appeal to target groups and strong linkages to the bank may be especially useful. The First National Bank of Minneapolis allocates 40 percent of its public relations budget to public attractions such as a Metropolitan Opera preview in the bank's lobby.[15] This and "upscale" publicity events are designed to enhance the bank's desired prestige bank image.

Personal Sales

Personal sales include the active person-to-person efforts of the firm to facilitate the sale of its products/services. Tom Ficquette, chairman of the BMA Training and Professional Development Council, concludes in a recent *Bank Marketing Magazine* article that the implementation of a strong sales orientation, sales management, and effective sales force can become the key to competition in the new banking environment. Mr. Ficquette feels that while many in banking may view personal sales as a high-pressure technique, an understanding of the sales function will cause bank managers to embrace personal sales as an element of the bank's promotional mix.[16] Rather than pressure, personal sales provides a one-to-one communication vehicle which can be customized to provide the right volume and complexity of information for each potential customer. Also sales calls can take many forms. We know of several banks with designated female representatives (i.e., sales personnel) to call on new arrivals in the community more or less as a bank welcome wagon. This soft-sell approach provides information only but can be quite effective if new residents are contacted before they establish a relationship with a local bank.

Retailers such as Sears, brokerage firms, insurance companies, and real estate firms, with which many banks are now competing, have historically emphasized personal sales. To be competitive the bank must learn to use personal sales as a part of its promotional and overall marketing strategy.

Most small- and medium-size banks do not have explicitly identified sales forces. Many banks, however, have begun to emphasize the sales capabilities of members of the operations personnel with customer contact functions. Business quotas and, in some cases, sales training are becoming more common for tellers and especially loan officers. Activities such as the acquisition of new deposits, business development for commercial accounts, trusts, and international services appear to be excellent opportunities for designated sales personnel and a sales manager and sales organization. Traditionally called *cross-selling,* such direct promotional activities can provide big benefits if systematically implemented. A midsize bank, for example, several years ago implemented a cross-selling program by beginning with a thorough reestablishment of its tellers as customer service representatives. New job descriptions, training in sales (including instruction in available services, costs of services, and sales techniques), and incentives for "selling" customers additional bank services were included in a comprehensive sales program. With top management support, buttressed by a coordinated advertising campaign, this initiative generated a successful long-term cross-selling program.

Types of Sales Efforts. Personal sales are simply communications aimed at satisfying consumer needs with the firms' products/services. Being interpersonal, this communication is extremely flexible and provides immediate feedback. Several basic types of sales activities and sales personnel can be identified. The most common salesperson is the *order taker.* As the name implies, the order taker's primary activity is to simply facilitate exchange. Order takers provide communication, but do little to offer solutions to consumer needs. Banks have traditionally used the teller function for this type of selling effort. A second type of salesperson is the *missionary* salesperson who does not take orders or actively close sales. The missionary salesperson's task is to provide information and to build goodwill for the firm and its products. The drug industry makes extensive use of missionaries to contact both physicians and pharmacists. The missionary influences rather than sells.

The essence of the personal sales activity is what is called *creative selling.* When engaging in creative selling, the salesperson aggressively seeks to satisfy needs. This requires a solid knowledge of the firm's products and an understanding of the customer. Unfortunately most bank personnel, including many designated customer service representatives, are order takers only. They do not aggressively sell or promote available bank services which can satisfy the customers' full range of financial needs, but rather just complete the transaction *initiated by the customer.* Further, one should be careful to differentiate true missionary selling activities from public relations. Many banks sponsor public information programs but few have true designated missionary selling efforts. A designated missionary salesperson will provide information much as in a public information program; however, the emphasis is on the bank's products/services in the context of customer needs. Bank officers are frequently in a position to act as a missionary sales force if in public speaking and other public and private activities they will include explicit references to their banks' activities.

Sales Training. Sales personnel are not born; they are trained and motivated. Of course, some individuals are better suited to selling than others. The first step in the development of the bank's sales force is the determination of what type of selling activity will take place and the level of product/service and customer knowledge necessary. As we discussed earlier, this may vary from using customer service personnel as order takers, to designating officers as missionary salespeople, to developing a designated creative sales force for particular products/services or markets. Particular attention to the target markets should also be given when one is deciding on the level of product/service training necessary for a particular selling task. This first step provides the basis for the selection and training program. Although hundreds of studies have been conducted, no single profile of the effective salesperson exists. In general, it appears that the successful salesperson will have a high energy level necessary to maintain a high level of interpersonal contact throughout the day, should possess a high level of expertise, and should resemble the customers of the target group in appearance, interests, and background. The effective salesperson will also possess the elusive factor of "presence"—the ability to gain the customer's attention and trust. No known test can match the manager's experience in gauging such factors.

Much of sales training will necessarily be directed at the obtaining of knowledge about the firm, the products/services to be sold, and the customers of the target market. A basic understanding of the selling activity itself, however, is necessary to provide a base for the development of planned personal sales efforts.

The sales interaction may be thought of as a series of steps, as shown in Table 8–7. With *prospecting* and *sales-calling planning*, the process begins *before the salesperson ever makes the first contact.* Prospecting is the identification of prospective accounts and the initial identification of criteria for qualifying the prospect as a potential buyer. While purchased lists and directories are frequently used, the best sources of prospects are your own bank's records and current customers. *Sales call planning* is frequently called the *pre-approach.* This method is the development of a plan to identify yourself and the firm and to gain the prospect's attention. The *initial contact* is a vital part of the sales process. In the first few seconds we gain what are generally lasting perceptions of the people we meet. The salesperson must establish a rapport with the prospect and gain the prospect's attention.

Establishing that the product/service will satisfy the needs of the prospect is the heart of creative sales. The effective salesperson today is not necessarily a good talker, but (s)he must be a good listener and must possess sufficient expertise to respond to the prospect's needs

TABLE 8–7 The Hierarchy of Communication Effects

Related Behavioral Dimensions	*Movement Toward Purchase*	*Examples of Types of Promotion or Advertising Relevant to Various Steps*
Conative. The realm of motives. Ads stimulate or direct desires.	PURCHASE CONVICTION	Point of purchase Retail store ads Deals Last-chance offers Price appeals
Affective. The realm of emotions. Ads change attitudes and feelings.	PREFERENCE LIKING	Competitive ads Argumentative copy Image ads Status, glamor appeals
Cognitive. The realm of thoughts. Ads provide information and facts.	KNOWLEDGE AWARENESS	Announcements Descriptive copy Classified ads Slogans Jingles Teaser campaigns

Source: R.J. Lavidge and G. A. Steiner, "A Model for Predictive Measurements of Advertising Effectiveness," *Journal of Marketing*, October 1961, p. 61. Used with permission.

with the appropriate solution. Solving a problem often means making a sale.

The next few steps in the process involve the actual closing of the sale. Many salespeople are not successful because they simply do not attempt to close the sale. In his book, *Increasing Your Sales Potential*, Leslie J. Ades recommends that one close the sale early and continually.[17] Resistance should be expected. The salesperson must meet objections by stressing product benefits and by assuming that the customer will buy. Ades stresses, "Assuming the sale is axiomatic to closing."

Note that the process does not end with the sale, but must extend to the postsale follow-up phase in which you ensure that the customer is satisfied. In the banking industry in particular repeat business is vital. These postsale activities are the start of repeat business. Remember the definition of marketing used in this book includes not only the identification and creation of demand but, equally important, the *servicing* of that demand.

Sales Promotions

Sales promotions include virtually any communication or sales promotion activity not previously included as advertising, publicity, or personal sales. Examples of sales promotions include point-of-purchase displays, demonstrations, trading stamps and premiums, coupon offerings, price discounts and free samples, and contests and sweepstakes. In the banking environment a free sample might take the form of a month's free service for an account or even a dollar in a new savings account. Some of these promotions are either related to the price/value attributes of specific products/services in order to directly stimulate demand, while others gain attention, and still other promotions are more institutional in nature. Many promotions are really an integral part of the product's attraction, as in the case of Crackerjacks.

Several years ago many banks attempted to utilize premiums to attract customers and deposits. These sales promotions ranged from house plants for opening a new account with $100 to Mercedes sports cars for deposits of $100,000 for five years. Prestone, Dwyer, and Rudelius explored the effectiveness of premiums in a study of matched groups opening time and deposit accounts both with and without premiums. New demand deposits opened during the premium promotions were found to perform as well as those opened without premiums. Retention rates were lower for premium period time deposits, but performance in terms of changes of six-month balance were equal between the two groups with the added number of customers offsetting the lower retention rate. In other words, premiums were found to be reasonably effective in gaining and keeping customers.[18]

More recently, with deregulation sparking an increase in competition, many bank managers have abandoned premiums. Premiums, however, are still being used effectively when targeted to both customers and firm needs. Major premiums such as televisions and personal computers are being offered for reasonably large long-term deposits. The Bank of Hartford, Connecticut, offered Commodore™ or Atari™ computers and color televisions with deposits of $2500 to $40,000 to produce $6 million in new deposits as a result of the promotional campaign.[19]

The big advantage of the sales promotion is that it may be targeted while rate competition may not. The cost of the sales promotion is generally very low compared to such price-oriented competition.

THE HIERARCHY OF COMMUNICATION EFFECTS

One way of understanding the various communication tools at the disposal of the market strategist should be applied through the hierarchy of communication effects (Table 8–7). This model of communication begins with the development of initial awareness of need and knowledge that a solution to the need exists. From a promotion viewpoint we are, of course, dealing with the needs and related products/services which are relevant for our bank. The individual moves through the hierarchy from "awareness" and "knowledge" to "liking" and "preference" of bank or product/service to "conviction." In "conviction" one becomes convinced that one competitor in the marketplace best meets his or her needs. Finally, "purchase or choice" follows this conviction stage. These six steps toward purchase are divided into three different types of behaviorally related processes, each of which calls for unique types of promotional activities. Knowledge and awareness are *cognitive.* These steps deal with thoughts about the product/service and needs or motives. Communications should provide information and facts which stimulate this initial thought process and direct it toward your communication and promotional goals. Preference and liking steps are *affective.* They deal with emotion. Communication messages must be aimed at developing positive feelings toward the bank and the specific product/service being promoted. For customers with existing attitudes or preferences for existing competitive offerings, attitude change should be a goal. Finally, the conviction and purchase steps are *conative.* They are related to actual behavior and appeal to motives directly related to behavior.

To use the hierarchy of communication effects, one needs to know enough about particular target markets to be able to determine the stage appropriate for a particular product/service offering. For brand-new products/services the market begins at the cognitive stage and moves through the stages over time.

As shown in the rightmost column of Table 8–7, each communication stage should be addressed with communication messages and media that best fit the appropriate behavioral dimension and purchase hierarchy step.

With the hierarchy of effects as a model we can now examine a total promotional campaign for a new product/service. Since we were dealing with a new product, we began by attempting to achieve initial awareness that a need was unfilled and that a solution to that need would be available. Attention-getting teaser campaigns were used to gain this initial impact, using outdoor billboards, newspaper ads, and even ads on local buses. The campaigns began with an all-black ad as a "teaser" one month before the introduction of the NOW account.

Two weeks before announcement the single word NOW and the bank's logo were added to the ads. At introduction the bank modified its campaign to provide complete information concerning NOW features and how NOW accounts meet customer needs in today's economic environment. Because of the reduction in regulatory restrictions represented by NOWs and their newness, public relations efforts were very effective, and the new product offering received wide attention in electronic and print media.

A key element in the campaign was to carry potential customers through initial knowledge and awareness in the affective stages. When the campaign was originally designed, it was decided that it would not be beneficial to attempt to make direct comparisons with competing banks with similar offerings or with nonbanks which had already been offering interest on "checking" account balances. Also note that the bank's goal was *not* to simply get current customers to move their money from noninterest-earning checking accounts, but to attract funds currently outside the bank. Thus the initial descriptive copy emphasized the ideas of "convenience" and "insured deposits" in addition to the interest income of the NOW account. At the same time a second message in all the promotional campaign communications emphasized that this new banking product was really right for only a select group of customers who kept a substantial premium balance in their account. This upscale message was emphasized with pictorial print ads and television commercials with a decided upscale tone. This double-barreled approach was desired to generate "affective" stage liking and preference through both logical appeals and an emphasis on image and status. This approach also reduced appeal to small-balance customers.

The third part of the campaign was designed to motivate behavior (conative stage). A mail appeal was made to selected individuals who might be currently using nonbanks for checking services in high-balance accounts. Lists of high-income-group individuals were purchased and checked against current customer lists. Lists of existing customers whose checking balances had decreased significantly were also obtained for bank records. The product was designed to include several package deals and "price" appeals to stimulate actual purchase.

The NOW product included free checking with a relatively small $500 minimum balance, free checks, free travelers checks, free notary service, no-bounce checking, free life insurance coverage with a $1500 minimum balance, and money market rather than passbook rates with $2500 average daily balance. This was backed up with personal sales training for bank employees and sales goals and incentives for employees acquiring new NOW customers.

SUMMARY

In this chapter we have presented the concepts of promoting the communication components of the marketing mix. As we emphasized in the beginning of the chapter, however, promotion is not just communication, but communication directed toward the goals of marketing strategy.

Today's bank marketer must select his or her communication tools from advertising, publicity, sales promotion, and personal sales. While advertising is the best-known and most widely used communication tool in bank marketing, publicity is the more believable communication vehicle, personal sales the most flexible, and sales promotion the most direct means of stimulating desired customer behavior. Almost all firms will adopt a promotional mix with each communication vehicle used as best fits each bank's strategy. In today's financial marketplace advertising has become a major component of promotional and competitive strategy for national and regional as well as local competitors. In designing the bank's advertising a campaign approach is most useful. In this campaign the advertising strategy is a component of the promotional mix, and an advertising mix of the various media is selected to best carry the campaign theme or message to the target market.

Through promotion the firm attempts to tell current and potential customers about itself and its offerings. Promotion provides the communication vehicle through which you must establish the position you have determined for the bank and communicate information concerning your products/services, your prices, and your distribution system. Using the personal sales component provides even greater flexibility with the opportunity to match the communication to the receiver/customer. Further, the personal sales effort provides an active means through which the bank may help solve the individual's financial needs with the firm's offerings.

Footnotes

[1]This model of communication is generally attributed to Wilbur Schramm, *The Process and Effects of Mass Communications* (Urbana: University of Illinois Press, 1955).

[2]Everett M. Rogers, *Diffusion of Innovations* (New York: Free Press, 1962).

[3]William Pride and O. C. Ferrell, *Marketing*, 3rd ed. (New York: Houghton-Mifflin, 1983), pp. 321–322.

[4]Sandra J. Teel, Jesse E. Teel, and William O. Bearden, "Lessons Learned from the Broadcast Cigarette Advertising Ban," *Journal of Marketing*, Vol. 43 (January 1979), pp. 45–50.

[5]Robert E. Pitts and James L. Wittenbach, "Tax Credits as a Means of Influencing Consumer Behavior," *Journal of Consumer Research*, Vol. 8 (December 1981), pp. 335–399.

[6]"100 Leaders Parry Recession with Heavy Spending," *Advertising Age*, September 8, 1983.

[7]William M. Pride and O. C. Ferrell, *Marketing* (New York: Houghton-Mifflin Co., 1983), p. 343.

[8]For a discussion of comparison advertising, see William L. Wilkie and Paul W. Farris, "Comparison Advertising: Problems and Potential," *Journal of Marketing*, No. 4 (October 1975), pp. 7–15.

[9]Jacob Hornik and Mary Jane Schlinger, "Allocation of Time to the Mass Media," *Journal of Consumer Research*, Vol. 7 (March 1981), pp. 343–355.

[10]Herbert Krugman, "What Makes Advertising Effective?", *Harvard Business Review*, Vol. 23 (March–April 1975), pp. 96–103.

[11]Howard Kamin, "Advertising Research and Frequency," *Journal of Advertising Research*, February 1978.

[12]For a discussion of these quantitative techniques see: Nariman K. Dhalla, "How to Set Advertising Budgets," *Journal of Advertising Research*, 1977.

[13]For an example of the application of advertising factors in regression models for advertising analysis in the banking industry, see: G. David Hughes, "Predicting Bank Deposits and Loans," *Journal of Marketing Research*, Vol. VII (February 1970), pp. 95–100.

[14]William P. Dommurmuth, *Promotion Analysis, Creativity* and *Strategy*, (Boston: Kent Publishing Company, 1981).

[15]Robert A. Pitner, "The Marketing Power of Special Events," *Bank Marketing*, June 1983, pp. 34–35.

[16]Tom Ficquette, "What It Takes to Transform Your Bank into a Vibrant Sales Organization," *Bank Marketing*, September 1983, pp. 10–14.

[17]Leslie J. Ades, *Increasing Your Sales Potential*. (New York: Harper and Row, 1981), pp. 200–228.

[18]Robert H. Preston, F. Robert Dwyer, and William Rudelius, "The Effectiveness of Bank Premiums," *Journal of Marketing*, July 1978, pp. 96–101.

[19]Kathryn Olfield, "Premiums: On Hold, but Making New Strides," *Bank Marketing*, August 1983, pp. 16–19.

9

pricing decisions

INTRODUCTION

One thing that all profit organizations have in common regardless of the nature of their business is the need to put a value on their products and services. Traditionally, marketers have felt that price was the most determining factor in consumer behavior. However, recent trends indicate that nonprice factors have increased in importance. But, in spite of the increasing trends in nonprice competition, the pricing variable is still an extremely important component of the marketing mix.

Economic interpretations of the price relationship to the quantity sold typically assumed an inverse relationship. That is, the lower the price of the product or service (within a relevant range), the greater would be the amount of that product or service sold. Marketers soon found that this relationship did not always exist. In fact, many marketers have found they could increase the number of products sold by increasing their price. Consider the range of prices for different bank products studied by the Consumer Federation of America (Table 9–1).[1] Depending on the particular market in which the products are sold, consumer willingness to pay for banking products varies considerably. These price ranges show the variability that exists in the pricing of products/services.

TABLE 9–1 How Bank Fees, Services Vary

	Low	*High*
Savings		
Minimum balance for interest	0.00	200.00
Monthly fee if below minimum	0.00	3.00
Regular Checking		
Bounced check	7.00	20.00
Returned deposit	0.00	12.00
NOW Accounts		
Minimum to avoid charges	50.00	2500.00
Monthly service charge if below minimum	2.00	8.00
Per check charge if below minimum	0.20	0.50
Other Checking		
Holds on nonpayroll checks from out of state	2 days	20 days

In the banking industry, price is the one component of the marketing mix that most likely will change in a more competitive industry. Bankers are going to have to develop a better understanding of pricing strategies and the effect the pricing variable can have on revenues and profits. Unfortunately, the pricing variable is one of the more complicated marketing variables to understand.

TRADITIONAL BANK PRICING APPROACHES

Two mechanisms explain the way in which bankers have traditionally—and to a certain extent still do—set prices. The first mechanism is called *bundling.* Bundling involves the aggregation of bank product/service offerings, such as checking accounts and loans, both credit and noncredit offerings, and pricing these bundles relative to compensating balances and a prime rate. From a cost standpoint, bundling required the banker to understand only total costs of bank services and to insure that the spread on loans was sufficient to cover these costs. This practice resulted in some bank products, most notably loans, subsidizing other bank products such as checking accounts. Bankers were also helped in their pricing task by federal restrictions governing interest rates payable. These restrictions provided a certain stability to the pricing decision by removing competitive uncertainty.

The second mechanism affecting the setting of prices in the banking industry is an *auction* mechanism. Banks wishing to make loans to both the commercial and retail segments auctioned their loan rates in a restrictively competitive market. Following the lead of large money center banks, most banks were able to establish a prime "price" for their services which was then adjusted by such factors as the creditworthiness of the customer, the balances of other accounts the customer had with the bank, and the relationship the bank had or wanted to have with the customer.

Several trends are operating to make the bundled, total-cost approach to pricing untenable in a less regulated and more competitive market. The first is a growing tendency among banks to establish profitability centers within banks. These profitability centers recognize the marginal contribution to overall profitability that certain products or departments can make. Profitability centers are a necessary but nonsufficient condition for a well-integrated marketing effort. In concert with the move to profitability centers was a changeover to a cost accounting system which enables bank managers to better understand the actual costs of providing specific product/service offerings, and hence, their profitability.

Externally, an increasingly competitive environment, thinner and more volatile spread, finer-tuned segmentation strategies, and an overall acceptance of the market concept are leading bankers to unbundle services and adopt, more and more, a fee-based pricing strategy. This unbundling does not mean that banks can't and shouldn't package different services into accounts which are targeted at specific market segments. Such approaches have been very successful in those instances where banks have done their homework and identified what segments really wanted from their banks. A good example is the tying of a checking account to a discount brokerage account. In other cases, where the bank has followed a me-too, copycat strategy, assuming that what worked in one market would work in another, packaged accounts have not been very successful. At the heart of the successful packaging approach is a better understanding of component costs. These costs can act as guidelines in the setting of the price. The real determinant of the final price will be the marketplace. Thus, we approach the setting of price from a market-oriented perspective.

PRICE SETTING BY OBJECTIVE

While fee-based pricing is gaining momentum and appears to be the wave of the future, the strategic marketing planner must incorporate one other component into the formula for price setting. Each product/service offering or package has the ability to accomplish certain goals or objectives for the bank. In some cases these goals and objectives will be the same and in some cases they will differ. A good example is the "goal difference" between safety deposit boxes and IRAs.

The latter has significantly greater profit potential for a bank, while the former has the ability to round out a product line and to attract customers. The more traditional total-cost approach essentially assumed the same objectives for all product/service offerings. Moreover, it did so within the same planning perspective, esentially a long-run horizon.

A strategic marketing perspective recognizes the differing potential of each product/service offering to do different things for the bank in different time periods. Consequently, the strategic marketing planner must specify at the outset what exactly these goals are for each product/service offering or package and then develop a pricing strategy which will enable the product/service offering to accomplish that goal. The product/service offering may have a short-term goal, or it may have a long-term goal. More than likely as the products move through their life cycle and the product mix expands and contracts, these goals will change. What strategic pricing objectives should be considered in the setting of prices for different product/service offerings?

Target Return Pricing

Target return pricing is a strategic option which focuses on either a prespecified level of profit (expressed perhaps as a rate of return on investment or absolute amount) or a level of sales revenue. In either case, the level of investment and risk must be incorporated into the determination of the price. Usually, the target is determined in the business analysis portion of the product development strategy. Break-even analyses, payback options, and internal rate of return estimates can then be made at different price levels.

Implicit in the use of this strategic pricing option is an understanding of the demand for the product under consideration. The demand for the product will be influenced by the price of the product. Assessing the demand for a brand-new product is more problematic than for a line extension or me-too type of product. In the latter cases the strategic marketing planner has a basis for determining a price and a demand. Slight adjustments in the price and resultant demand can be made by assessing the degree of difference between the newer introduction and the existing product. When the brand-new product is considered, the strategic planner has to rely upon market research, market testing, judgment, and a trial-and-error approach to pricing. After introduction, the strategic planner must examine any variances in return from what was targeted. Product adjustments, promotional adjustments, distribution adjustments, as well as pricing adjustments may be necessary to achieve the targeted return. Sometimes, too, the strategic marketing planner has put the targeted return rate too high. Reality may dictate that no matter what adjustments are made in the marketing mix, the anticipated return will never be reached.

Stabilizing Prices

This is a decidedly short-term pricing objective which is found in those industries, like banking, which are essentially oligopolistic in nature. Pricing competition may produce an unstable, fluctuating price, which makes it extremely hard for managment to plan. Price fluctuations are also detrimental to customer perceptions of individual banks and the entire industry. This is particularly true for those banks which have established a premium image strategy.

Price fluctuations can be stabilized by the emergence of a leader in the industry or market that takes a firm stand on prices. This is the role the Fed essentially performs by adjusting the discount rate for federal funds. Banks will tend to follow suit, perhaps not at the same price level but at one which is relative to their market position. There is a fine line between this type of strategic consideration and price collusion, which is illegal. Many customers wonder how banks respond to the "silent signals" for stabilizing prices without some explicit, less than tacit understanding's having been reached. Perhaps this is why most banks and organizations would prefer to compete on a nonprice basis.

Maintain/Improve Market Share

This is a strategic option available to banks which are attempting to increase the market share for a specific product/service offering or a package of services. Typically a short-run objective, banks will seek to increase their market share, realizing that long-term profitability is related to market share. Price reductions, if perceived as real reductions, can increase market share significantly. If a bank offers free checking to any account maintaining a $50 minimum balance, the bank may soon find that it has many small checking accounts. The problem with this type of strategy is that if volume increases cannot compensate for margin losses and the bank is forced to increase its price after awhile, many customers may choose to bank elsewhere. In other words, the gain in market share by lowering price may evaporate once and if a bank has to increase its prices. This should be carefully considered before such a strategy is implemented.

Another consideration in such a strategic undertaking is the reaction of competition. Competition can be expected to make certain retaliatory moves, which could produce a situation where any gains that are experienced because of price cutting may be short-lived.

This particular strategy is perhaps most beneficial in the introduction of a new product/service offering or package. Market penetration strategies have been discussed in the chapter on products. The pricing component of the strategic action is, of course, a very important consideration.

Maximize Profits

This is perhaps the most common pricing objective and is necessarily the only objective that can be considered to be long-term in nature. This particular objective is most applicable at the product-mix level, where the strategic planner is concerned with profit maximization of the entire product mix. This point was discussed in Chapter 6. It will be recalled that viewing the product mix as a system suggests that some product/service offerings may be more profitable than others, yet even those product/service offerings which are not as profitable may have an important role in overall product profitability.

Marketers have long realized the benefit of certain products which have the ability to draw attention and customers. This is especially true if these "loss leaders" are priced at an extremely attractive level. The low price has the ability to attract customers, who can then be sold additional products at their normal selling price. Such has been the case with trust services in many banks. Trust services were a product that was "given away" by many banks as a free service to its customers. Recognition of the potential profitability of the trust department has changed some of the thinking in this regard. In fact, trust services were some of the first banking products to be sold on a "fee" basis. However, other loss leaders may be attractive inducements to banking customers. These loss leaders can be incorporated into packages of other more profitable products and marketed accordingly.

CAVEATS ON ESTABLISHING STRATEGIC PRICING OBJECTIVES

It should be kept in mind that these are objectives and accordingly must conform to the rules of objective setting established in Chapter 2. Pricing, in general, is a heuristic process, one marked by continued adjustment over the life cycle of the product/service offering. The establishment of pricing objectives provides the strategic marketing planner with a control mechanism by which (s)he can monitor the product's contribution to overall bank profitability.

The trend to fee-oriented services will make the pricing task much more difficult. Individual costs and demands for each product/service offering must be estimated. When these are better understood, the strategic marketing planner can make more effective use of the price variable.

PRICING STRATEGIES

Given the pricing objectives identified above, we can identify two major pricing strategies which have been used during product introduction. These are called *skimming* and *penetration* strategies.

Skimming the Market

Skimming is a pricing strategy that recognizes that there exists a portion of the market which is willing to pay higher prices for a new product. Roughly, this portion of the market tends to coincide with the innovator and early adopter categories discussed in the preceding chapter. Skimming seeks to maximize profit from the outset of product introduction. It is designed to decrease the payback period of a product and achieve product profitability at an early stage.

The idea behind skimming is that the product is introduced at a high price. As demand at that price level tapers off, the price is reduced somewhat, thereby making the product accessible to a different market. We have defined a market as consisting of people with an ability and a willingness to buy. A skimming strategy explicitly recognizes these aspects of a market and attacks the market on an incremental basis.

Skimming is something of an extension of multiple segmentation approach. It segments the market on a price sensitivity basis. Skimming makes the product accessible to the least sensitive segment, the next least sensitive segment, and so forth. Typically, the product changes very little. By this we mean that the product undergoes certain adjustments imposed by time and competition, but no changes in product are made to attract different segments. Segments are attracted on the basis of price. Skimming can be useful when the bank is not facing a price-sensitive market where high price may be an attractive signal to competition. In addition, skimming has the ability to convey a premium product image, as many customers will regard price in certain product lines as a cue for judging product quality.

Penetration Pricing

While the objective of a skimming strategy is profitability, penetration pricing seeks to acquire market share. Penetration pricing allows the firm to enter the market at a relatively low price and to buy market share. Penetration pricing is particularly useful in those markets characterized by intense competition and allows the bank to acquire market share before competition has an opportunity to retaliate. Market share is related to long-term profitability, so that the early purchase of market share represents an investment in future profitability.

Penetration pricing requires sufficient promotional resources and distribution capability. Market demand can quickly exceed a bank's ability to supply the product/service offering or service it. When this happens, consumer dissatisfaction can cause a negative backlash and can work against the image of the bank. Many banks experienced this during the rush for IRA business. They attracted more accounts than they had the personnel or computer software capability to handle. Where skimming regulated demand through the pricing mechanism, penetration pricing is volume-oriented. Many banks typically use a penetration strategy when introducing new products. For example, when NOW accounts were introduced, many banks offered the product with low minimal balances only to find later that they had to adjust these upwards when market share objectives were achieved.

Penetration pricing is especially applicable when the market is price-sensitive. In addition, this strategy may be useful in encouraging actual and potential competition.

PERCEIVED-VALUE PRICING

A relatively new strategic pricing approach, one which is supplanting the more traditional commodity or total cost approach used in banking, is a value-added strategy. According to Edward E. Furash, a Washington, D. C. bank consultant, value-added pricing is "based on the concept that the service rendered has a combination of tangible and interpretable values that add up to more than the commodity service price."

Unfortunately this is a particularly difficult pricing strategy to implement. However, by recognizing the interactive nature of price and the perceived image of the product/service offering and the effect of this interaction on perceived value, several different perceived-value strategies can be identified. These are summed up in Table 9–2.

Most of the product/service image and price combinations suggest useful strategies for the pricing of different services. While banks may be somewhat hesitant to admit or accept a low product service image, such an image for an individual product/service offering may actually exist. This may be true for those less than glamorous product/service offerings such as Christmas Club accounts, safety deposit boxes, distribution of welfare checks, equipment leasing, and a large number of nontraditional banking services.

For the medium to high image offerings, the pricing guidelines suggest both short- and long-term strategies. Several of these have already been discussed. For example, many banks have used a premium strategy when positioning packaged accounts. Such products in the President's Account or Group One Accounts carry high image connotations with a higher price. On the other hand, Christmas Club accounts utilize a low price-low image or a cheap value strategy. Generally, most bankers are leery of low-value image products, since banking pivots on a sense of trust and security. Consequently, most perceived value pricing strategies presently used by banks typically shy away from low-value product images. However, as public policy issues continue to emerge over so-called "ignored" segments (lower socioeconomic banking customers) some banks may find fruitful application for the low-value image strategies. The reader can see how some of the other combinations may prove useful.

The key is that market-oriented pricing strategies will be useful tools for achieving objectives for individual product/service offerings. And, while obviously costs cannot be ignored, they should be included into an objective-driven market strategy whereby adequate margins provide profitability.

TABLE 9–2 Perceived Value Pricing Strategies

Intended Product Image	*PRICE* High	*PRICE* Medium	*PRICE* Low
High	Premium strategy	Penetration strategy	Super-bargain strategy
Medium	Overpricing strategy	Average-value strategy	Bargain strategy
Low	Hit and run strategy	Low-value strategy	Cheap value strategy

Philip Kotler, *Marketing Management,* 3rd ed. (Englewood Cliffs, N.J.: Prentice-Hall, Inc., 1976), p. 49.

A WORD ON COSTS

The different pricing strategies discussed in the chapter are designed to accomplish specific marketing and bank goals. The long-term pricing goal, really the only long-term goal, is profit maximization. In order to accomplish this, banks must understand their cost structure. While many banks are moving to more exacting and detailed costing procedures, most banks do not know how much it costs them to provide specific products. As was mentioned before, this is a legacy of regulation. Developing the appropriate cost accounting procedure is essential to effective pricing strategies. While pricing below cost may produce increases in market share in the short run, it would prove disastrous in the long term. As a guide, bankers should look at product costs in three categories—development costs, delivery costs, and allocated overhead costs.

Development costs include all the expenses incurred in developing a particular product: research costs, material costs, labor costs, machine costs, etc. These costs must be carefully noted and rendered.

Delivery costs are those costs associated with the delivery of the product—labor costs, marketing costs, material costs, etc.

Finally, allocating overhead costs to a specific product may represent the greatest challenge to bank accountants. Whereas in the past when costs were allocated to divisions or departments on square footing basis or some other relative delineation, allocating costs to specific products may prove more difficult. However, a fee-oriented pricing system rquires it. These costs must be estimated during product development and examined in the economic analysis portion of the process.

SUMMARY

A marketing orientation brings with it a need for changing the ways in which banks set prices. A focus on the individual costs of product/service offerings coupled with an objective-driven pricing procedure will characterize pricing in the banking industry. These changes will place greater demands on the strategic marketing planner. In addition, the increasing number of product/service offerings will require a more coordinated systematic approach to pricing.

Strategic bank planners will have to adopt a market adjustment approach to pricing where the initial price is recognized as a first offer to be adjusted in the light of actual demand and competition. Nonprice competition will continue to be important in the banking industry, where battles for market share will be fought primarily on the basis of product/service offerings and to a lesser extent on the basis of prices. Yet, in this time of transition and perhaps because of it, the pricing variable will take on new importance. Freed from the restrictions of regulations, bankers will begin to understand the utility that the pricing variable can provide in profit considerations.

Footnotes

[1]Nationwide Survey Conducted by the Consumer Federation of America, April, 1984.

10

distribution decisions and marketing strategy

INTRODUCTION

The actual delivery of the product⁄services which the bank chooses to provide is a key part of marketing strategy. In contemporary marketing literature this delivery system is called the *channel of distribution* to reflect the concept of a flow of goods and services through several levels from producer to consumer. Although many bank managers have historically viewed this delivery process as a single-step, retail-oriented process, contemporary banking practices are producing a much more complex environment. In this chapter we will use a marketing channel approach to explore the unique demands currently being placed on the delivery system in the banking industry. For most banks the key decisions will involve the number and types of locations at which specific services will be offered. A basic element in the strategy, formulated to deliver the bank's products⁄services to the potential customer, is the location of main office, branches, and automated teller installations providing the service window for interaction with the customer.

The importance of location and office hours as a means of meeting competition and demand will be explored in detail, and a model of branch location will be discussed. The impact of new technologies on distribution decisions will also be discussed. Finally, we will address the importance of forecasting demand and its timing in service-based industries, and will examine techniques for matching product/service supplies to meet the demand at the customer interface.

THE MARKETING CHANNEL

The marketing channel is the path that a product/service takes as it moves from the producer to the consumer. In the historical banking environment the concept of a marketing channel was not particularly relevant, as each bank produced and sold its own services/products.[1] In today's highly competitive environment, the channel concept is very relevant to the way the bank conducts its everyday business. As Nelson A. Valverde points out in a recent article in *Bank Marketing*,[2] today financial institutions are beginning to specialize as manufacturers, wholesalers, or retailers for financial products/services (see Table 10–1).

As the environment changes and bank specialization increases, the members of the channel face new responsibilities and new relationships with which they must deal. Most commercial banks are in fact retailers for many products/services such as credit cards, travelers checks, and loan placements. National and regional banks have become manufacturers for the above products and other services such as the Chemical Bank's Chemlink information system. The secondary-mortgage market and commercial lending are but two prime examples of the wholesale activity that is growing rapidly in the new banking environment. With this new and changing environment, it is vital that the bank marketer understand the basic principles which underlie the operation of the interfirm relationships on which the marketing channel is based.

The channel of distribution exists because of specialization and the efficiencies of specialization and concentration of superior resources. National credit cards have grown from regional and local credit programs. National firms such as Visa International and MasterCard have the resources to promote the product on a national level and to offer the efficiency and convenience of an internationally accepted product/service. It is likely that manufacturing and wholesaling levels

TABLE 10–1 Evolution of the Financial Services Industry

Historical:	Manufacturer	+	Wholesaler	+	Retailer	→	Consumer
Emerging:	Manufacturer	→	Wholesaler	→	Retailer	→	Consumer

Source: Nelson A. Valverde, "Developing Profitable Strategies that Don't Box You In," *Bank Marketing*, June 1983, p. 8.

of the channel will be dominated by major international, national, and regional firms such as American Express, Sears, and Merrill Lynch, companies with the necessary resources, economies of scale, and market presence. Regardless of specialization and the complexity of the marketing channel, the basic activities of marketing must be accomplished. The majority of small- and medium-size banks in the financial industry have their main strengths in their direct contacts with consumers at the retail level.

SERVICE DISTRIBUTION DECISIONS

The marketing considerations involved in arraying the number and assortment of facilities for consumer interaction and the products/services to offer at these facilities are the major considerations in channel strategy for the bank. While such decisions have historically been closely regulated, the banking environment is rapidly moving toward deregulation of retailing activities. In anticipation of this deregulated environment we will explore the question of matching banking distribution facilities to demand from a free market viewpoint. As Table 10–2 shows, many major banks are already truly national (and international) in scope. BankAmerica, for example, has offices in 40 states and the District of Columbia, while American Express's international banking subsidy has established a branch on the Queen Elizabeth II to offer a variety of services, including cashing checks, currency exchange, funds transfer, and, of course, replacing lost American Express cards. The only bank on a cruise ship cannot operate in the United States and can

TABLE 10–2 Out-of-State Offices of 10 Large Bank Holding Companies

	Nonbank Subsidiary Offices	*Banking Offices*	*Total Offices*	*Total States*
Manufacturers Hanover	471	7	478	30
Security Pacific	427	7	434	35 & DC
Citicorp	419	25	444	39 & DC
BankAmerica	360	15	375	40 & DC
Chemical	135	6	141	23
First Chicago	13	14	27	10
Chase	13	4	17	15 & DC
Continental Illinois	9	12	21	10
Bankers Trust	1	8	9	4
J. P. Morgan	1	5	6	4

Reprinted by permission of the publisher from "The New Reality," Manufacturers Hanover Corporation from *Journal of Business Research*, May 14, 1981, by Elsevier Science Publishing Co., Inc.

only operate when the Queen Elizabeth II is outside the 12-mile territorial limit.

The ability to match the supply of services to their demand is vital in a service industry. Use of physical facilities and personnel within the delivery boundaries of the distribution channel is critical if consumers are to be satisfied and profits maintained. Unlike manufactured products, the core services of the bank cannot be inventoried, but must be supplied upon demand.[3] Even services, such as lines of credit, which are established at one point in time require accounting and other activities when actually used by the customer.

The expansion of branch banking, automated tellers, and telecommunication innovations, such as home banking, have dramatically expanded the window of time and location through which services may be provided. Each of these delivery alternatives provides unique opportunities and unique problems for the bank. Further, many banks have applied a "more is always better" and a "follow the leader" approach without examining the impact of the delivery alternative on bank marketing strategy or examining the cost/benefit characteristics of a new branch or ATM. A checklist for improving productivity in the distribution function is presented in Table 10–3.

Automatic teller machines have been touted as a means of improving banking productivity and of extending historically short service hours at low cost for routine transactions. From their inception in 1967 in British banks to today's highly advanced machines, the automatic tellers have gained increasing acceptance by both the banking community and the consumer. The most successful installations, however, have been those that have considered consumer needs and concerns. Christopher Lovelock of the Harvard Business School and Robert Young of Northeastern University point to such factors as a special-customer service staff that may be available on a 24-hour basis to deal with ATM problems, multiple machines to ensure availability, and designs that return rather than keep invalid cards as examples of this customer orientation.[4]

Across the nation several banks have moved to the extensive use of the lobby ATM as a distribution strategy for low potential/high personal service cost customers. Customers falling below specified account minimums are "encouraged" to use ATMs to free customer contact personnel for maximum interaction with high potential customers in the bank's selected target market.

Branch office and ATM distribution decisions will generally include regulation requirements, services to offer, market area location, and site selection. The key question, however, is how many facilities of each type are economically justifiable and the marginal impact of the development of an additional product/service or distribution unit. In

TABLE 10–3 Identifying Opportunities for Improving Productivity

- Do your customers have time on their hands as they wait for service? Is there something they could do to speed the service delivery process?
- Are your customers and service personnel meeting face-to-face unnecessarily? Could such contacts be handled instead by mail, phone, or computer terminal?
- Are there significant peaks and valleys in the demand for your service? If so, what is the root cause? Can you do anything to change or modify these demand patterns?
- Are your customers trying to bypass service personnel and doing the work themselves?
- Are customers asking your personnel for information that is readily available elsewhere (e.g., in a directory)? If so, why is this?
- Are your customers being subjected to needlessly bureaucratic forms and requests for personal data? Are such data necessary to your operations? Could they be gathered and recorded through alternative means?
- Is the efficiency of your operations being impaired by a minority of customers who appear ill-informed about the nature of your service and how to use it? If so, is there perhaps something wrong with your information dissemination efforts?
- Do customers show a high level of interest in the knowledge about the tasks being performed by your service personnel? Perhaps they would like to do some of these tasks themselves?
- Is there any reason, other than tradition, why you should provide certain personal-service "extras?" Which would do most for your competitive position—to continue offering these extras or to eliminate them and share the savings with your customers?
- Could you efficiently delegate all or part of your service functions—especially information, reservations, and payment—to third-party organizations already used by your customers?

Source: Christopher H. Lovelock and Robert F. Yury, "Looking to Customers to Improve Productivity," Christopher H. Lovelock, ed., *Services Marketing* (Englewood Cliffs, N.J.: Prentice-Hall, Inc., 1984), p. 268. Used with permission.

other words, will the total operating profit of the firm be increased by the addition of a new ATM? Frequently a new location, for example, will gain revenue and customers that were already part of the customer base. Such cannibalization is always a possibility and may be accepted at even higher levels when total profit and/or a bank's competitive strategy is considered. Further, many authorities suggest that decisions of this type be analyzed by using net present-value methodologies that allow the analysis of alternative uses of the funds, which would be considered in expansion of service locations.

For many banks the distribution channel for some products/services has already evolved beyond the framework of branches or ATMs. Money market funds, credit cards, and some loan services are today being transacted across state lines and with almost exclusive use of mail or 800 telephone service for customer contact. Thus a decline in the total number of conventional branches nationwide is expected in the future. The larger banks, however, are expected to offer full-service branches in key financial centers.[5] Such competition requires that distribution location decisions be made carefully and with full use of the tools available to contemporary marketing management.

At the time this book is being written, the nation's largest banks have plans for more than 30 so-called "nonbank" banks across the nation which will offer either checking accounts or commercial loans but not both. Such location expansions in the past have been associated with fast-growing grocery retail and fast food chains, but certainly not with banks.

LOCATION AND DISTRIBUTION DECISIONS

A systematic approach to bank location is presented in Table 10–4. Of course, as we have indicated already for a sizable portion of the market, location convenience is paramount. This need does not mean that the construction of a new facility will necessarily provide enough marginal increase in business to break even with the additional costs. There are occasions, however, when a firm will add distribution sites to protect its market position against new competition or will attempt to block potential competitiors' access to the area or site.

In "Formulating Retail Location Strategy in a Changing Environment," Ghosh and Craig[6] of New York University suggest a cost comparison between the incremental outlet and the expected gain in revenue. A number of mathematical modeling techniques have been proposed for the prediction of the expected revenue gain of this additional facility. In general, these techniques call for the determination of a facility performance model for selected competitive and market fac-

TABLE 10–4 Systematic Approach to Bank Location Strategy

1. Determine number of distribution points needed, i.e., impact of incremental addition to bank profits.
   a. Compute expected revenue for additional facility
   b. Expected profit = Revenue expected − costs for facility
2. Examine distribution goals and strategy.
   a. Generate invested profits
   b. Tap new market area
   c. Block competition
3. Select location within market area.

tors. An example of this type of performance modeling is shown in a following section. The performance model is then used to project incremental revenue increases and total system revenues under a number of facility alternatives, including number and location of facilities. Linear programming or iterative heuristic programming techniques are used to determine optimum distribution-facility alternatives.

We must stress that the object of distribution strategy is not to minimize short-term costs, but to maximize the firm's profits in the long run. For most firms the facility decision can be analyzed by using a break-even approach. Again, however, the development of sound distribution planning requires the estimation of revenue for a given facility.

The location decision is one of the most important long-run decisions in the marketing mix for most banks. A good location provides the retail bank with strategic advantages that the competition may find very difficult to overcome. The capital investment necessary to build in today's market requires that careful consideration be given to any location decision, and that the full impact of future environmental conditions be considered.

It is estimated that more than half of all commercial banking retail customers are extremely convenience-oriented, and select a bank that may be incorporated into their normal shopping schedules. This large convenience-oriented market segment views banking goods and money as an undifferentiated product and is relatively immune to many patronage appeals other than convenience.[7]

Despite the obvious importance and investment associated with the location decision for a bank, relatively little has been published in banking literature about the location of either main office or branch banks. While most location decisions appear to be based on the assumption that banking location decisions are more an art than a science, the basic approaches appear to be centered on the volume of vehicular or pedestrian traffic from which customers may be drawn and to match the competition on a location-by-location basis. The tendency to match every possible competitor and to attempt to maximize locational convenience has led to situations where the population per branch office has declined to less than 4000 in some markets.[8] The trend toward more and more branches has been alleviated somewhat by the newer trend of placing automatic tellers in locations with high shopper traffic, such as shopping centers, office complexes, and even university student-activity centers. Further, as deregulation allows expanded product offerings and geographical scope, many banks are reevaluating the number and placement of many marginal branches. Funds saved by closing or selling branches with limited profit potential can provide the dollars needed for new initiatives in an expanded environment. Thus we may expect to see expensive branch offices replaced with multitudes of ATMs in a bank's existing market area. Funds and capital used for the branch offices could then be applied to expansion into other geographical areas. This, of course, is a vastly simplified example which assumes that current branch offices can be easily sold so that the capital invested in the location may be recovered and that retail bank customers will continue to accept increasing reliance on ATM service. Further, the very act of closing a number of branches may produce a negative image of the bank's financial and business solidity.

A SYSTEMATIC APPROACH TO MARKET AREA LOCATION DECISIONS

The location decision is actually part of a complex set of strategic decisions concerning the firm's desire to serve particular market segments, the members of the segment's work and shopping patterns, and, of course, the bank's demands for return on its distribution facility investments. Location decisions should be viewed as involving two separate decisions, one macro, the other micro. The first decision is whether a new branch or even a new bank can be supported by the market area being considered. In other words, how many branches or facilities are needed? The micro decision must then be directed toward the best specific location within the subject area for the new banking facility. For most banks the idea of a macro location decision is very new and has only come into importance with deregulation of the industry. Opportunities in interstate banking and expanded intrastate opportunities in many states will require the bank to increase the scope of its location analysis to explore new opportunities.

A combination of local population characteristics, local competition characteristics, and the characteristics of the branch being considered may be used to predict branch performance (Figure 10–1).[9]

The market area population characteristics to be examined will generally include:

1. Income characteristics
2. Employment in the area
3. Rental vs. ownership of homes in area
4. Housing values and ownership
5. Savings or other banking use data on a per capita basis
6. Population by age categories

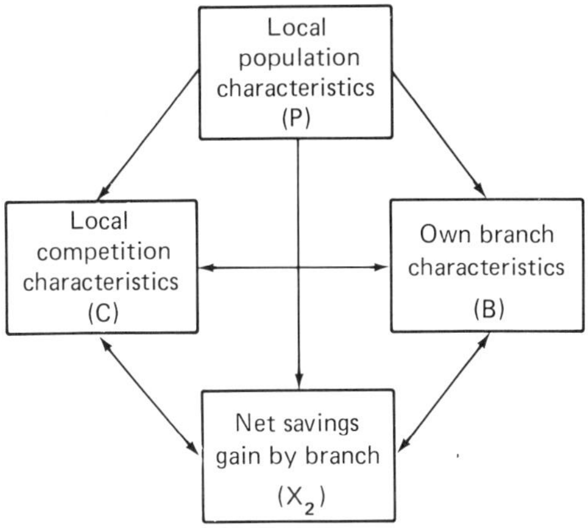

Source: *C. Joseph Clawson, "Fitting Branch Locations, Performance Standards and Marketing Strategies to Local Conditions," Journal of Marketing, Vol. 38, (January 1974), p. 10.*

FIG. 10–1. Performance in a local retail financial market.

Competitive characteristics may include:

1. Number of existing competing bank facilities
2. Number of competing S & L facilities
3. Measure of population per S & L and banking facility
4. Measure of market share of competition in market area

Branch variables may include a number of measures of the site and facility-related factors, including:

1. Retail square footage in market area
2. Retail sales within some area around the proposed site
3. Specific site characteristics such as free standing or as part of a shopping center
4. Parking availability
5. Retail square footage in branch[10]

A key need is obviously the ability to find relevant characteristics for each of the three major factors influencing branch performance, and to relate the expected impact of each factor to performance measures. By necessity the decision to add a new branch takes on very different dimensions as the size of the branch operation increases. For the relatively small bank with several branches, the decision to open a new branch may actually be a location decision rather than a market area decision. That is, all branches of the bank draw from the same market area, and new branches are attempts to maximize marginal convenience. The small number of branches and the single market area precludes the possibility of deriving significant quantitative statistical models of branch performance. The relationship of the branch and market area characteristics of the branch performance are very much related to the unique characteristics of the area being studied.

For the larger bank with a number of existing branches statistical multiple regression techniques may be used to relate the characteristics of existing branches and market areas to performance. The regression equation may then be used to predict performance potential of proposed branches and to set performance standards at existing facilities.

The Regression Approach to Location Decisions

Lola Olsen and Dennis Lord of the University of North Carolina[11] provide an example of the use of regression analysis of market area characteristics and branch performance. This study examines the characteristics of 12 branch bank locations and savings and checking account balances. In this application of the branch performance model, the variables were categorized as either supply or demand variables, as shown in Figure 10–2.

The demand variables include purchasing power (obtained by multiplying the mean household income by the number of households within a radius of one and one half miles of the branch), median household income, and employment in the area. Retail square footage was used as a surrogate for the number of shoppers in the area who might bank at a branch on a shopping trip. Percentage of rental housing was thought to be negatively related to savings deposits. The external competition variables were expressed as the number of competitors within one mile of the branch, while the internal measure indicated whether or not another of the bank's branches was within one and one half miles of the branch.

The results of stepwise multiple regression analysis conducted with 7 of the independent variables, checking account deposits, and saving deposits respectively are shown in Table 10–5.

Note that the use of the stepwise method of multiple regression produces a model which explains the maximum amount of variance in the performance variable, producing the "best" possible model with the smallest number of independent variables. This is very important when the number of observations (branches) is small.

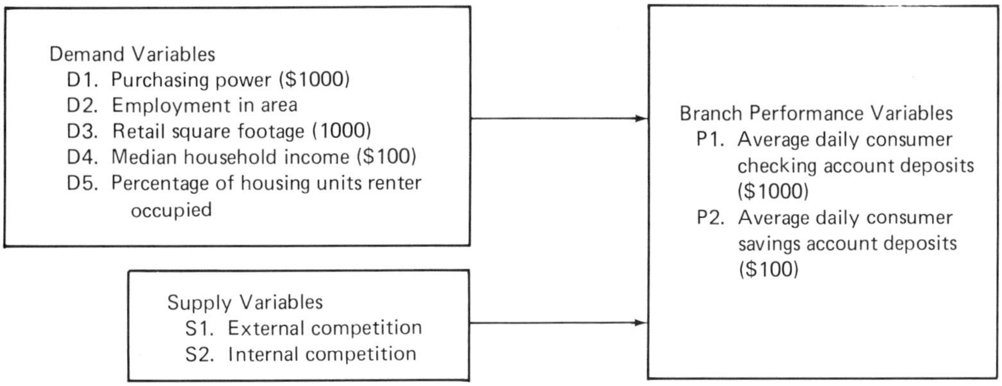

Source of Data:

D1. Population estimates obtained from the National Planning Data Corp. 1974 census tract figures were used. Measured by multiplying the number of households by the mean household income.
D2. Local planning commission and Chamber of Commerce for the year 1975.
D3. Local planning commission for the year 1975.
D4. Urban Decision Systems, Inc., 1974 estimates.
D5. Urban Decision Systems, Inc., 1974 estimates.
S1. Field survey of the market area, 1975. Measured as the number of competing branches in the area.
S2. Subject firm's records, 1975. Measured as a binary scaled variable to indicate if the service area of the branch overlapped with the service area of another branch of the subject bank.
P1. Survey conducted by the subject bank, 1975.
P2. Survey conducted by the subject bank, 1975.

Source: Lola M. Olsen and J. Dennis Lord, "Market Area Characteristics and Branch Bank Performance," Journal of Bank Research, Summer 1979.

FIG. 10–2. Example of application of rejection analysis for predicting market area performance.

The regression coefficients are standardized in Table 10–5, so that the impact of each independent variable on the dependent variable may be made by a simple comparison. To determine the expected impact of a variable on the dependent measure, you multiply the regression coefficient times the standard deviation of that variable. For example, an increase in an area's purchasing power of one standard deviation ($22,695,149) should produce additional daily savings deposits of $47,660.

Olsen and Lord conclude that their results indicate that for this bank and its branches, different factors influence checking and savings deposits in a market area. In the case of checking accounts the presence of a competitor causes a major reduction in deposits.

Again we must emphasize that the results presented are for a specific bank under unique competitive and market situations. A unique performance model should be developed for the specific branches of the bank being studied.

The use of this procedure may provide a base from which the core business of the branch may be estimated. The analysis may be extended to other important sources of revenue, or estimates may be de-

TABLE 10–5 Results From Market Area Analysis Models

Model	*Relevant Variables*	*Regression Coefficients*	*Cumulative* R^{2*}	*Increase in* R^2
Checking account deposits P1 ($1000)	Median household income D4 ($100)	1.2706† (3.26)	.55	.55
	Retail square footage D3 (1,000)	0.2365† (3.36)	.72	.17
	External competition S1	−8.6889 (1.37)	.77	.05
Savings account deposits P2 ($100)	Purchasing power D1 ($1,000)	0.0021† (6.25)	.57	.57
	Employment D2	0.0375† (3.93)	.77	.20
	Percent renter D5	−1.2973† (2.00)	.81	.04

*R^2 values have been adjusted for bias due to the loss of degrees of freedom as additional variables are entered into the regression equation.

†Statistically significant at the .05 level.

t values of regression coefficients are in parentheses.

Source: Lola M. Olsen and J. Dennis Lord, "Market Area Characteristics and Branch Bank Performance," *Journal of Bank Research,* Summer 1979.

rived as percentages of the basic deposit analysis. These estimates of revenue may then be compared with appropriately estimated branch costs to determine the expected profitability of the branch.

The regression approach may also be applied to available data at the market area level to determine the attractiveness of a particular area for the development of a new bank or the attractiveness of merger or acquisitions. For this analysis, published data at the local level would be analyzed along with measures of bank performance. Because this analysis is across different banks rather than within the same branch system, variables to measure each bank's marketing mix should be included. Such measures as the number of branches and expenditures for promotion if available should be incorporated for each bank included in the analysis.[12]

Site Evaluation

Site evaluation is the next step in the location decision process. For the small community bank the location decision for branches and for automated-teller systems without full branch services is a site decision within a market area. Many banks have applied multiple sites as a means of maximizing convenience without careful evaluation of the full impact of the trade-off between the business generated by the branch

TABLE 10–6 A Site Evaluation Checklist

Rating: E G F P*

1. Trading area potential
   a. Public utility connections (residential)
   b. Residential building permits issued
   c. School enrollment
   d. New bank accounts opened
   e. Advertising linage in local newspapers
   f. Retail sales volume
   g. Sales tax receipts
   h. Employment—specific
   i. Employment—general
2. Accessibility
   a. Public transportation (serving site)
   b. Private transportation (serving site)
   c. Parking facilities
   d. Long-range trends (transportation facilities)
3. Growth potential
   a. Zoning pattern
   b. Zoning changes
   c. Zoning potential
   d. Utilities trend
   e. Vacant-land market (land zoned for residential use)
   f. Land use pattern (in areas zoned for other than residential)
   g. Retail-business land use trend
   h. Retail-building trend (building permits issued for new retail business construction)
   i. Retail-improvement trend (permits issued for remodeling expansion, etc., in existing properties)
   j. Retail-location trend (changes in occupancy of retail-business locations)
   k. Income trend for average family unit
   l. Plant and equipment expenditure trend
   m. Payroll trend
4. Business interception
   a. Location pattern—competitive businesses between site and trade area
   b. Location pattern—competitive businesses between site and trade area (served by and sharing traffic arteries with site)
5. Cumulative attraction potential
   a. Neighboring business survey
6. Compatability
   a. Compatability factors
7. Competitive-hazard survey
   a. Competitive pattern—competitors within 1 mile of site (nonintercepting)
   b. Competitive pattern—potential competitive sites
8. Site economics
   a. Cost and return analysis
   b. Site efficiency
   c. Natural description
   d. Adjacent amenities (for both vacant-land and existing building sites)

*Excellent, Good, Fair, Poor.

Source: Richard Nelson, *The Selection of Retail Locations* (New York: McGraw-Hill, 1958), p. 66. Used with permission.

and its full costs. With the decision to add a branch or ATM, full consideration must be given to the specific site for the facility.

While highly quantitative site location methodologies are available, most firms turn to a qualitative approach for site evaluation. Key factors such as the compatibility of surrounding business, competition in the area, and access to the facility are examined in detail. The use of ATMs and "after dark" banking hours require consideration of customer and bank security. Future conditions should also be considered with careful analysis of future zoning, building, and street or road development for the site.

A checklist such as that in Table 10–6 is generally developed by management so that several available sites may be fairly compared.

SUMMARY

In this chapter we have examined the distribution decisions facing the bank manager in a highly competitive environment. Bank strategy today must address the complexity of channel relationships linking several levels of the distribution system for many financial products. Each of the banks in these ever more complex systems must attempt to accomplish its individual objectives while working with other members of the channel to satisfy consumers' needs.

The distribution decision for the retail bank includes the macro components directed toward the number of facilities and array of the services the bank will place in a particular marketplace. The number of branches or detached ATM units the market can support at profitable levels is a key aspect of the macro component of distribution analysis. The micro component is the determination of a specific location within the market area. More qualitative checklist approaches are generally used to select specific locations for facilities.

Footnotes

[1]See: Edwin B. Cox and Sandra M. Spies, "Messages from the Market Place," *Banker's Magazine,* Vol. 165 (July–August, 1982), pp. 22–25.

[2]Nelson A. Valverde, "Developing Profitable Strategies that Don't Box You In," *Bank Marketing,* June 1983, pp. 8–14.

[3]Christopher H. Lovelock, "Why Marketing Management Needs to be Different for Services," *Services Marketing,* (Englewood Cliffs, N.J.: Prentice-Hall, Inc., 1984).

[4]Christopher H. Lovelock and Robert F. Young, "Look to Consumers to Improve Productivity," *Services Marketing,* (Englewood Cliffs, N.J.: Prentice-Hall, Inc., 1984), pp. 260–271.

[5]George Kaufman and Larry Mote, "Implications of Deregulation for Product Lines and Geographical Markets of Financial Institutions," *Journal of Bank Research,* Spring 1983, pp. 8–24.

[6]Avijit Bosh and Samuel Craig, "Formulating Retail Location Strategy in a Changing Environment," *Journal of Marketing*, Vol. 47 (Summer 1983), pp. 56–68.

[7]W. Thomas Anderson, Eli P. Cox III, and David G. Fulcher, "Bank Selection Decisions and Market Segmentation," *Journal of Marketing*, Vol. 40 (January 1976), pp. 40–45.

[8]Lola M. Olsen and J. Dennis Lord, "Market Area Characteristics and Branch Bank Performance," *Journal of Bank Research*, Summer 1979, pp. 102–110.

[9]C. Joseph Clawson, "Fitting Branch Location Performance Standards and Marketing Strategies to Local Conditions," *Journal of Marketing*, Vol. 38 (January 1974), pp. 8–14.

[10]See Clawson, op. cit., p. 10 and Olsen and Lord, op. cit., p. 105.

[11]Olsen and Lord, op. cit.

[12]See Gosh and Craig, op. cit., for a discussion of the application of quantitative location models.

11

marketing organization and implementation

INTRODUCTION

Throughout this text we have stressed the importance of the integration of the marketing function as part of the operational and planning structure of the bank. The complete integration of the marketing function is a fundamental precept of the marketing concept. This structural integration may take many differing forms to best serve the needs of the bank's marketing environment but typically grows out of the need to sell and distribute products and services. As a new bank grows and adds customers and products, the need for a functionally oriented marketing department is generally recognized. However, a marketing structure is not designated, in many existing bank organizations. Even in larger banks with a marketing department, marketing usually serves as a staff-planning and research unit rather than as a part of the line-profit-producing structure of the bank. In this chapter we will explore the marketing function and its organization and implementation in the modern bank. After establishing a general foundation in other business settings, the application of these approaches to the needs of the banking organization will be presented. Finally, a plan for the implementation of marketing in the banking organization will be offered.

ORGANIZATIONAL OBJECTIVES AND ORGANIZATIONAL STRUCTURE

Peter Drucker[1] suggests that the organizational structure of the firm will not evolve simply, but that analysis and a systematic approach to organizational development are required. Drucker contends that structure must follow strategy to be truly effective and should consider three types of work: operating, top management, and innovative work. In order to better understand the implementation of marketing in the banking environment, it is necessary to explore briefly how these work elements have evolved into the various structures which may be observed in almost all organizations.

Types of Organizational Structures

The simplest organization in the typical business firm is the line structure, as shown in Figure 11–1. The operating elements of the organization are arrayed in a simple structure with a line of authority from the

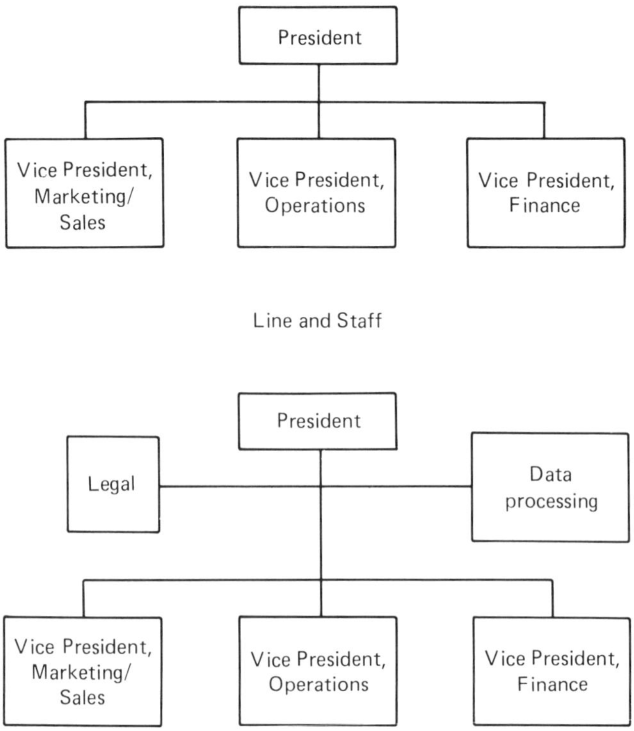

FIG. 11–1. Basic organizational structures.

top executive to the lowest operating employee. As the firm grows, the need for specialization and expertise leads to the addition of a staff of specialists, which does not have authority or responsibility over the operational units but which advises top management.

A variant of the line-staff organization is the functional organization, as shown in Figure 11–2, advocated by Fredric W. Taylor in the early 1900s. Taylor's functional organization establishes multiple specialist-managers for every major identified function influencing the operative activity. Of course, the basic flaw of this structure is the imposition of multiple supervisors, which violates the "unity of command" principle. While this organizational structure provides a supervisor who may be considered an expert in a particular part of a subordinate's activities, the overall goals of the organization may be lost in supervisory detail, and conflicting orders may be given by the various area supervisors.

New organizations generally begin with a basic structure designed to (1) manage the production of goods or services, (2) provide marketing and sales activities, and (3) provide the financial resources needed. As they grow, most organizations, whether of a product or a service orientation, find it necessary to structure the organization around the major distinctive characteristics of the products/services produced or the markets to which products/services flow.

Typical Bank Organizational Structure

In the small bank, the organization is generally structured on a product basis. That is, the divisions of the bank are organized around particular product/service offerings such as trust and cashier, as shown in Figure

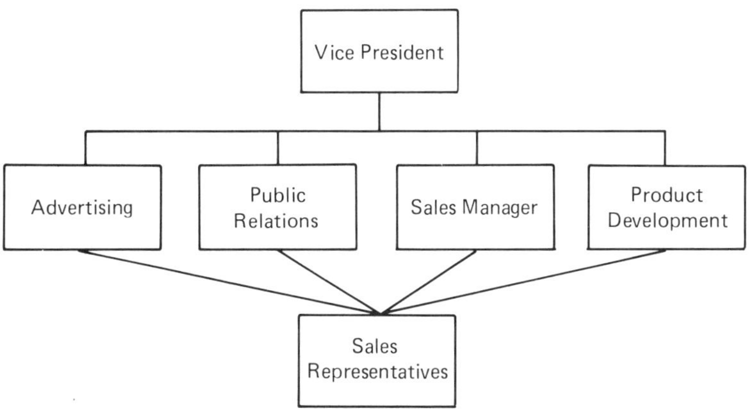

FIG. 11–2. Functionally organized marketing division.

11–3. In larger banks, it is quite common for a marketing vice president to head up a corporate level marketing activity while each division possesses its own marketing structure, much as in the smaller firm. This approach allows the overall coordination of marketing policy and the ability to make use of a highly skilled corporate staff while still emphasizing the integration of marketing in the division structure to facilitate exchange.

As the size and complexity of the bank grows, as in the structure shown in Figure 11–4, the marketing division in a typical branch-banking system remains under the president.

In the branch-banking organization structure shown, a market-oriented structure is presented with the commercial branch group, install-

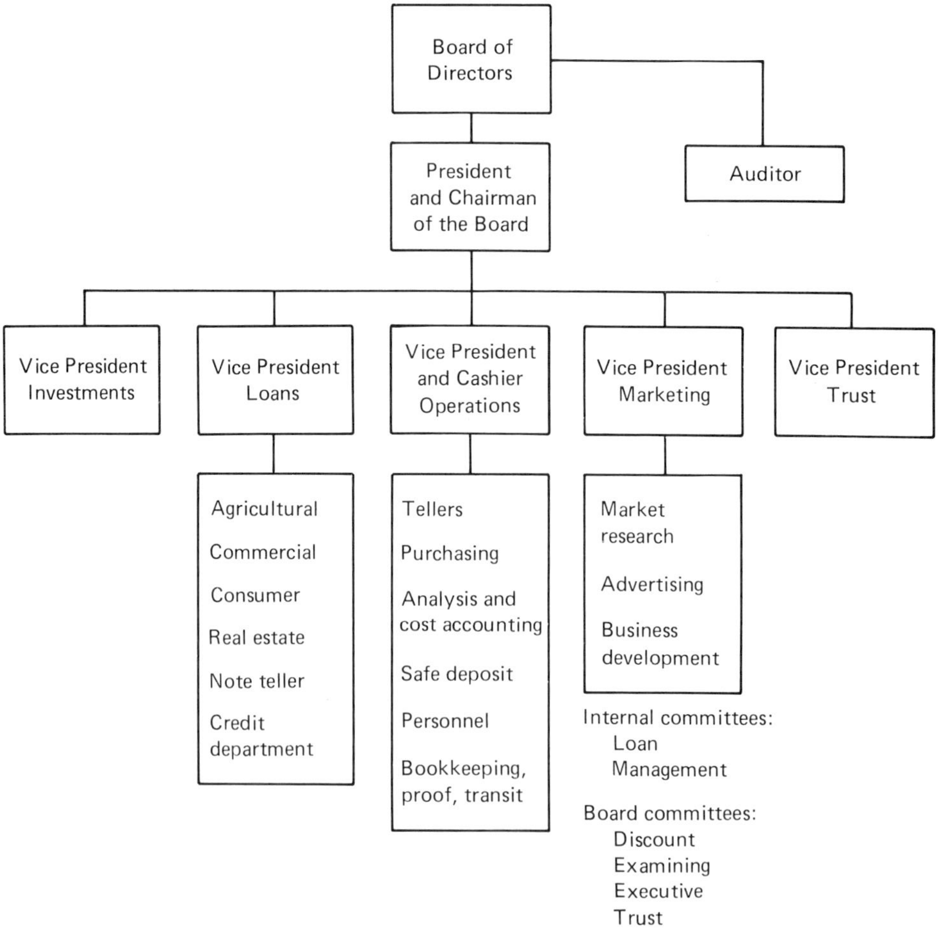

FIG. 11–3. Hypothetical organization of a small bank.

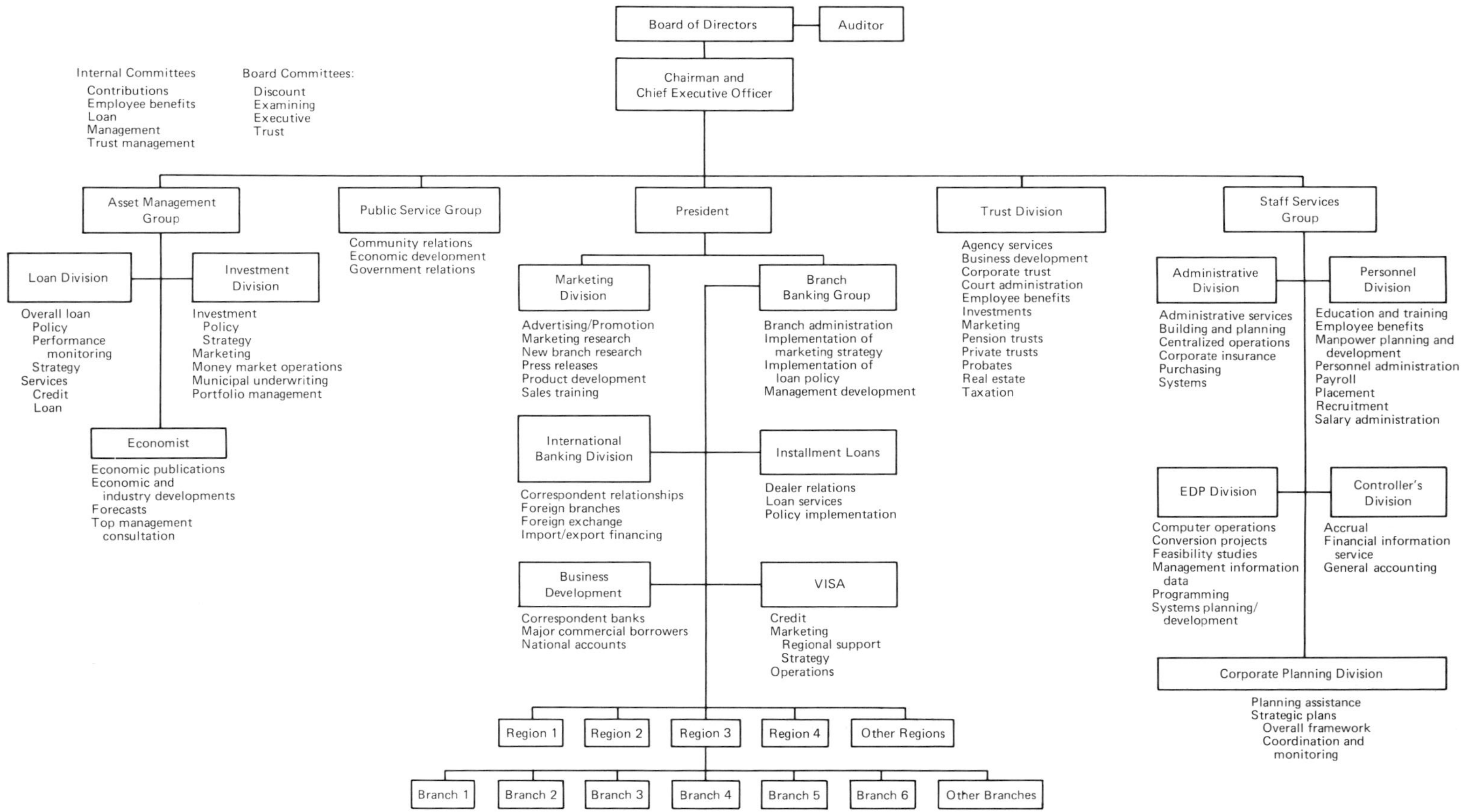

Source: Edward W. Reed, Richard V. Cotter, Edward K. Gill, and Richard K. Smith, *Commercial Banking*, 3rd ed. (Englewood Cliffs, N. J.: Prentice-Hall, Inc., 1984).

FIG. 11–4. Hypothetical organization for a branch banking system.

ment loan division, international banking division, Visa, and business-development groups emphasizing specific markets as well as the particular product for that market.[2] This type of structure represents a major realization in the line type structure of the small bank to meet the needs of specific segments of the market.

We should also note that the large branch-banking organization shown explicitly includes separate marketing activities in the Visa and branch banking divisions. Unlike the typical manufacturing firm, the typical bank may have numerous groups with operational tasks (such as asset management and trust) who report directly to the chairman. These groups/divisions have their own marketing activities, as shown. However, a corporate-level marketing structure to coordinate the bank's total marketing activities is not present, but is needed.

We discussed in the promotion chapter, Chapter 8, how the existing customer-contact interface in the commercial banking organization has caused many banks to ignore the need for separate sales personnel and sales organization. We must emphasize that the need for this important activity still exists, even though customer-interface personnel may efficiently perform both their service and communication/sales functions. As the bank extends its activities and especially when entry into nontraditional areas is contemplated, the organization must be modified to incorporate sales personnel.

MARKETING ORGANIZATION

In the typical business firm, the marketing activities of the firm will be organized under a vice president for marketing. Under this vice president, the various activities necessary for marketing will be arrayed in a fairly "flat" organizational structure. Generally, only the sales activity and distribution will require extensive substructures, such as geographical or market subdivisions, to reach the firm's customers.

While the geographical division of the sales function is the easiest to use, the sales activity may also be structured around the products/services offered or customer types. The product/service differentiated structure allows the sales organization to emphasize its product/service expertise. Overlap and duplication of effort, however, occurs frequently, with several salespeople serving the same customers. Dividing the marketing organization among customer types provides the maximum level of customer knowledge, which may be applied to need satisfaction. Each salesperson must possess a great range of product/service knowledge, and travel and other costs may be high if customers are dispersed geographically.

It is important to emphasize that in the marketing organization, the marketing division, including sales and distribution, is a component of the operative-line part of the organization. That is, the marketing division is an operative, profit-generating part of the firm. In a product or a service firm, the exchange facilitative functions of the marketing activities are as vital as the production of the product or service.

As shown in Figure 11–5, the organization of a typical bank with a marketing group generally follows this approach, but with one major exception. In the typical structure depicted, the vice president for marketing has no responsibility or authority for the banking activities through which the marketing activities we have presented are achieved. In effect, marketing is simply a staff activity. The organization shown is really overstating the position given marketing in many banks. Frequently, marketing activities are limited to a staff advertising department.

As the number of products/services grows, the firm frequently finds that no individual responsibility for a particular product/service exists, and that the diversity of the firm's products requires that a means of managing each product be provided. Many consumer goods producers, such as Procter and Gamble, which is generally credited with popularizing the idea, have thus turned to *product managers* within

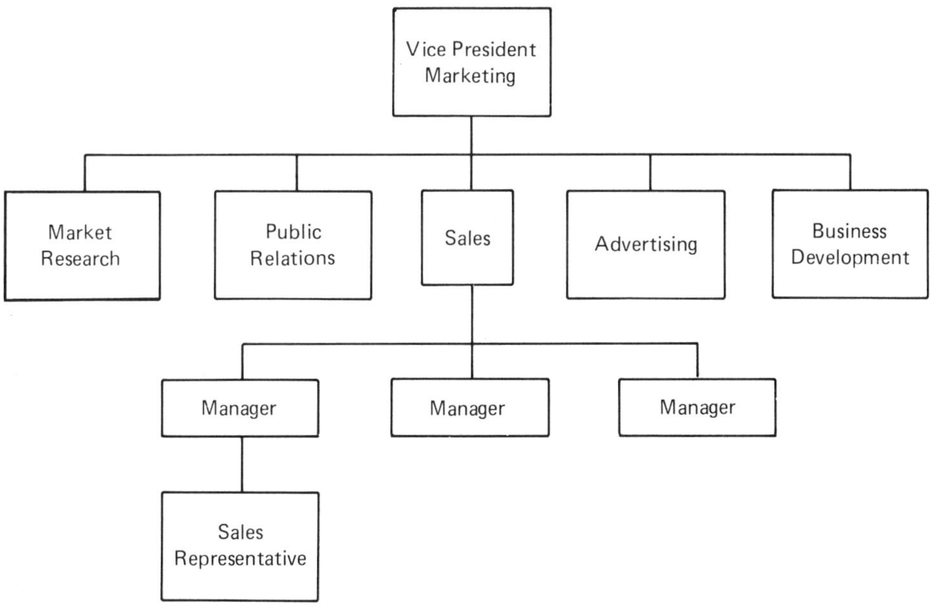

FIG. 11–5. Hypothetical marketing/sales organization.

the existing marketing structure. In the simplest terms, the product manager is given the responsibility of managing a particular product. As can be seen from Figure 11–6, the product manager is an addition to the structure rather than a change in activities. The product manager attempts to coordinate the activities of the marketing function to best serve his particular product. This arrangement is used when the firm sells many products in a single market.

Other firms are faced with the reverse problem. They offer a single product or product line to multiple heterogenous markets. In this situation, *market managers,* as shown in Figure 11–6, are often used. The marketing manager attempts to manage the firm or SBU's efforts as they relate to a single market or distribution channel.[3]

Because of the desire to match personal-sales efforts to the target market, an important distinction between these two ways of organizing within the marketing area soon appears. Product managers have no direct control of the sales force which promotes their product, while the market manager frequently evolves into a separate marketing division for important markets, as shown in Figure 11–7. In each case the objec-

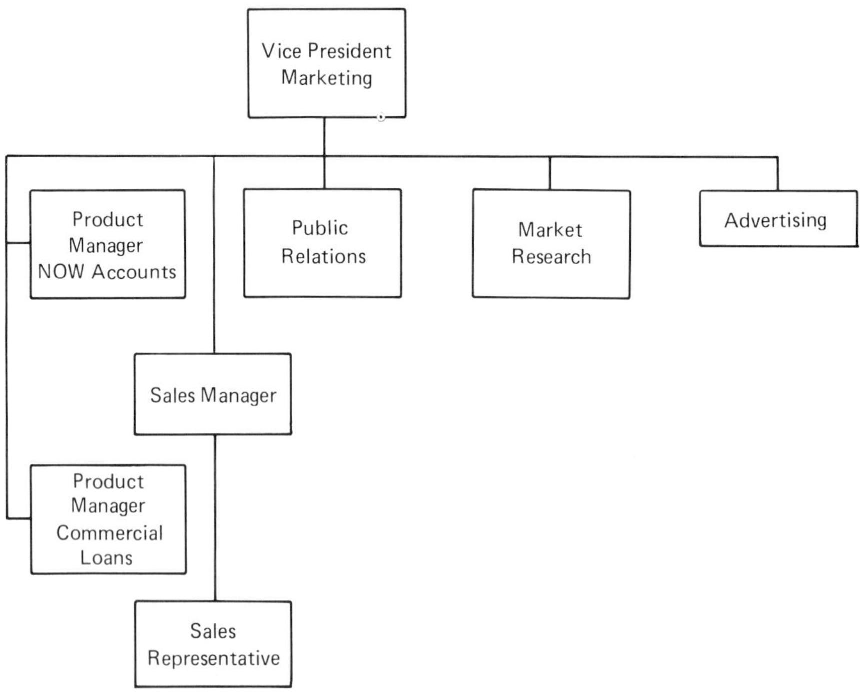

FIG. 11–6. Hypothetical bank marketing organization for a small bank with product managers.

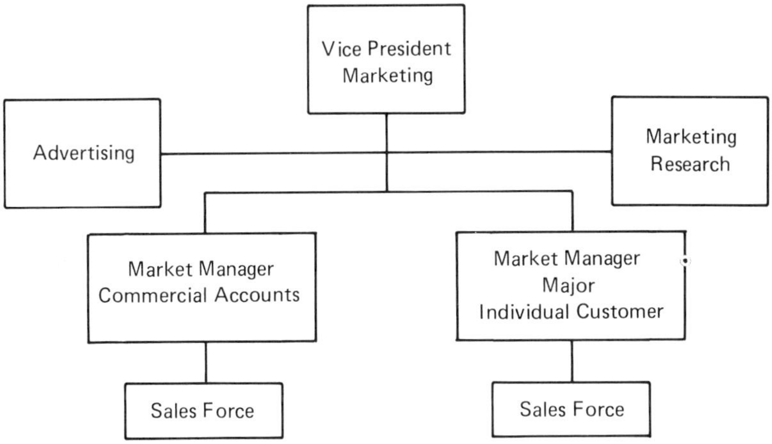

FIG. 11–7. Hypothetical bank marketing organization with market managers.

tive is to emphasize the distinctive characteristics of either product or market.

While one of the above organizational structures should be selected in the light of the organization's products and markets, other alternatives may be very useful to meet special needs. The matrix organization has been widely touted as a means of cutting across functional lines to draw on needed skills. The *venture team,*[4] an application of the matrix approach, is especially useful for the introduction of new products or services (Figure 11–8). The venture team is drawn from the existing personnel of the organization's various departments as need develops to bring the new product/service to the marketplace. The team is separated from the rest of the organization and the marketing structure to create an entrepreneurial environment. This task force is given a broad market-based mission and will normally report to the highest level of the firm. Thus, individuals may be freed from normal duties and may be given wide flexibility to devise new solutions and products and services.

MARKETING IMPLEMENTATION IN THE BANKING INDUSTRY

Most authorities agree that only a few American firms, such as Procter and Gamble, IBM, and McDonald's are truly marketing-oriented, rather than sales-oriented.[5] This orientation is even more of a problem in the banking environment, where both marketing and the sales activity have historically received less emphasis than operations. Many

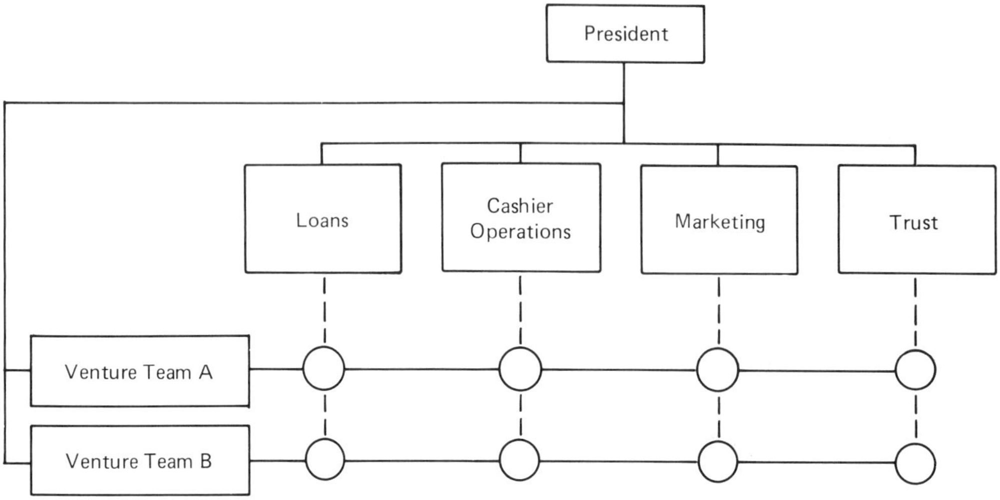

FIG. 11–8. Venture teams in bank organizations.

banks have responded to increased competition with increased promotional emphasis without fully becoming marketing-oriented. A marketing orientation in planning, operations, and communications, and modification of the existing structure to emphasize markets/products rather than operations are major but needed changes in most bank organizations (see Table 11–1). These changes are the basis for a reorientation from an operations culture to a marketing culture. A number of steps are necessary for the creation of a marketing "culture" within the organization.

1. Presidential leadership. The integration of marketing into the active planning and operation of all phases of the firm requires that top management embrace a marketing approach.
2. Marketing task force. Key officers of the firm are given the task of developing and implementing a plan for focusing on true marketing.
3. Outside marketing consultant. An outside consultant is usually necessary to serve as a change agent. The consultant brings new ideas, an unbiased view of the firm, and experience in marketing thought to the firm.
4. A corporate marketing department. Emphasis on the commitment to marketing is provided through a corporate level marketing department, which coordinates marketing activities in the SBUs and divisions of the firm. Later each major division is organized with a strong marketing structure.

TABLE 11–1 Marketing Integration Check List[7]

A. Implementation of Marketing in the Organization

1. Does your bank aim any of the following training programs toward the marketing concept?

			Scoring
_____	Company-run meetings and conferences	2 points	
_____	On-the-job training	1 point	
_____	University executive development programs	4 points	
_____	Special lectures (business consultants)	3 points	_____
		Total	

2. Please mark an "X" in the appropriate column indicating the primary professional background of the following key individuals or groups in your bank. If your bank has more than one group executive, place as many "Xs" as appropriate in the columns.

	Accounting	*Finance*	*Marketing*	*Academic*	*Legal*	*Banking*	*Other*
Board chairman	____	____	____	____	____	____	____
Vice board chairman	____	____	____	____	____	____	____
President	____	____	____	____	____	____	____
Chairman of the executive comm.	____	____	____	____	____	____	____
Group executive	____	____	____	____	____	____	____

One point for each check in the marketing column.

3. Is your top marketing executive a member of the following committees or groups?

_____ New product/service planning
_____ Executive

_____ Board of directors
_____ Finance
_____ Asset
_____ Liability management   Total _____
Scoring:
One point for each checked.

4. Indicate the level of responsibility each of the following departments or functional areas has concerning the strategic planning process.

	Very Much Responsibility	*Very Little Responsibility*
Business development	_____	_____
Marketing	_____	_____
Commercial lending	_____	_____
Account/auditing	_____	_____
Research and development	_____	_____

TABLE 11–1 *(continued)*

Consumer lending	_____	_____
Personnel administration	_____	_____
Legal	_____	_____
Real estate lending	_____	_____
Public relations	_____	_____
Asset/liability management	_____	_____
Correspondent banking	_____	_____
Bank operations	_____	_____
Trust	_____	_____
Investment	_____	_____

Scoring: For Very Much Responsibility column, 10 points if *only* marketing is checked, 5 points if marketing and another department(s) is checked, and 0 points if marketing is *not* checked.

B. Adoption of Marketing Orientation in the Organization.

1. What is the title of the top marketing executive in your bank?

____

Scoring: If vice president or higher, 5 points.
If the word marketing is used in title, add an additional 5 points.

2. Which of the following functions are the responsibility of your top marketing executive or his/her staff? Please mark an "X" in the appropriate column.

	Very Much Their Responsibility	*Shared Responsibility*	*Not Their Responsibility*
Advertising	_____	_____	_____
Market share analysis	_____	_____	_____
Promotional activities	_____	_____	_____
Marketing research	_____	_____	_____
Customer relations	_____	_____	_____
Pricing of services	_____	_____	_____
Correspondent relations	_____	_____	_____
Product/service planning and development	_____	_____	_____
Public relations	_____	_____	_____
Credit extension	_____	_____	_____

Scoring: For Very Much Responsibility column, 3 points. Shared Responsibility, 1 point; Not Their Responsibility, 0 points, for each checked.

TABLE 11–1 *(continued)*

3. Please mark an "X" in the appropriate column indicating how frequently the following methods are used to coordinate the activities of the marketing department with the activities of other departments.

	Very Frequently Used	*Not Frequently Used*	*Not Used*
Interdepartmental meetings	____	____	____
Headquarters staff	____	____	____
Committees	____	____	____
Job training program	____	____	____
Joint field operation	____	____	____

Scoring: Very Frequently Used, 3 points. Not Frequently Used, 1 point; Not Used, 0 points, for each method checked.

4. Which methods of communication are generally used to coordinate activities within your marketing department?

	Very Frequently Used	*Not Frequently Used*	*Not Used*
Formal			
Reports of actual vs. planned results	____	____	____
Approval of operating budgets	____	____	____
Reports of planned activities	____	____	____
Statements of policy	____	____	____
Informal			
Periodic and special staff meetings	____	____	____
Nonperiodic exchange of information (office meetings, coffee, meals)	____	____	____
Voluntary exchange of information (copies of correspondence)	____	____	____
Special-purpose committees	____	____	____

Scoring: Very Frequently Used; 3 points. Not Frequently Used, 1 point; Not Used, 0 points.

5. In-house marketing seminars. Training and planning sessions are conducted by the newly hired marketing personnel.
6. Hiring marketing talent. The firm should hire new talent from existing marketing-oriented firms.

For example, the Apple Computer Company hired the president of Pepsi-Cola to provide a new and needed marketing culture from the top down. Here many bankers may become very restrictive to marketing in an industry that has generally recruited and hired from within. Larger banks with marketing departments, however, have turned to more marketing-oriented industries for help. Kotler notes that Citibank hired several product managers from General Foods to further the development of its marketing orientation.

7. Promoting marketing-oriented executives. Promoting marketing-oriented executives fosters the marketing culture in many ways. Subordinates will view the marketing orientation as the correct path to advancement. Also, advancing the marketing-oriented manager reinforces what was a top-down orientation into a bottom-up orientation. Individuals who have advanced through their marketing skills are unlikely to neglect marketing in the future. Reed Wriston's selection as the chairman of Citicorp is widely held to be because of his marketing skills.[6]
8. Install a formal marketing planning system. Requiring that managers explicitly consider the environmental trends, target market, and mix considerations in the firm's planning process is a highly effective tool for fostering marketing thought. A formal marketing-planning system provides a mechanism through which the integration of marketing into the organization may be monitored.

SUMMARY

In this chapter we have presented the elements of redirecting a firm through its formal organization and through a systematic appraisal of change. The basis of a marketing-oriented formal organization is an examination of the marketplace in which the bank's products/services will be offered. The firm must then organize itself to best interface with the target market. Such change is not easy to accomplish, but a planned strategy like that suggested by Kotler offers a systematic approach to implementing marketing orientation throughout the firm.

As you can see, change in an organization is not an easy process. It requires careful planning, top management commitment, and an outside "change agent." Further change does not come as quickly as frequently desired. Real change toward a marketing-oriented banking firm is a long-term process which will be truly accomplished only when every employee sees his or her job from a marketing viewpoint.

Footnotes

[1]Peter Drucker, *Management: Tasks, Responsibilities and Practices* (New York: Harper and Row, Publishers, Inc., 1974), pp. 610–638.

[2]For an example of an organization change to address consumer market segments, see Richard J. Matteis, "The New Bank Office Focuses on Customer Service," *Harvard Business Review,* March–April 1979, pp. 146–159.

[3]John P. Carroll, "How Change Will Impact the Organization," *Journal of Bank Research,* Autumn 1974, pp. 165–169.

[4]Richard M. Hill and James O. Hlavack, "The Venture Team: A New Concept in Marketing Organization," *Journal of Marketing,* Vol. 36 (July 1972), pp. 44–50.

[5]This discussion of implementation and the eight steps to implementing marketing in the firm are drawn from Philip Kotler, *Marketing Management: Analysis Planning and Control* (Englewood Cliffs, N.J.: Prentice-Hall, Inc., 1984), pp. 734–736.

[6]"What Made Reed Watson the Choice at CITIBANK," *Business Week,* July 2, 1984, pp. 25–26.

[7]Adapted from Carlton P. McNamara, "The Present Status of the Marketing Concept," *Journal of Marketing,* Vol. 27 (January 1972), pp. 50–57.

12

controlling the bank's marketing activities

INTRODUCTION

An integral part of marketing management is control. The elements of control provide a means of evaluating the effectiveness of services of marketing activity. This process of continual and systematic evaluation is vital if marketing strategy and tactics are to be effective in meeting changing conditions. Today's banking environment, with rapidly changing regulatory, competitive, and economic conditions provides new challenges almost daily.

The very structure of a typical banking organization places a premium on effective evaluation of the bank's marketing activities. The traditional financial orientation of banking management with funds management as the key to profitability must always be integrated with the marketing orientation of consumer need and response. Further, unlike many firms with well-defined marketing activities, many of the bank's promotion and distribution activities are integrated as part of the responsibilities of operative customer-contact personnel. Such personnel will require strong marketing control to ensure that the marketing part of their activities receives the necessary emphasis.

MARKETING EVALUTION FOR MANAGERIAL CONTROL

Table 12–1 identifies four types of marketing evaluations for managerial use: annual planning, profitability evaluation, efficiency evaluation for distribution and promotion, and the strategic marketing audit.[1] Each of these will be discussed and their use applied to the banking firm in the following sections.

Annual Plan

The annual plan is a detailed evaluation of the performance of a specific product/service for the past 12-month period and an even more detailed plan of marketing activities for the next 12 months. The annual plan normally includes forecasts of expected revenue and a budget for marketing expenditures. For many firms the annual planning process is the mechanism through which marketing strategy is formulated, evaluated, and approved on a regular basis.[2] The annual plan forms

TABLE 12–1 Types of Marketing Control

Type of Control	*Prime Responsibility*	*Purpose of Control*	*Approaches*
1. Annual-plan control	Top management Middle management	To examine whether the planned results are being achieved	Sales analysis Market-share analysis Sales-to-expense ratios Financial analysis Attitude tracking
2. Profitability control	Marketing controller	To examine where the company is making and losing money	Profitability by: product territory customer group trade channel
2. Efficiency control	Line and staff management Marketing controller	To evaluate and improve the spending efficiency and impact of marketing expenditures	Efficiency of: sales force advertising sales promotion distribution
4. Strategic control	Top management Marketing auditor	To examine whether the company is pursuing its best opportunities with respect to markets, products, and channels	Marketing audit

Source: Philip Kotler, *Marketing Management* (Englewood Cliffs, N.J.: Prentice-Hall, Inc., 1984), p. 744. Used with permission.

the guidelines for the evaluation of the firm's efforts for the next year. In effect, each year's plan is an application of the marketing planning process detailed in earlier chapters of this book. In the first steps of the plan, the responsible manager will review the last year's sales and profit figures and present relevant research on the target market. The overall strategy of the firm is used as a base from which the plans for each product/service are developed. This is generally accomplished by having a series of annual plans with each plan built on the plans of subordinate units.

Although many firms develop annual plans on a crash basis to meet some arbitrary budget deadline, the annual planning process should be a year-round activity. Top management input is necessary at the early stages of the plan's development to provide guidance for the final plan. Input into the plan should come from marketing and financial units of the firm and from line operational units.

Expenditure Plan

One element of the plan will be a detailed expenditures plan for the coming period. In a recent *Bank Marketing* article, Gordon Bleil[3] suggests that the three basic questions in capital budgeting are

1. How much will be spent? (cash outlay)
2. How much will be returned? (cash received)
3. What is timing of the transactions?

These three factors may then be used to examine alternative uses of the bank's resources through the application of payback, return on investment, and discounted cash flow analysis techniques (Table 12–2). Payback is simply the estimation of the period in which the bank will recover its initial investment and begin to make a profit in the funds expended. Basically, projects with early payback periods are preferred because of money's time value. Many banks will establish payback guides against which all uses of resources will be evaluated during the planning process.

Return on investment (ROI) used the same data as payback analysis, but rather than a simple comparison of the timing of the break-

TABLE 12–2 Capital Budget Analysis

Payback.	Time period until investment is repayed
Returned on investment (ROI).	Percentage of return to investment by year.
Discounted cash flow.	Cash flow for each period is discounted to base period.

even point, a percentage return is computed. In this manner the flow of funds into the bank through time is evaluated, and competing plans may be compared on a standard basis. This technique, however, does not allow for the impact of cash flow timing and thus ignores the time value of funds.

The use of net present-value analysis in discounted cash-flow analysis provides a mechanism through which the timing of cash flows may be related to the time value of money. Flows for each period are adjusted to their "present value" using a specified rate of return and the net outflows compared to net inflows. This approach is modified somewhat by many banks through the use of internal rate of return or the annualized yield of all cash flow. As Bleil points out, this is the rate that would ". . . give a zero net present value in the calculation of a series of cash flows."[4] This rate may be used to compare projects and to evaluate projects against the bank's cost of funds for each project.

Once the plan is developed and approved, it becomes the basis for the evaluation of marketing efforts and bank performance for the next planning period. The bank's information system should be designed to provide the necessary information for timely evaluation of the product/services performance. Kotler suggests five analytical tools to monitor plan performance: sales analysis, market-share analysis, marketing expense to sales analysis, financial analysis, and customer attitude tracking.[5]

Before we discuss these analyses, a framework for effective information analysis for marketing control and a source for comparative data is necessary.

Variance Analysis

The performance-versus-plan approach is the basis for most annual planning and evaluation. In an article entitled "A Strategic Framework for Marketing Control," Hulbert and Toy[6] emphasize that identification of variance is only the first step in the controlling activity. Diagnosing the problems which generated the favorable or the unfavorable variance requires both managerial expertise and market knowledge.

Variances may be caused by changes in total market size, market share, and price/cost relationships. The observed variance should be decomposed into these elements, then the root causes of each decomposed difference examined. In effect, two different types of variance must be considered. *Planning variance* is variance in expected and actual market conditions. *Performance variance* is caused by the impact of the marketing mix in the marketing environment. The decomposition procedure allows the manager to compare variances to the original plan levels so that planning variances may be controlled and performance variances examined in depth.[7]

CONTROL AND THE ANNUAL PLAN

An integral part of the development of the annual plan is the application and examination of control techniques which are keyed to long-term performance. Although the plan has a one-year horizon, we must frequently look backward and forward in time to examine trends which indicate problem areas for the bank. We should be especially cognizant of controllable marketing factors, that is to say, measures which allow us to examine our marketing performance from a comparative viewpoint. Two such factors are market share and customer attitude.

Market Share and Sales Analysis

Strategic marketing management requires that we evaluate entire market segments. Examination of this basic planning unit in marketing provides the bank manager with the "big picture" which may be observed on a target market and product/service. We are talking about not being able to "see the forest for the trees" unless you deal with aggregations-market segments.

While the evaluation of sales or revenue figures are basically straightforward, meaningful control consideration requires that the numbers be compared to the total market, not simply to the bank's results. In this manner it can be determined whether the plan is working, or if the results are simply a function of overall changes in the market. FDIC data can be used to evaluate the overall marketplace and direct competitors.

Market-share analysis is an important control tool used to monitor changes in market position for individual products. Many authorities contend that share, rather than actual profits/losses, is the best indicant of long-term viability in a market segment. While profit/loss may be very volatile and due to factors outside the control of the manager (such as economic conditions or cost of funds), share provides an indication of a bank's relative performance with competitors facing similar *external* environments.

Often, a product's market share is obscured by overall market volume and the bank's volume of business for a given product. The result is that while market volume for a product may be increasing, the bank's share of a growing market may actually be dropping. Market-share analysis is designed to permit the marketing manager a closer look at market changes.

Table 12–3 shows the type of matrix which is used to conduct the analysis. For the purpose of explication a NOW account analysis is used, shown in Table 12–4. The marketing manager needs two levels of information. First, aggregation for NOW accounts for *all relevant competition* must be acquired. This information can and should be estimated through market surveys that track product movements. Total deposits for a past year are used for a benchmark, in this case 1983. The marketing manager also needs estimates for the present (1985) and projections for all relevant competition for 1987.

Second, the marketing manager needs NOW account deposit history for his or her bank for the year 1983, present deposits for 1985, and projections for 1987. As Table 12–4 indicates, market volume for NOW accounts has been increasing and is expected to increase in 1987. Moreover, the marketing manager notes that the bank's deposit volume for NOW accounts is also up. However, looking at the bank's share of the market indicates that while market volume has exhibited a healthy increase, the bank's share of that volume has not been increasing at the same rate. In fact, the bank is losing market share and is expected to keep losing share for NOW accounts unless something is done.

The share analysis matrix alerts the marketing manager to actual and potential losses in share. It signals the need for an audit of several possible bank trouble spots. For example, new product extensions to existing NOW accounts may be necessary. New competitive versions may be targeted to lower-income segments. Price reductions in the form of lower minimum deposits may also be a necessary step. It may be a promotional problem, where the bank's NOW account messages are not communicating with the right households. The share analysis matrix can be a useful tool for identifying possible problems in loss of share, can suggest potential solutions, and is a powerful control tool.

TABLE 12–3 Market Share Analysis Matrix (NOW Accounts)

Total market deposits	Past market deposits ($)	Present market deposits ($)	Potential market deposits ($)	Increase Decrease No change
Bank's deposits	Past bank deposits ($)	Present bank deposits ($)	Potential bank deposits ($)	Increase Decrease No change
Bank share of market	Past market share (%)	Present market share (%)	Potential market share (%)	Increase Decrease No change

TABLE 12–4 Share Analysis Matrix: NOW Accounts

	Past (1983)	*Present (1985)*	*Future (1987)*	*Trend*
Total relevant market deposits	$24,754,000	$40,325,000	$52,250,000	Up
Bank deposits	4,506,950	5,887,450	6,531,250	Up
Bank share of relevant market	17.5%	14.6%	12.5%	Down

Customer Attitude

Robert Person contended in a recent *Banking Magazine* article entitled "Losing Customers, Keeping Customers"[8] that every 20 months the typical bank will lose 30 to 50 percent of its retail customers. As shown in Table 12–5, *poor service* is the primary controllable factor in the customer equation. Person found that bank employees assumed that the customer complaining about an error was wrong 75 percent of the time. We agree with Person that the "most important customers to any bank are the ones the bank already has." Marketing-oriented managers should install a conscientious and systematic tracking procedure to determine problem areas before they cost the bank customers. The best approach is the development of a single sampling procedure and questionnaire which can be mailed to selected customers with their monthly statements or other regular communications. These surveys are excellent tools for pinpointing problem areas on a continuing basis.

PROFITABILITY CONTROL

Profitability analysis is at the heart of the marketing plan analysis. What are necessary, however, are not quarterly or yearly financial reports, but more timely and more detailed statements. Such profit-and-

TABLE 12–5 Why a Customer Leaves a Bank

Poor service	20%
Service charges	10%
Loan-related problems	5%
Moved	45%
Changed job locations	10%
Changed travel pattern	10%
	100%

Source: Robert J. Person, "Losing Customers, Keeping Customers," *Retail Banking*, Vol. 67 (October 1975), pp. 92, 94, 96. Reprinted with permission.

loss statements should be developed with respect to the target market, the branch, the service/product unit, or other basis appropriate for the individual bank.[9] As in the analysis of the annual plan elements, the elements making up profit or loss should be analyzed to determine the cause of both high profits and loss (Table 12–6). Further, those measures relevant to the level of profitability for committed assets should also be examined.[10]

TABLE 12–6 Profitability of Insured Commercial Banks in 1982
Report of income, all insured commercial banks, 1978–82
Millions of dollars, except as noted

Item	*1978*	*1979*	*1980*	*1981*	*1982*
Operating income, total	**113,170**	**149,795**	**190,109**	**247,932**	**257,188**
Interest, total	102,706	137,364	174,416	228,675	235,121
Loans	75,948	101,942	126,663	163,171	166,589
Balances with banks	6,662	10,561	16,035	23,935	23,857
Federal funds sold and securities purchased under resale agreement	3,664	6,106	8,750	12,236	11,316
Securities (excluding trading accounts)					
Total income	16,432	18,755	22,968	29,333	33,359
U.S. Treasury and U.S. government agencies and corporations	9,335	10,630	13,400	18,037	21,022
States and political subdivisions	6,003	6,928	8,131	9,671	10,612
Other[1]	1,094	1,197	1,437	1,635	1,725
Trust department	2,138	2,375	2,738	3,179	3,604
Direct lease financing	862	1,073	1,371	1,746	1,943
Service charges on deposits	2,039	2,517	3,173	3,905	4,573
Other charges, fees, etc.	2,930	3,635	4,352	5,302	6,203
Other operating income	2,495	2,831	4,059	5,116	5,715
Operating expenses, total	**98,104**	**131,950**	**170,675**	**227,714**	**238,016**
Interest, total	59,198	87,570	119,758	169,268	168,553
Time and savings deposits	50,054	71,693	98,130	138,977	141,097
Time CDs of $100,000 or more issued by domestic offices	11,693	18,105	24,753	39,034	37,359
Deposits in foreign offices	14,559	24,523	34,941	46,696	41,746
Other deposits	23,802	29,065	38,436	53,248	62,029
Federal funds purchased and securities sold under repurchase agreement	7,247	12,218	16,707	23,786	20,618
Other borrowed money[2]	1,452	3,162	4,380	5,894	6,188
Capital notes and debentures	445	497	541	611	650
Salaries, wages, and employee benefits	18,654	21,465	24,565	27,927	31,218
Occupancy expense[3]	5,559	6,255	7,325	8,566	9,960
Loan-loss provision	3,499	3,764	4,453	5,059	8,291
Other operating expenses	11,194	12,796	14,573	16,962	19,953
Income before taxes and securities gains or losses	15,067	17,843	19,435	20,149	19,172
Applicable income taxes	4,155	4,736	5,009	4,611	3,639
Net securities gains or losses (−) after taxes	−225	−350	−492	−861	−661

TABLE 12–6 *(continued)*

Item	*1978*	*1979*	*1980*	*1981*	*1982*
Extraordinary charges (−) or credits after taxes	45	39	17	54	68
Net income	10,731	12,797	13,950	14,731	14,940
Cash dividends declared	3,714	4,449	5,091	5,831	6,529
MEMO					
Number of banks	14,380	14,352	14,421	14,400	14,121
Average fully consolidated assets (billions of dollars)	1,418	1,593	1,768	1,933	2,101

1. Includes interest income from other bonds, notes and debentures, and dividends from stocks.

2. Includes interest paid on U.S. Treasury tax and loan account balances, which were begun in November 1978.

3. Occupancy expense for bank premises net of any rental income plus furniture and equipment expenses.

Source: Barbara N. Opper, "Profitability of Insured Commercial Banks," in 1982; Federal Reserve Bulletin, July 1983 (Vol. 69–2), p. 501. Used with permission.

$$\text{Profit margin} = \frac{\text{income before taxes}}{\text{total operating income}}$$

$$\text{Asset productivity} = \frac{\text{total operating income}}{\text{total assets}}$$

$$\text{Operating return on assets} = \frac{\text{income before taxes}}{\text{total assets}}$$

This analysis should also be applied at the division and branch levels. At the product/service, market, and customer levels, the measures are generally related only to those assets and costs that can be allocated. As one can see from Table 12–7, these measures vary greatly by bank size.

TABLE 12–7 Bank Size and Earnings Characteristics (1969–1979)

	Bank Size ($ in Millions)		
Ratios	*10*	*100*	*1000*
Operating income to total assets	6.66%	6.93%	6.77%
Standard deviation of operating income	.51	1.29	1.71
Operating expense to total assets	5.50	5.89	5.78
Standard deviation of operating expenses	.55	1.21	1.77
Income prior to taxes and other securities gains and losses to total assets	1.16	1.04	.99
Correlation of operating expenses and income prior to taxes and other	(.28)	.09	(.22)

Source: Ronnie N. Anderson, William C. Handorff, and Michael P. McCarthy, "Bank Size and the Management of Capital Ratio," *The Bankers Magazine*, Vol. 165 (January–February 1982), p. 69.

In "Analyzing Branch Office Profitability," David Bupp[11] of the Bank of Hanover and Trust Company provides a procedure for branch-level analysis. The first step is the calculation of cost of funds for the office from the weighted average cost of money. Next, branch profitability, as shown in Table 12–8, is calculated. The calculation is straightforward; however, the reader should consult Bupp's article in *Bank Administration* for the details of Hanover's use of the form.

When developing the profitability analysis procedure, the marketing manager should remember that approximately two-thirds of the average commercial bank's operating income is generated by interest on loans, with the remaining one-third coming from a variety of sources such as balances with banks, federal funds, exchanges under resale agreements, securities trust, lease and service, and other fees.

There is evidence that many banks charge some large depositors less for loans than the offsetting impact of required compensating balances. That is to say, many so-called "preferred" customers who appear to be important sources of profit because of the activity in their accounts are actually costing the bank money. Thus, many customers may not, in fact, be profitable for the bank.

ACCOUNT EVALUATION

Today more progressive banks are combining everyday records and bank reports within a computer-based management information system framework to conduct profit/loss analyses of individual accounts. This analysis should include not only the expenses incurred in servicing the account from the cost accounting system and any payment for their expenses from billing, but also earnings derived from the loanable portion of the average daily balance (Table 12–9). Of course, most banks are accustomed to account maintenance charges and other charges, but most banks do not really have a cost accounting system through which they effectively evaluate the *true* cost to the bank of handling deposits and paying drafts, much less the costs of such services as stop payments, cash payrolls, credit investigation, night depository, or lock box. Most charges are, in fact, very arbitrary and may not cover true costs even when the customer is billed for the service. Effective analysis will require comprehensive and competent cost accounting procedures in each bank's cost area.

The determination of the bank's potential earnings from holding an account is relatively straightforward but, like true cost numbers, requires a systematic evaluation of account activity. While many banks may evaluate the average daily balance for an account, this is generally an inflated evaluation of actual funds available to the bank from the

TABLE 12–8 Branch Profitability Analysis

Office Profitability Analysis Form

PERIOD ______________________ OFFICE ____________

			Line No
Retail Funds Supplied			
1) Demand		$______	1
2) Savings (Passbook–Statement)		______	2
3) Time		______	3
4) Clubs		______	4
5) Equity		______	5
6) TOTAL FUNDS SUPPLIED		$______	6
Retail Funds Used			
7) Installment Loans		$______	7
8) Mortgage Loans		______	8
9) Revolving Credit Loans		______	9
10) TOTAL FUNDS USED		$______	10
Income			
11) Installment Loans	____	$______	11
12) Mortgage Loans	____	______	12
13) Revolving Credit	____	______	13
14) Surplus Funds	____	______	14
15) TOTAL INCOME		$______	15
Expenses			
16) Cost of Funds Supplied	____	$______	16
17) Loan Administration	____	______	17
18) Executive Admin.	____	______	18
19) Direct Salary Expense	____	______	19
20) Direct Charge-Off Exp.	____	______	20
21) Overhead Expense	____	______	21
22) TOTAL EXPENSES		$______	22
23) NET INCOME (LOSS)		$______	23
24) RETURN ON ASSETS		$______	24

account. Float for the account should be evaluated on a daily basis for each account for the period evaluated, and the average daily balance should be reduced by the actual float amount applicable to activity in the account to give an *average daily collected balance.* Expected earnings from the account are determined by applying the Federal Reserve re-

TABLE 12–8 *(continued)*

Cost of Funds Form

PERIOD ____________ OFFICE ____________

Type	Column 1 **Amount**	Column 2 **% in Non-Earning Assets**	Column 3 **Contribution to Earning Assets**	Column 4 **% of Earning Assets**
Demand				
Savings				
Time				
Clubs				
Equity				
TOTAL				

Type	Column 5 **Handling Cost (%)**	Column 6 **Interest Rate**	Column 7 **Total %**	Column 8 **Adjusted Cost**
Demand				
Savings				
Time				
Clubs				
Equity				

Type	Column 9 **Adjusted Cost**	Column 10 **Weight**	Column 11 **Weighted Average Cost**
Demand			
Savings			
Time			
Clubs			
Equity			

TOTAL COST ____________
COST OF CAPITAL ____________
RAW INTEREST COST ____________

Source: David Bupp, "Analyzing Branch Office Profitability," *Magazine of Bank Administration,* March 1981, p. 46. Used with permission.

TABLE 12–9 Account Profit/Loss

Expected Account Revenue			
	Average daily balance	________	
	Float (subtract)	________	
	Average daily collected balance		________
	Federal Reserve requirement (multiply)	________	
	Average daily available to loan		________
	Annualized treasury bill rate (multiply)	________	
A.	Expected revenue		________
B.	Actual *costs* of account activity		________
C.	Billed charges for account activities		________
D.	Adjustment for uncollected balance		________
	Profit/Loss = $A - B + C - D =$		________

quirement to the average daily collected balance and then applying the annualized ninety-day treasury bill rate.

The account evaluation procedure should also consider whether the account has an average uncollected balance. If so, the account's expected revenue should be reduced by some rate greater than that applied in the expected earnings computation. This amount may or may not be actually charged to accounts which are billed for true costs of services, depending on your bank's practices.

The key to using the account evaluation described is the ability it affords to pull together information from existing bank records that are normally not linked. Once the necessary information is brought together, the procedure is straightforward. Many banks evaluate every commercial and correspondent account with detailed analysis provided to management on an *exception* basis determined by the billing status of the customer and whether a profit or loss resulted for the account each month.

More elaborate methods have been proposed to evaluate customer profitability over a period of several months or even years. In a recent *Journal of Bank Research* article, Professor Daniel White[12] of Georgia State University presents a present-value approach, using linear programming techniques to evaluate customer profitability. White's approach emphasizes the differential cost of funds over the typical business cycle and a long-term rather than short-term approach to evaluating customer profitability. The methodology may also be applied to determine the true cost of doing business with a customer over time and the differential rate at which loans should be priced to each customer.

The procedure used by White is to set up customer activity over a 48-month period as the input into a linear-programming algorithm as follows:

Maximize: U_t

Subject to: $a_{it}xW_t - BOR_t + INV_t < E_t$

$C_i < 1$

where U_t = the discount factor for a period

W_t = withdrawals for each period

C_t = each customer

a_{it} = each customer's net cash flow

BOR_t = 1 + the borrowing rate for funds in each period

INV_t = 1 + the investment rate for funds in each period

E_t = new equity invested in each period

The linear programming output is inspected to determine if a customer was accepted or rejected in the analysis. Accepted customers' value to the bank may be determined from the "dual value of the constraint." The opportunity cost is used to determine a bank's loss of doing business with customers not accepted by the model. White provided results for a number of actual customers of a major commercial bank for a 48-month period, as shown in Table 12–10. He points out that the bank's traditional customer accounting system indicated that all the customers were profitable in the last period.

TABLE 12–10 Comparison of Single Month with Discounted L/P Methodology for Customer Analysis

Last Month Profitability	*48-Month Value of Customer*
Customer	
1. 4773	4,427,224.69
2. 3906	525,866.31
3. 2863	−2,156,373.33
4. 920	105,555.16
5. 663	−50,170.98

Adapted from: Daniel L. White, "The Present Value Approach to Selecting Bank Customers," *Journal of Bank Research*, Summer 1974, pp. 96–101. Used with permission.

EFFICIENCY CONTROL

Efficiency control is the ongoing evaluation of the relative performance of the variable cost elements of the marketing mix. Sales force, advertising, sales promotion, and distribution components should be evaluated to determine if these elements of the marketing mix are within expected ranges.

Sales force measures such as contacts per representative per day, sales and revenue per contact, and cost per contact should be tracked on, at least, a monthly basis. These measures are available through the bank's records and may be developed at relatively low cost by marketing management. Sales promotion evaluation may include simple analysis of revenue due to the promotion and relative cost of the promotion to revenue realized.[13]

Measures of distribution efficiency in the bank may be derived from branch and ATM use and cost data. Cost per transaction and operating profit measures should be evaluated in the light of past performance and other similar distribution points. This will be valuable input into future product/service development decisions. (See Chapter 7.)

The above efficiency controls generally use data that is internally available to bank management. In like manner, advertising efficiency may be tracked by asking new customers the source of their interest in a product/service and if they have seen the bank ads. Simply keeping records of the number of inquiries about newly advertised products/services allows the determination of efficiency measures in terms of cost per inquiry. Measuring the efficiency of advertising expenditures, however, frequently requires the collection of data to determine the level of exposures and the advertisement's impact on attitudes and intentions. Measures of knowledge about and attitudes toward the bank and its services/products may be taken before and after the advertisement. A useful method for evaluating the effectiveness of print media is the *Starch Readership Report.* This service evaluates reader advertisement recall for almost 200 general magazines, business publications, and newspapers. Personal interviews are used to evaluate the major sections of each ad in the publication in terms of aided recall. Starch also provides readers-per-dollar and "cost ratios" comparisons for advertisements within a particular publication.[14]

MARKETING AUDIT

The financial/accounting audit is a common part of every bank's business practice. In many banks the marketing audit is joining the more commonplace financial/accounting audit as a tool for control. The bank marketing audit is a systematic review of every aspect of the bank's marketing operations. The audit is broad in scope, as Table 12–11 shows, and should cover every level of the bank.

The audit should address the bank's objectives, its strengths and weaknesses, the environment, policies, and practices in every aspect relevant to the marketing activity. As Abe Schuchman, one of the pioneers of the audit concept, points out, the audit is a ". . . search for opportunity as well as for malfunction."[15]

The marketing audit is the primary strategic marketing analysis and control mechanism within the bank. The other control tools presented in this chapter are of an ongoing nature and generally provide data for tactical or daily decisions concerning the marketing operations of the bank. Even the annual plan is to some extent tactical in orientation in that it operationalizes the bank's marketing plans for the coming year rather than actually providing a framework for a broad strategic examination of the bank's total marketing activities.

The marketing audit should be used by top management to provide a regular review of the bank's marketing operation. Often data for the audit will be collected through interviews and surveys of both the bank's members and its customers. The audit may be conducted by an auditing team from within the various functional divisions of the bank. The matrix organization structure suggested for the venture team is frequently applied to the marketing audit team. Outside consultants are

TABLE 12–11 Components of a Marketing Audit

Part I. Marketing Environment Audit	
	MACROENVIRONMENT
A. Demographic	1. What major demographic developments and trends pose opportunities or threats to this company?
	2. What actions has the company taken in response to these developments and trends?
B. Economic	1. What major developments in income, prices, savings, and credit will affect the company?
	2. What actions has the company been taking in response to these developments and trends?
C. Ecological	1. What is the outlook for the cost and availability of natural resources and energy needed by the company?
	2. What concerns have been expressed about the company's role in pollution and conservation, and what steps has the company taken?
D. Technological	1. What major changes are occurring in product technology? In process technology? What is the company's position in these technologies?

TABLE 12–11 *(continued)*

	2. What major generic substitutes might replace this product?
E. Political	1. What laws are being proposed that could affect marketing strategy and tactics?
	2. What federal, state, and local actions should be watched? What is happening in the areas of pollution control, equal employment opportunity, product safety, advertising, price control, and so forth, that affects marketing strategy?
F. Cultural	1. What is the public's attitude toward business and toward the products produced by the company?
	2. What changes in consumer and business lifestyles and values have a bearing on the company?
	TASK ENVIRONMENT
A. Markets	1. What is happening to market size, growth, geographical distribution, and profits?
	2. What are the major market segments?
B. Customers	1. How do customers and prospects rate the company and its competitors on reputation, product quality, service, sales force, and price?
	2. How do different customer segments make their buying decisions?
C. Competitors	1. Who are the major competitors? What are their objectives and strategies, their strengths and weaknesses, their sizes and market shares?
	2. What trends will affect future competition and substitutes for this product?
D. Distribution and Dealers	1. What are the main trade channels for bringing products to customers?
	2. What are the efficiency levels and growth potentials of the different trade channels?
E. Suppliers	1. What is the outlook for the availability of key resources used in production?
	2. What trends are occurring among suppliers in their pattern of selling?
F. Facilitators and Marketing Firms	1. What is the cost and availability outlook for transportation services?
	2. What is the cost and availability outlook for warehousing facilities?
	3. What is the cost and availability outlook for financial resources?
	4. How effective are the company's advertising agencies and marketing research firms?
G. Publics	1. What publics represent particular opportunities or problems for the company?
	2. What steps has the company taken to deal effectively with each public?

TABLE 12–11 *(continued)*

Part II. Marketing Strategy Audit

A. Business Mission	1. Is the business mission clearly stated in market-oriented terms? Is it feasible?
B. Marketing Objectives and Goals	1. Are the corporate and marketing objectives stated in the form of clear goals to guide marketing planning and performance measurement?
	2. Are the marketing objectives appropriate, given the company's competitive position, resources, and opportunities?
C. Strategy	1. Is management able to articulate a clear marketing strategy for achieving its marketing objectives? Is the strategy convincing? Is the strategy appropriate to the stage of the product life cycle, competitors' strategies, and the state of the economy?
	2. Is the company using the best basis for market segmentation? Does it have sound criteria for rating the segments and choosing the best ones? Has it developed accurate profiles of each target segment?
	3. Has the company developed a sound positioning and marketing mix for each target segment? Are marketing resources allocated optimally to the major elements of the marketing mix—i.e., product quality, service, sales force, advertising, promotion, and distribution?
	4. Are enough resources or too many resources budgeted to accomplish the marketing objectives?

Part III. Marketing Organization Audit

A. Formal Structure	1. Does the marketing officer have adequate authority over and responsibility for company activities that affect the customer's satisfaction?
	2. Are the marketing activities optimally structured along fuctional, product, end-user, and territorial lines?
B. Functional Efficiency	1. Are there good communication and working relations between marketing and sales?
	2. Is the product management system working effectively? Are product managers able to plan profits or only sales volume?
	3. Are there any groups in marketing that need more training, motivation, supervision, or evaluation?
C. Interface Efficiency	1. Are there any problems between marketing and manufacturing, R&D, purchasing, finance, accounting, and legal that need attention?

Part IV. Marketing Systems Audit

A. Marketing Information System	1. Is the marketing intelligence system producing accurate, sufficient, and timely information about marketplace developments with respect to customers, pros-

TABLE 12–11 *(continued)*

	pects, distributions and dealers, competitors, suppliers, and various publics? 2. Are company decision makers asking for enough marketing research, and are they using the results? 3. Is the company employing the best methods for market and sales forecasting?
B. Marketing Planning Systems	1. Is the marketing planning system well conceived and effective? 2. Is sales forecasting and market potential measurement soundly carried out? 3. Are sales quotas set on a proper basis?
C. Marketing Control System	1. Are the control procedures adequate to ensure that the annual-plan objectives are being achieved? 2. Does management periodically analyze the profitability of products, markets, territories, and channels of distribution? 3. Are marketing costs periodically examined?
D. New-Product-Development System	1. Is the company well organized to gather, generate, and screen new-product ideas? 2. Does the company do adequate concept research and business analysis before investing in new ideas? 3. Does the company carry out adequate product and market testing before launching new products?
Part V. Marketing Productivity Audit	
A. Profitability Analysis	1. What is the profitability of the company's different products, markets, territories, and channels of distribution? 2. Should the company enter, expand, contract, or withdraw from any business segments and what would be the short- and long-run profit consequences?
B. Cost-Effectiveness Analysis	1. Do any marketing activities seem to have excessive costs? Can cost-reducing steps be taken?
Part VI. Marketing Function Audits	
A. Products	1. What are the product-line objectives? Are these objectives sound? Is the current product line meeting the objectives? 2. Should the product line be stretched or contracted upward, downward, or both ways? 3. Which products should be phased out? Which products should be added? 4. What are the buyers' knowledge and attitudes toward the company's and competitors' product quality, features, styling, brand names, etc.? What areas of product strategy need improvement?

TABLE 12–11 *(continued)*

B. Price	1. What are the pricing objectives, policies, strategies, and procedures? To what extent are prices set on cost, demand, and competitive criteria? 2. Do the customers see the company's prices as being in line with the value of its offer? 3. What does management know about the price elasticity of demand, experience curve effects, and competitors' prices and pricing policies? 4. To what extent are price policies compatible with the needs of distributors and dealers, suppliers, and government regulation?
C. Distribution	1. What are the distribution objectives and strategies? 2. Is there adequate market coverage and service? 3. How effective are the following channel members: distributors, dealers, manufacturers' representatives, brokers, agents, etc.? 4. Should the company consider changing its distribution channels?
D. Advertising, Sales Promotion, and Publicity	1. What are the organization's advertising objectives? Are they sound? 2. Is the right amount being spent on advertising? How is the budget determined? 3. Are the ad themes and copy effective? What do customers and the public think about the advertising? 4. Are the advertising media well chosen? 5. Is the internal advertising staff adequate? 6. Is the sales promotion budget adequate? Is there effective and sufficient use of sales promotion tools such as samples, coupons, displays, sales contests? 7. Is the publicity budget adequate? Is the public relations staff competent and creative?
E. Sales Force	1. What are the organization's sales-force objectives? 2. Is the sales force large enough to accomplish the company's objectives? 3. Is the sales force organized along the proper principles of specialization (territory, market, product)? Are there enough (or too many) sales managers to guide the field sales representatives? 4. Does the sales-compensation level and structure provide adequate incentive and reward? 5. Does the sales force show high morale, ability, and effort? 6. Are the procedures adequate for setting quotas and evaluating performances? 7. How does the company's sales force compare to competitors' sales forces?

Source: Philip Kotler, *Marketing Management: Analysis, Planning and Control,* 5th ed. (Englewood Cliffs, N.J.: Prentice-Hall, Inc., 1984). Used with permission.

also frequently employed to assist in the audit, since consultants can provide a view of the bank unhindered by everyday association or personal interest in existing activities. This external approach provides more objectivity, may generate information from internal personnel who might not confide in a superior or rival, and allows more time for the audit without disrupting ongoing activities. The audit should produce a formal written document which evaluates the bank, its environment, its competitors, and its marketing mix, identifies problems, and suggests solutions.

SUMMARY

Control is a vital part of the marketing management process in banking and begins with the bank's objectives. Planning and implementation are only the beginning of the development of the marketing culture in the bank. The activities must be effectively monitored, evaluated, and, where necessary, modified to meet constantly changing competitive, economic, and regulatory conditions.

Footnotes

[1]The framework for this chapter is drawn from Philip Kotler's *Typology of Marketing Control;* Philip Kotler, *Marketing Management Analysis: Planning and Control,* 5th ed. (Englewood Cliffs, N.J.: Prentice-Hall, Inc., 1983), pp. 743–763.

[2]For a discussion of annual marketing planning in several settings, see Stanley F. Stasch and Patricia Lanktree, "Can Your Marketing Planning Procedures Be Improved?" *Journal of Marketing,* Vol. 44 (Summer 1980).

[3]Gordon B. Bleil, "Capital Budgeting in Marketing," *Bank Marketing* (January 1983), pp. 9–11.

[4]Ibid, p. 10.

[5]Philip Kotler, *Marketing Management: Analysis Planning and Control,* 5th ed. (Englewood Cliffs, N.J.: Prentice-Hall, Inc., 1984), p. 744.

[6]James M. Hulbert and Norman E. Toy, "A Strategic Framework for Marketing Control," *Journal of Marketing,* April 1977, pp. 12–19.

[7]See Frank H. Mossman, Paul M. Fischer, and W. J. E. Crissy, "New Approaches to Analyzing Marketing Profitability," *Journal of Marketing,* Vol. 38 (April 1974), pp. 43–48.

[8]Robert Person, "Losing Customers, Keeping Customers," *Banking Magazine,* October, 1975.

[9]See V. H. Kirpalani and Stanley S. Shapiro, "Financial Dimensions of Marketing Management," *Journal of Marketing,* Vol. 37 (July 1973), pp. 40–47.

[10]Edward W. Reed, Richard V. Cotter, Edward K. Gill, and Richard K. Smith, *Commercial Banking,* 3rd ed. (Englewood Cliffs, N.J.: Prentice-Hall, Inc., 1984), p. 226.

[11]David C. Bupp, "Analyzing Branch Office Profitability," *Bank Administration,* March 1981, pp. 44–48.

[12]Daniel L. White, "The Present Value Approach to Selecting Bank Customers," *Journal of Bank Research,* Summer 1974, pp. 96–101.

[13]See Porter Henry, "Manage Your Sales as a System," *Harvard Business Review,* March–April 1975.

[14]For information concerning the Starch Media Services, contact Daniel Starch & Staff, Inc., Mamaroneck, New York.

[15]Abe Shuchman, "The Marketing Audit: Its Nature, Purposes and Problems," *AMA Management Report,* No. 32. "Analyzing and Improving Marketing Performance," 1959, American Management Association. As quoted in *The Great Writings in Marketing,* Howard A. Thompson, ed. (Tulsa, OK: PPC Books, 1977), p. 135.

13

marketing and public policy issues in the 1980s

INTRODUCTION

As we look back over the last 25 years, it is evident that the banking industry has emerged relatively unscathed from the turbulence of consumer activism and public policy problems that have marked other industries.[1] Many of the banking industry's consumer goods counterparts were not so lucky.

Toy manufacturers, lawn mower makers, the funeral industry, the drug industry, cereal manufacturers, the automobile industry, soft drink producers, fast food chains, the insurance industry, and a host of other industries were targeted by consumer groups and government agencies for scrutiny concerning a number of different practices. At the same time the banking industry appeared to enjoy a certain immunity from the investigatory actions of consumerists.

That is not to say the banking industry was untouched by the consumerist activity. Such legislation as the truth-in-advertising and truth-in-lending legislation has had an indirect effect on industry practices, but really no more than on other industries. The point is, the so-called consumer movement of the 1970s and the occasional public policy issues that have emerged have not been a major impetus for changing banking practices in this same time period.

There are, however, signals of a growing concern over emergent public policy issues catalyzed by the advent of deregulation that may prove to have significant impact on banking. Consumer groups are beginning to question the presence of several banking practices and the lack of other practices.

In Pittsburgh a coalition of ministers and labor leaders are bringing pressure to bear on Mellon Bank to develop and support an economic plan aimed at saving dying steel communities. Their methods are somewhat attention-getting. For example, dead fish have been placed in safe deposit boxes, and branch operations have been interrupted by activists spilling bags of pennies.

The Consumer Federation of America, based in Washington, has set as a high priority the influencing of banks to adopt a new code for disclosing financial information to consumers, and to provide basic "lifeline" services to the less affluent.

A bank in Boston pleaded guilty to a felony charge of failing to report to the government $1.22 billion in transatlantic bank-to-bank case transactions. A $500,000 fine was paid by the bank, which faced new allegations of a linkage to organized crime. Thus, a wide range of practices and occurrences promises to draw increasing attention from a number of different quarters.

This chapter examines those factors which we feel shielded the banking industry from the concern of consumer activists and public policy groups and how deregulation is changing these factors and making the industry vulnerable to potential public policy concerns. In addition, we identify what we consider to be potentially significant and threatening issues facing the industry and what bankers can do to assuage the negative impacts of these issues.

THE PROTECTIVE VEIL OF BANKING

For the nearly 50 years preceding 1980, commercial banking was the archetype of the consistently profitable, stable industry. This was primarily the result of governmental intervention in response to the banking crisis in the late 1920s and early 1930s. There were basically three important underpinnings that afforded commercial banking some protection that were not available to most other industries: (1) Banks possessed an exclusive product franchise. Banks, by virtue of their ability to offer checking accounts, effectively forced nearly every household and business to use the services of a bank to access the payment system. (2) Banks had a protected geographic territory. Commercial banks were among the few businesses in the country that could not conduct business across state lines and in some cases were not allowed to branch at all. (3) Banks were restricted as to the rates they could pay savers. This was an unusual constraint placed on banks in the acquisition of their raw materials. Through Regulation Q, the Federal Reserve dictated interest rate ceilings above which a bank could not pay.[2]

We believe that within this context of industry structure, several factors can be identified that have operated to veil the banking industry from the prying eyes of consumers and public policy action groups.

The Nature of Bank Products

Bank products are different from consumer goods in a number of key ways. First, they require no physical packaging. The so-called undue proliferation of package size of consumer products has been the *cause célèbres* of consumer groups and has even provided impetus to the Fair Packaging and Labeling Act.

Second, bank products are immune from the "faulty products" issue. Writing in 1972, Richard Shaffer pointed out:

> Products that don't work as they should, which now rival automobile accidents as the nation's number one cause of litigation, were responsible for an estimated 500,000 court cases last year, compared with 10,000 five years ago, and many expect the annual total to reach one million by 1985.[3]

Faulty products are also linked to safety issues, repair/maintenance problems, warranties, and guarantees; they also give rise to product recall situations.

Bank products do not have the same potentially issue-provoking characteristics of packaging, safety, repair, and maintenance that many consumer goods have. This is due to their intangible nature.[4] This reduces significantly the potential for complaining, litigation, and regulation that have been witnessed in other industries.

Nonaggressiveness of Bank Activity in the Retail Market

Aggressive marketing activity by consumer-goods firms has given many companies a visibility they had not anticipated and, in retrospect, may not have desired. Puffery, exaggeration, nonexistent additives, and deceptive advertising were at one time defended as necessary activities in a competitive market. The hard sell was the hallmark of consumer goods marketing, where many companies adopted the ethos of caveat emptor.

Banking, on the other hand, and relative to the insurance industry for example, carried on what might be referred to as nonaggressive marketing of its products, using a soft sell, if any sell was used at all. Traditional bankers were inside order takers content for the most part to accept their market share, keep a clean loan portfolio, and keep the stockholders happy. When bankers did venture out of their offices, they were more desirous of enhancing their community image than selling bank products. The traditional banker perceived the nature of bank products as requiring very little sales efforts. There was little provocation in this type of activity relative to consumer advocate groups.

Lack of Consumer Knowledge of Banking Operations

Within the confines of a highly regulated industry, information relative to the detailed operations of a bank was not forthcoming and was not, for the most part, required by the consumer. There was a perceived standardization of banks and bank products and services. Consumers' knowledge of banking activities did not appear to exceed that of understanding that banks collected deposits and made loans. Many banking practices were not questioned, or, one would suspect, even noticed. For example, there was little need for consumers to inquire into a bank's pricing of deposit services, because these services were either free or priced very low. There was little reason to question interest rates paid to savers, because these rates were fixed. Consequently, there was little need for consumers to pressure bankers to explain their operations. The questions just weren't a top-of-the-mind issue for most consumers, because they were not controversial by nature.

A recent survey of bank customers, household and business, revealed a lack of consumer knowledge of banking operations. Very few of the respondents could correctly answer questions concerning bank products. Examples of subjects questioned were the definition of compounding, the purpose of the Federal Reserve System, the current FDIC insurance maximum, and the description of a NOW account. The knowledge that consumers displayed with respect to specific bank products was consistently low.[5] Another study indicated that consumers fall short of an optimum level of consumer awareness.[6]

Knowledge of the annual percentage rate (APR) being charged has increased since the passage of the Truth-in-Lending Act, but consumers cannot translate this APR into a reasonably accurate dollar finance charge even when the finance charge is clearly disclosed on credit contracts.[7]

It appears that this lack of information was a factor in the distance that banks kept from the consumerist issue. The lack of sophistication on the part of the consuming public, taken in concert with other factors, afforded the banking industry some added protection.

Simple Product/Service Mixes

Consider the typical product mix of a retail bank in the 1970s. Consumers could choose from such products as noninterest-bearing checking accounts, savings accounts, 30-year mortgage notes, safety deposit boxes, trust services, and maybe a bank card. Product mixes were simple and, perhaps equally important, standardized. Products and interest rates had remained relatively fixed for many years.

Not so for consumers entering a supermarket, for example. Consumers had to choose from among a large assortment of brands, many in different-sized packages, with different types of product information and different prices. For example, in 1937 Charles Wyand estimated there were 250,000 distinct types of consumer goods marketed. Eugene Beem, in a more recent commentary, argues:

> The Sears-Roebuck and Company catalogues, alone, describe between 90,000 and 100,000 types of commodities. On top of this baffling assortment of goods from which to choose, consumers are confronted with a myriad of competing qualities for most every product which they wish to buy. Philadelphia families, in a recent year, were using 64 brands of packaged coffee, 86 of butter, 39 of fresh milk, 52 of laundry soap, 122 of face powder, 49 of safety razor blades, 32 of automobile tires, 71 of electric toasters and 51 [of] vacuum cleaners.[8]

These practices brought much attention from consumer activists, who claimed the consumer was disadvantaged in the face of so many different and complex choices. Banking, on the other hand, usually offered a basic mortgage, maybe a couple of variations of a checking account, etc. The toughest and most complex decision facing banking consumers was choosing check designs and the color of the checkbook. Moreover, many of these products were free, subsidized by other products, primarily loans.

The "Halo Effect" of Bankers

Bankers and banks were typically considered pillars of society. Conservatism, the three-piece suit, and high community involvement were the trademarks of the industry. Such an image extended to banking operations and practices. The industry tacitly frowned upon flamboyant behavior and high-profile individuals. Much of this "halo effect" was, and still is, for that matter, attributable to a highly regulated image. The SEC, the FDIC, the Comptroller of the Currency, the Federal Reserve Board, and other august regulating bodies inspired trust, security, confidence, and a feeling that your banker was a friend who was working for you and would not let you down. This, of course, was the legacy of a successful image-building campaign waged by the industry since the depression years. Consumers trust banking and bankers, in whom they place a great deal of confidence, higher than for any other industry.[9]

DEREGULATION IS LIFTING THE PROTECTIVE VEIL

The forces of deregulation are a catalyst for change in the banking industry. One by-product of this change is seen in the diminution of those protective factors which we feel shielded banking from sticky public policy issues and consumer activism in the past. While deregulation will mean expanded opportunity, it also means opportunity at a cost. One cost will be the greater potential for public policy issues and closer scrutiny as this protective veil is lifted. What follows is a brief description of four major changes promising to exacerbate potential public policy issues facing the industry. These are summarized in Table 13–1.

Increased Efforts Toward Segmentation

Banks are devoting increasing amounts of their time and energy at developing market segmentation strategies in order to increase profits. The long-held belief that 20 percent of your customers provides 80 percent of your funds is taking on increased meaning as bankers develop strategies for delivering services to this more affluent 20 percent. The chasing of the "carriage trade" at the expense of the less affluent mar-

TABLE 13–1 The Changing Climate of Banking

From	*To*
Restrained competition	Increased competition
Market aggregation	Market segmentation
Personalization of service	Depersonalization of service
Consumer ignorance	Consumer awareness
Narrow role of regulators	Broadened role of regulators
Social passivism	Social activism

ket segments will be a potential threat to bankers who respond inappropriately. Affluent customers are typically the most profitable, and it is understandable from an economic standpoint why they are targeted. To do so at the exclusion of the less affluent consumer is to invite criticism and problems for civil rights groups and consumer groups.

For example, at this writing a California group is challenging the targeting of affluent customers as unfair to the less affluent, maintaining that basic and necessary life-line banking services will no longer be made available to many customers who desparately need these basic financial services.

Increasing Competition

The trend toward an increase in competition for the retail customer will continue as structural barriers to competition are removed or relaxed between banks and other bank-like institutions. There are some 50,000 firms providing financial services of one type or another in this country.[10] As competition increases, so too will the visibility of banking.

One aspect of this competition which may prove problematic is the growing complexity of product mixes. Consider increases in the number and types of mortgage loans. No longer is there just a 30-year fixed-rate conventional loan. Now banks offer different variations of adjustable rate mortgages (ARMs), graduated payment mortgages (GPMs), graduated equity mortgages (GEMs), balloon notes, and bridge notes, and, for the consumer, this increased choice is often confusing, bewildering, and even costly. Not understanding the "fine print" of the agreement and thinking (s)he has a nonescalating note can result in a mortgage that the consumer can't pay and the loss of a house. So-called payment shock—"a dreaded new economic disease meaning loss of life, liberty, and perhaps the house"—increases the likelihood of attracting the attention of a growing number of consumer watchdogs.[11]

Increasing Depersonalization of Services

Increased competition often means an increased cost of doing business. Bankers are turning to automated product delivery systems as less expensive alternatives to more expensive human transactions. As banks get larger and rely more heavily on automation, bank customers may find themselves dealing with a cold, monolithic institution from which no redress of grievances is possible. Research with consumers shows that all too often, consumers see computers and automated systems installed to accommodate the bank, not them.[12] This leads to frustration and reaction.

Citicorp experimented with a policy of requiring minimum balances of $5000 in order to transact with a human. Below that amount Citicorp's customers were to carry out their transactions via machine. The bank's management was finally forced to change its policy in the face of massive discontent and negative publicity that such a move produced. Moreover, forcing certain types of consumers (the handicapped and elderly, for example) to use these "nonhuman tellers" may be dangerous to these consumers. This produces a David and Goliath type of situation, one which is easily exploited by consumer groups.

Push Toward Social Activism

Banks, because of their considerable financial clout, occupy pivotal social positions. This power, in the past, has gone relatively unexercised except for typical community public relations types of activities. Socially minded reform groups will demand greater social activism from banks than banks have demonstrated in the past. Banks will become increasingly appealing targets for groups that would like them to use their power to advance more socially responsible causes. This social activism will greatly heighten their visibility.

There is also some evidence that regulators are broadening their view of their role. For example, the FDIC has proposed to publish and make publicly available the names of banks and bank officials against whom it has issued enforcement actions. The FDIC said that public disclosure is intended to subject banks and their managements to greater public scrutiny with the goal of increased market discipline. This is clearly an expanded role for the FDIC and is seen as being consistent with the mood of consumerist groups to observe banks more closely in the future.[13]

FOUR MAJOR PUBLIC POLICY ISSUES OF THE 1980s

These changes are giving rise to a number of public policy issues that will manifest themselves in the remainder of this decade. These issues will pose either threats or opportunities, depending on the reaction of individual banks and, for that matter, the entire banking industry. We do not offer these as being exhaustive, only significant.

Pricing of Services

There is increasing criticism of banks that their pricing structures bear disproportionately on the poor. That is to say, pricing structures set by banks are geared to the more affluent and, in fact, discriminate against the poor. For example, a current issue is the so-called *lifeline* account. The idea behind this issue is that there is a large segment of the population that cannot afford a basic checking account from a bank because of excessive minimum balance restrictions or excessive maintenance and service charges.

Already manifestations of this issue are beginning to emerge. A coalition of California-based consumer and civil rights groups has filed a petition with that state's superintendent of banking. The petition asks for a "restructuring of California banking laws that the group contends discriminate against poor and moderate income consumers."[14] This group says that banking charges have increased 115 percent and are gouging moderate- to low-income consumers. This potential problem is even more accentuated, because most banks do not know what their cost structures are for certain products. Thus, when a bank attempts to justify a NSF charge on a cost basis, it may find itself on thin ice.

Moreover, the Cooperative Association, a Washington-based public interest group, has applied to the Comptroller of the Currency for a charter to provide "lifeline banking services." This move is in response to the neglect the banking industry has shown the less affluent banking customer.[15]

The opportunity is clearly present in this issue for banks to address a perceived and actual need and to develop products and delivery mechanisms to meet this need profitably. Discount retailers emerged in response to a similar situation in the retailing industry. Many of the discounters have found it extremely profitable to serve the less affluent market.

Delivery of Services

Some banks have made attempts to further serve customers through increased technological delivery of service. An attempt has even been made, quite unsuccessfully, to place a minimum balance restriction on the use of a "live" teller, thus forcing further technological delivery to a larger segment of consumers by the use of automated teller machines.

As psychologists tell us, in this increasingly impersonal age people want to communicate on a one-to-one basis, particularly where such important elements as money are concerned. Further, consumers perceive inefficiencies in an electronic system; it is believed that computers err more frequently than humans. It is also believed to be more difficult to rectify computer error than human error.[16]

Personalized service remains an important issue even with those consumers who are prone to use an automated teller machine. This group, while responsive to a bank's effort to develop a higher level of technological delivery of servicing, still demands high-quality personal service.[17]

Financial institutions that seek to displace personnel with automated teller machines may be making a serious miscalculation. ATMs and other technological means to deliver service hold great potential for increasing the productivity of a financial institution if consumer banking habits change on a time-consistent basis. To date, in its haste to be more productive, technology appears to have advanced faster than consumers are willing to accept. This holds great challenge to bankers as they attempt to streamline their operations and operate more efficiently.

Another potential public policy issue relative to the delivery of service is that of closing unprofitable locations. This issue is more complex than just a decision to operate or close an unprofitable branch bank. This, unfortunately, tends to impact disproportionately on the less affluent segment of consumers. While we would not suggest continuing the operation of a location at a loss, we are suggesting that there is an opportunity present to structure an alternative delivery system where this segment may be served profitably. Such an opportunity may be leasing of unneeded space to other businesses. The overall opportunity lies in the development of appropriate delivery systems with the realization that, for a large segment of consumers, the preference tends toward personal service.

Communication with Consumers

Deregulation, as we pointed out earlier, has caused a great proliferation of products and services from banks and also from other providers of financial services. This has proved to be very confusing to consumers in their attempt to evaluate their increased alternatives for financial services. Consumer educators must revise their communication strategies because of the blurring between savings, investing, and insurance. It is becoming increasingly difficult to tell the difference between the local bank and the Sears-Roebuck store.

Consumer communication and education should be aimed at increasing consumer awareness, which should be the first line of defense against consumer problems.

The communication of instructions as to how these increasingly complex products work is essential. While many of the products may be easily understood by bankers, consumers have relatively less experience and contact with these products.

A few of the questions consumers may have are (1) Are savings accounts stated in a manner that allows easy comparison among competing plans? (2) Are savers clear about the penalties for premature withdrawal of principal? (3) Do consumers understand statements about methods of compounding interest? (4) Do they understand loan agreements? (5) Do consumers understand all associated costs with the origination of a mortgage? (6) Do consumers understand the complexities of adjustable rate mortgages? (7) Do consumers understand pricing differences between your bank and competing banks? (8) Are package accounts fully explained? (9) Do consumers understand minimum balance requirements of demand deposit options? The opportunity is present for bankers to communicate more clearly and concisely with consumers about product offerings. Bankers need to take an active role in the education of consumers concerning banking products.

Employment of Deposits

With geographic and structural restrictions being lifted, which will ultimately allow banks to operate in expanded geographic areas, an issue bankers must address is the employment of deposit dollars. Will deposits be taken from one area and be employed in another nonlocal area? The issue is one of degree of service and commitment to the community from which deposits are taken. The opportunity here is the strategic definition of service to communities.

> Ten years ago in a west Texas city of 100,000, there were two independent banks of similar size and growth rates. About 85–95% of their loan portfolios were of local origin. Seven years ago, one bank sold to a Houston holding company. A recent check showed the remaining independent banks with the same high level of local lending, but the holding company affiliate's portfolio had only 25% of local loans.[18]

Company support and community involvement is an issue for banks, especially with the current trend toward geographical expansion. Consumer activism may result if a bank attempts to gather deposits from one area and employ them in another to the economic detriment of the area where the deposits were gathered.

PUBLIC POLICY ACTION PLANS

Obviously there are other public policy issues that bankers will face in this decade. We have made no attempt here to totally define the range of issues that impact on the way banks do business in the future. We have, however, identified four important issues that bankers must be prepared to address. Bankers should view these issues as opportunities allowing them to better serve their markets. Some action programs banks should consider in addressing these issues are

1. Make sure your bank understands the effects of deregulation from the consumer perspective.
2. Provide a person-oriented contact point within the bank for the resolution of consumer grievances and questions.
3. Bring bank managment into closer contact with bank customers. Initiate management call programs designed to aid in the strategic definition of service.
4. Become more heavily involved in the education of consumers on money management matters and how banks may assist them. The goal is solid financial knowledge with which to make reasoned decisions.
5. Consider consumer needs and wants in the design of product formats. Consider eliminating redundant services so as to provide a simplified array of product alternatives.
6. Introduce technology only within the framework of the consumer's ability to accept it. Fight depersonalization through the empathetic use of technology and through sound personnel selection and training.
7. Develop an increased sense of community support and commitment, especially with respect to economic development and sustenance.
8. Strive to address social responsibility issues fairly and objectively through rational pricing structures and delivery mechanisms.

There is nothing to suggest that the banking industry will remain immune to public policy issues under deregulation. On the contrary, we feel, as many bankers do, that deregulation will provide the impetus for and catalyze public policy issues for the remainder of the decade.

Bankers are in a position to head off several of these issues by *proactive* programs aimed at defusing the potential threat posed by them. This is the enlightened approach. However, if bank managements operate as did their counterparts in the consumer goods industries, one can expect to see the industry *reacting* to these problems. This will put the banking industry on the defensive at a time when it can ill afford to adopt such a position.

Footnotes

[1]This chapter is adapted from a working paper entitled "Potential Public Policy Issues Facing the Banking Industry: Threats or Opportunities?" by M. Ray Grubbs and R. Eric Reidenbach, University of Mississippi working paper, series 1984.

[2]G. L. Parker, "New Management Will Make or Break the Bank," *Harvard Business Review*, November–December 1981.

[3]Richard Shaffer, "More Customers Press Lawsuits Against Firms Selling Faulty Products," *Wall Street Journal*, November 3, 1972.

[4]Philip Kotler, "Marketing's Role in the Age of Consumerism," *Proceedings of the ABA National Marketing Conference*, 1973, New Orleans, Louisiana.

[5]Thomas O. Stanley, "Inadequate Product Information," *The Bankers Magazine*, Vol. 167, No. 2 (March–April 1984).

[6]Virginia H. Dickinson and James P. Shaver, "A Test of Consumer Awareness for Adults," *Journal of Consumer Affairs*, Vol. 16, No. 2.

[7]Arnold A. Heggestad, *Regulations of Consumer Financial Services* (Cambridge, Mass.: ABT Books, 1981).

[8]Eugene Beem, "The Plight of the Consumer," *New Consumerism: Selected Readings*, William T. Neely, ed. (Columbus, Ohio: Grid, Inc., 1973).

[9]Kotler, ibid.

[10]David Cohen, "The Flaws in 'Lifeline' Banking Concepts," *Bank Marketing*, February, 1985.

[11]Raoul D. Edwards, "The ARM Issue," *United States Banker*, October 1984.

[12]Daniel Yankelovich, "Priorities in the Age of Consumerism," *Proceedings of the ABA National Marketing Conference*, 1973, New Orleans, Louisiana.

[13]*ABA Bankers News Weekly*, Vol. 4, No. 8 (February 19, 1985).

[14]"California Coalition Says Banking Hurts Poor, Seeks Changes," *Wall Street Journal*, August 10, 1985.

[15]Phil Battey, "Is This the Bank of the Future?" an interview with Richard Hurt in the *ABA Journal*, February 1985.

[16]Paco Underhill, "The Sins of Bank Retail Marketing" *United States Banker*, October 1984.

[17]Thomas S. Stanley and George P. Moschis, "The ATM-Prone Consumer: A Profile and Implication," *Journal of Retail Banking*, Vol. 5, No. 1 (1983).

[18]Jane Faut Nelson, "Community Bank Perspectives on Interstate Banking," *United States Banker*, September 1982.

index